Casebook in Child Behavior Disorders

FIFTH EDITION

CHRISTOPHER A. KEARNEY
University of Nevada, Las Vegas

WADSWORTH
CENGAGE Learning·

Australia • Brazil • Japan • Korea • Mexico • Singapore • Spain • United Kingdom • United States

WADSWORTH
CENGAGE Learning

Casebook in Child Behavior Disorders, Fifth Edition, International Edition
Christopher A. Kearney

Publisher: Jon-David Hague

Executive Editor: Jaime Perkins

Developmental Editor: Jessica Alderman

Senior Marketing Communications Manager: Laura Localio

Marketing Program Manager: Janay Pryor

Art and Cover Direction, Production Management, and Composition: PreMediaGlobal

Manufacturing Planner: Karen Hunt

Rights Acquisitions Specialist: Roberta Broyer

Text Researcher: Pablo D'Stair

Cover Image: Petrenko Andriy/ Shutterstock

International Edition:

ISBN-13: 978-1-133-49137-8

ISBN-10: 1-133-49137-5

Cengage Learning International Offices

Asia
www.cengageasia.com
tel: (65) 6410 1200

Australia/New Zealand
www.cengage.com.au
tel: (61) 3 9685 4111

Brazil
www.cengage.com.br
tel: (55) 11 3665 9900

India
www.cengage.co.in
tel: (91) 11 4364 1111

Latin America
www.cengage.com.mx
tel: (52) 55 1500 6000

UK/Europe/Middle East/Africa
www.cengage.co.uk
tel: (44) 0 1264 332 424

Represented in Canada by Nelson Education, Ltd.
www.nelson.com
tel: (416) 752 9100/(800) 668 0671

Cengage Learning is a leading provider of customized learning solutions with office locations around the globe, including Singapore, the United Kingdom, Australia, Mexico, Brazil, and Japan. Locate your local office at: **www.cengage.com/global**.

For product information and free companion resources: **www.cengage.com/international**.
Visit your local office: **www.cengage.com/global**.
Visit our corporate website: **www.cengage.com**.

Printed in the United States of America
1 2 3 4 5 6 7 16 15 14 13 12

To my clients and students

Contents

Preface

With the explosion of knowledge about childhood behavior disorders comes a heightened sense of responsibility to appreciate the problems these disorders create for children, their parents, and others who address these children. One goal of this casebook is to synthesize current thinking about childhood behavior disorders with the cases of specific children and their significant others, whether at home, school, or in other settings. My purpose is to show how the lives of the children and their families are both painful and disrupted on a daily basis.

Representing the Breadth of Children's Psychopathology

I present a wide variety of cases to illustrate the continuum of psychopathology in youth. The cases represent internalizing and externalizing disorders and mixed symptomatology (diagnoses?). Cases in Chapters 1, 14, and 15 purposely omit diagnoses so instructors can discuss possibilities. Instructors can access case solutions in a special supplement. A student can derive a clinical picture for each case by reading about symptoms, major assessment methods, risk factors and maintaining variables, developmental aspects, and treatment strategies. These sections represent types of information professionals find most important when addressing a particular case. Each case concludes with questions to stimulate student review or group discussion. The breadth of these cases is reflected as well by the fact that children's presenting symptoms often differ from DSM-IV-TR criteria and by substantial differences in treatment outcome.

Real Cases Can Be Used in Different Settings, in Different Ways

This casebook was primarily designed for undergraduate and beginning graduate students in psychology, but the text is written so people of other disciplines and interests may find the material useful and appealing. The cases are based on actual case histories or composites of cases seen by different mental health professionals. The names and some of the details of the cases were changed to protect the confidentiality of the people involved. Resemblances to actual people are coincidental because details were altered.

An Empirical Approach

This casebook generally reflects an empirical approach derived from a cognitive-behavioral-family systems orientation. This does not imply, however, that other forms of treatment are invalid for a certain population. An intricate combination of biological and other interventions is often needed to successfully resolve a particular case of child-based psychopathology.

About the Author

Christopher A. Kearney is Distinguished Professor of Psychology at the University of Nevada, Las Vegas. He is also the Director of the UNLV Child School Refusal and Anxiety Disorders Clinic in Las Vegas. Dr. Kearney received his B.A. from the State University of New York at Binghamton and his M.A. and Ph.D. from the State University of New York at Albany. He completed his internship at the University of Mississippi Medical Center. Dr. Kearney's research focuses primarily on the classification, assessment, and treatment of school refusal behavior and internalizing disorders in children and adolescents. He also works with adults with severe developmental disabilities. Dr. Kearney has authored several books on anxiety disorders and school refusal behavior in youth; in addition, he has written numerous journal articles and book chapters. Dr. Kearney is a Fellow of the American Psychological Association and the recipient of the Harry Reid Silver State Research Award and Distinguished Teaching Award from the University of Nevada, Las Vegas.

Chapter 1

Mixed Case One

Symptoms

Michael Rappoport was a 9-year-old European American male referred by his parents to an outpatient mental health clinic. Michael was in fourth grade at the time of his initial assessment. His parents, Mr. and Mrs. Rappoport, referred Michael for what they described as "difficult" and "unruly" behavior. During the telephone screening interview, Mrs. Rappoport said Michael was not listening to her or to his teacher, was failing subjects at school, and was occasionally aggressive toward his 5-year-old sister. She hinted that the family was experiencing conflict and financial problems since Mr. Rappoport lost his job several weeks before. The Rappoports were scheduled for an intake assessment session that week but the family either postponed or failed to show for their appointment three times before attending.

A clinical psychologist who specialized in childhood behavior disorders interviewed Michael and his parents separately. The psychologist interviewed Michael first and found him to be polite, social, and responsive to most questions. Michael went into detail about his pets, soccer team, and neighborhood friends. When asked why he thought he was at the clinic, however, Michael shrugged and said his parents did not like him very much. He said his parents often yelled at him and that his father "hits me when I'm bad." The psychologist asked Michael how his father hit him and how often this occurred, but Michael again shrugged and did not answer.

The psychologist then asked Michael about behaviors his parents considered bad. Michael said he would often run and hide in his room when his parents fought, which was often, and that his mother did not like running in the house. He was usually in trouble for failing to do his homework and for getting poor grades in school. Michael struggled with most of his subjects. He also said he and his little sister "didn't get along."

Michael complained his teachers "yell at me for everything." His teacher often reprimanded Michael for not staying in his seat, paying attention, or completing homework assignments. Michael said the work was too difficult for him,

1

especially reading assignments, and that he could not concentrate on them. He usually had to sit close to his teacher during the day because of these problems and often missed recess to complete past work.

The psychologist noticed, as the conversation turned to misbehavior, that Michael's mood became more downcast and his interaction with her more withdrawn. Michael cried at one point and said he often felt "lonely and sad." He felt deprived of time with friends at school and was embarrassed to bring his friends to his house to play. He was sad his parents often fought and worried about what would happen in the future. Michael denied thoughts about harming himself but did muse about what his parents would think if he were dead.

The psychologist concluded her initial interview with Michael by asking him what he would like to see different in his life. Michael said he wished his father were out of the house because of the constant fighting there. Michael said he wished he did better in school and could avoid trouble. The psychologist asked Michael as well if he wanted to feel differently but Michael simply shrugged.

The psychologist then interviewed Mr. and Mrs. Rappoport. The two were clearly irritated with one another. Mrs. Rappoport apologized for earlier scheduling postponements and indirectly blamed her husband. Mr. Rappoport rolled his eyes in response and said, "Let's get on with this." The psychologist asked both parents what brought them to the clinic. Mr. Rappoport shrugged but Mrs. Rappoport quickly listed a series of problems regarding Michael.

Mrs. Rappoport said Michael was "impossible to control." He was argumentative, boisterous, and noncompliant. Mrs. Rappoport complained that Michael would not listen to instructions and would often yell obscenities at her when she asked him to do something. Michael would also run around the house during a tantrum, which occurred almost every day. His tantrums – which included yelling, crying, and punching something – often occurred after parental commands or when Mr. and Mrs. Rappoport were "discussing something." Michael would often end up in his room or be spanked by his father after these tantrums. This did little to control his behavior, however. In addition, Michael was becoming aggressive with his 5-year-old sister – he was caught slapping the child on several occasions. Michael could no longer spend time alone with her.

Mrs. Rappoport said Michael was doing poorly at school. He was failing almost all subjects and had problems with reading and spelling. This was somewhat surprising because Michael had been a good student up to the middle of third grade (last year). Michael was difficult to control in the classroom, often throwing tantrums and complaining the work was too difficult. He often refused to do his homework and had to sit near his teacher so she could better monitor his behavior. Michael's academic problems and misbehavior grew so bad his teacher, Mrs. Greco, suggested a referral to special education. Mr. and Mrs. Rappoport strongly resisted this suggestion, however.

Mrs. Rappoport finished her comments about Michael by saying he was often sullen and sometimes "quirky" in his behavior. Michael would often cry when upset and withdraw to his room. He was also concerned about contracting

AIDS (acquired immune deficiency syndrome). One of Michael's classmates returned to class following a bout with hepatitis and this triggered a fear of AIDS and other diseases in Michael. He thus washed his hands about 10 times a day to prevent possible contagion.

The psychologist then asked Michael's parents about other family matters. Mrs. Rappoport again did most of the talking and said her husband recently lost his job and the family had financial problems. She admitted she and her husband fought "sometimes" but did not feel this led to Michael's behavior. She insisted that the focus of the interview and later therapy be on Michael, who was displaying the most problematic behavior. Despite several gently prodding questions, she and her husband did not provide more detail regarding their marriage or disciplinary style.

The psychologist spoke with Michael's teacher, Mrs. Greco, with parental permission. She said Michael had been a relatively good student during the first month of the year but that his grades and behavior worsened since then. Mrs. Greco said Michael was struggling with many of his assignments even though he was intelligent and could do the work easily if motivated. This seemed particularly true for assignments involving extensive reading and writing. Mrs. Greco said she never recommended Michael for special education, as claimed by Mr. and Mrs. Rappoport, but did feel that Michael's parents needed to take a more active role to address their son's academic problems. She also speculated that Michael's parents, who were difficult to address in their own right, were a primary cause of many of Michael's problems.

Mrs. Greco said Michael's misbehavior was becoming intolerable as well. She complained her student was often noncompliant, inattentive, and disruptive. She described how Michael refused to do assigned work by throwing papers, crying, and stomping his feet around the room. She thus sent him to the principal's office about once a week. Michael was overactive and needed reminders to sit in his seat. He demanded a substantial amount of attention from Mrs. Greco, who said her ability to attend to the rest of her class was suffering.

The psychologist felt Michael and his family had several problems that needed treatment. Michael had a combination of internalizing, externalizing, and academic problems. His family was marked by substantial conflict and intense life stressors. Potential abuse from corporal punishment was also an issue the psychologist believed she would have to explore further.

Assessment

The general purpose of assessment, or collection of information on children and their families in a clinical setting, is to answer three basic questions:

1. What is the behavior problem?
2. Why is the problem continuing to occur?
3. What is the best treatment for the problem?

These questions may seem straightforward but are sometimes difficult to answer. This is especially so in a complicated case like the Rappoports'.

The first question – What is the behavior problem? – might raise several additional questions. Is there an actual behavior problem that needs to be addressed? Was Michael referred for treatment because his behavior was truly abnormal or because he upset his parents and teacher? Some of his behaviors might be developmentally appropriate for a 9-year-old. What if a child's behavior problem understandably results from family variables such as conflict, disarray, abuse, or negative parent attitudes? What if the "behavior problem" lies more with the family than with the child? Michael's sadness may have been due to his parents' fighting. A psychologist does not automatically assume a child is the one who needs the bulk of attention during treatment.

Deciding upon the behavior problem can also be difficult if one person, such as a child, says no problem exists and other people, such as parents, disagree. A therapist should look for behaviors that clearly interfere with a child's daily functioning. Several of Michael's behaviors did so and therefore needed to be addressed. If a child does have behavior problems, then a decision must be made as to which behaviors are most severe and should be addressed first. Different symptoms from different disorders overlap in many youths referred for treatment. Michael certainly had several overt symptoms but his acting-out behaviors might have been linked to more serious internalizing problems, such as anxiety or depression.

The second question to be answered from an assessment – Why is the problem continuing to occur? – is fraught with difficulty as well. A therapist must determine what *maintains* each behavior problem in a child. These maintaining variables, as mentioned throughout this casebook, include sensory reinforcement, attention, escape from aversive situations, and tangible rewards such as money. Different variables maintain different behaviors, as may have been true for Michael. His tantrums and aggression toward his sister could be a way to get attention; his hand washing could be a way to escape or reduce worry about contamination; his noncompliance could be a way to solicit bribes from his parents.

These questions – What is the behavior problem? and Why is the problem continuing to occur? – refer to form and function of behavior. Knowing the form *and* function of a child's behavior makes answering the last major question easier; that is, What is the best treatment for the problem? Suppose Michael's most severe behavior problem was his tantrums at home and school (form). Eliminating this behavior problem might help reduce other behavior problems, such as general noncompliance. Suppose also that Michael's tantrums were motivated by attention from parents at home but escape from work at school (function). Michael's parents might wish to ignore his tantrums at home, but Michael's teacher might wish to work through his tantrums at school and not allow him to leave class.

Mental health professionals use various assessment methods to answer these questions; these methods are described in this casebook. Common methods include interviews; self-report and cognitive measures; self-monitoring; physiological and medical procedures; role-play; parent or family and teacher measures;

sociometric ratings; direct observation; and intelligence, achievement, and personality tests. A multidimensional approach to assessment is often necessary to evaluate different areas of functioning (e.g., social, academic, intellectual, emotional) that may be problematic.

Michael and his parents were administered versions of the Anxiety Disorders Interview Schedule for DSM-IV, a semistructured interview that covers various internalizing and externalizing disorders (Silverman & Albano, 1996; Silverman, Saavedra, & Pina, 2001). The psychologist diagnosed Michael with three disorders indicated in the *Diagnostic and Statistical Manual of Mental Disorders* (DSM-IV-TR) (American Psychiatric Association, 2000). One disorder involved an internalizing problem, the second involved an externalizing problem, and the third involved an academic problem. The psychologist rated each disorder as moderate to severe. Michael also endorsed fears of medically related stimuli (e.g., sickness, germs, hospitals, injections), social and evaluative situations (e.g., large crowds, being criticized), and parental arguing.

Michael completed self-report measures such as the Multidimensional Anxiety Scale for Children (MASC) and Revised Child Anxiety and Depression Scales (Chorpita, Moffitt, & Gray, 2005; March, 1997). Michael indicated he was often tearful, indecisive, shy, and unhappy in school. He worried about schoolwork, evaluations from others, the future, what his parents would say to him, and bad things happening to him. He had nightmares, trouble concentrating, and various somatic complaints such as feeling sick to his stomach. Michael believed terrible things would happen to him, that he was alone, and that he could never be as good as other kids. Michael seemed anxious and depressed about different areas of his life. Areas of most concern included his current family situation, medical status, social evaluations, and future events.

Michael's parents completed the Child Behavior Checklist (CBCL) (Achenbach & Rescorla, 2001), Family Environment Scale (FES) (Moos & Moos, 1986), Parental Expectancies Scale (PES) (Eisen, Spasaro, Brien, Kearney, & Albano, 2004), and Dyadic Adjustment Scale (DAS) (Spanier, 2001), which is a measure of general marital satisfaction. Mr. and Mrs. Rappoport endorsed high levels of attention problems and aggressive behaviors on the CBCL. They emphasized their son's impulsivity, nervousness, poor school performance, arguing, meanness, disobedience, screaming, temper tantrums, and demands for attention. They endorsed few internalizing symptoms. Mr. and Mrs. Rappoport rated their family as conflictive and detached on the FES and confirmed their high expectations that Michael should take much responsibility at home on the PES.

Mr. and Mrs. Rappoport indicated on the DAS that they frequently disagreed with one another in several areas, especially finances. They rarely had positive conversations with one another or showed affection. These responses contrasted somewhat with their verbal reports during their interview. The Rappoport family was clearly in distress but Mr. and Mrs. Rappoport continued to see Michael's externalizing behaviors as the main problem. They referred especially to his noncompliance and disruptive behavior.

Other assessment instruments in this case included the Teacher's Report Form (TRF) (Achenbach & Rescorla, 2001), a continuous performance test, and the Wechsler Intelligence Scale for Children (Wechsler, 2003). Michael's teacher, Mrs. Greco, completed the TRF and emphasized Michael's social and attention problems, especially his regressive behavior, crying, lack of concentration, impulsivity, disorganization, and underachievement. A continuous performance test, which measures impulsivity, indicated that Michael's speed of response resembled that of children with attention deficit/hyperactivity disorder (ADHD). Michael's intelligence test score was in the high average range, suggesting that his academic problems were not because of intellectual deficit. Michael was instead performing far below his ability.

The psychologist believed Michael had various behavior problems that were not well defined. Different functions maintained many of these problems as well. On top of all this, Michael's family situation involved marital tension, conflict, financial stress, and possible abuse. Any treatment program would thus likely have to involve the entire family and a complex strategy.

Risk Factors and Maintaining Variables

Several models have been proposed to explain causes of childhood behavior disorders. Psychodynamicists emphasize inborn sexual drives and intrapsychic personality conflicts as precursors to later psychopathology. Attachment theorists speculate that a caregiver's failure to provide for an infant's needs could lead to future psychopathology in that child. These models may have some relevance for youth but the validity of both remains an open question.

A more widely held etiological model, and one mentioned throughout this casebook, is a behavioral one. Behaviorists claim children learn or receive reinforcement for abnormal behaviors. Examples include parents who inadvertently reward noncompliance, family members who provide sympathy for depressive behaviors, and peers who reward delinquent behaviors. Social learning theorists propose that children imitate or model inappropriate behavior of others. Examples include increased child aggression following parental spanking and substance abuse after watching others drink alcohol or use illegal drugs.

Learning models did seem to apply to Michael's behaviors. Parental attention reinforced his aggression. Social learning triggered Michael's medical anxieties, fear of AIDS, and hand washing. Several of Michael's classmates discussed the student who had hepatitis, describing his hospital stay, isolation from others, injections, and constant need for cleanliness. Like many 9-year-olds, they exaggerated the stories. Michael took them seriously, however, and thus became fearful and compulsive in his hand washing.

Cognitivists believe child psychopathology relates to distorted thought processes that trigger or maintain behavior problems. Examples include anxiety and depression from irrational thoughts of negative evaluations from others and eating disorders maintained by irrational beliefs about beauty and weight loss. Affective theorists claim that some people have difficulty regulating their emotions and subsequently have trouble with motivation, behavior organization, or communication with others. Someone who was abused may experience ongoing anxiety or arousal from cues that remind her of the abuse and this may lead to posttraumatic stress disorder.

Distorted thought processes were not clearly an issue for Michael but he did worry about present and future events. His emotional state was excitable and Michael therefore had problems regulating his behavior. Because of his excitability and impulsivity, he had difficulty concentrating on his schoolwork, organizing materials, maintaining conversations with others, and controlling temper tantrums. These problems subsequently led to poor grades, feelings of isolation, and punishment for disruptive classroom behavior.

Child psychopathology clearly relates as well to biological factors. Biological risk factors include genetic predispositions, chromosomal aberrations, central nervous system changes, neurochemical imbalances, and stress and temperament. Evidence supports a genetic predisposition for several disorders, such as depression. Chromosomal aberrations such as Down syndrome often lead to moderate mental retardation. Central nervous system changes can lead to specific developmental disabilities such as learning disorder or pervasive disabilities such as autism. Neurochemical imbalances, stress, and difficult temperament influence problems as diverse as social anxiety and ADHD. A medical examination revealed no outstanding problems for Michael. Less obvious problems, such as subtle brain changes or ongoing stress, however, might partly explain his misbehaviors.

Family systems models may help explain childhood disorders that result from inconsistent parenting or family dysfunction. The Rappoports' ongoing conflict might have sparked Michael's behavior in several ways. The stress of the conflict could have triggered his sullenness, withdrawal, and isolation. His parents' verbal threats to one another regarding harm or divorce might have fueled Michael's worries about the future. Such depression and worry could then lead to difficulties in concentration, lack of motivation, and poor schoolwork. Mr. and Mrs. Rappoport's fighting also took time away from disciplining Michael for his behavior. Michael's tantrums and other disruptive behaviors were often ignored until they became severe.

Each of these models – psychodynamic, attachment, behavioral, social learning, cognitive, affective, biological, and family systems – holds that specific causal pathways lead to childhood behavior disorders. No one model successfully explains all aspects of a childhood disorder, however. The complexity of childhood disorders instead demands an integrative approach. Combinations of variables from these different perspectives, or multiple causal pathways, are needed to explain fully the etiology of a disorder. Different child, parent, peer, and teacher factors influenced Michael's behavior. The presence of multiple causal pathways suggests as well that successful treatment for children with behavior problems must involve many targets.

Developmental Aspects

Developmental psychopathology refers to study of antecedents and consequences of childhood behavior disorders and how the disorders compare to normal behavior development (Hudziak, 2008). An important task of developmental psychopathologists is to identify pathways that lead to normal development, mental disorder, or some fluctuation of the two in children. A developmental psychopathologist may wish to discover what child and family factors lead to depression. He or she might also want to know what factors prevent the development of depression, what factors help a person with depression return to mental health, and what factors maintain depression over time.

An important task in developmental psychopathology involves discovering whether childhood behavior problems are stable over time and whether they lead to problems in adulthood. Some childhood behavior problems are *very* stable over time. Consequently, they usually interfere with functioning in adulthood. Examples include autism, profound mental retardation, and aggressive forms of schizophrenia. Severe forms of late adolescent problems, such as conduct disorder or substance abuse, may carry into adulthood and create ongoing difficulties.

Other childhood behavior problems remain *fairly* stable over time. They may or may not lead to problems in adulthood depending on severity of the disorder and whether early intervention occurs. Examples include ADHD, learning disabilities, aggression, school refusal behavior, eating disorders, pediatric conditions, and effects from abuse.

Other childhood behavior problems tend to be *less* stable over time. These problems may dissipate but could still cause problems over time if aggravated by negative environmental events. Examples include fear, anxiety, depression, and elimination disorder.

Childhood behavior disorders may be stable over time but symptoms of the disorders may not remain the same. Children with ADHD tend to become less overactive as they mature, but ongoing restlessness and difficulty concentrating as well as lagging social development create other problems in adolescence. Similarly, a child who wants to coerce items from family members may do so using noncompliance in childhood but aggression in adolescence. A child behaviorally inhibited as a preschooler may avoid new social situations in childhood and become depressed in adolescence.

Symptom change was evident for Michael. His problem behaviors at age 9 years differed somewhat from his preschool days but some of his general behavior *patterns* remained the same. His parents described Michael as an "ornery" child who was fussy and who complained about what he had to eat. Mrs. Rappoport also said Michael was a "very sensitive child" who overreacted to criticism and inadvertent contact from others. These general characteristics were somewhat imbedded in Michael's current behavior problems. His temper tantrums were a regressive way of coping with stress and his sudden fear of disease was an overreaction to his classmates' stories. Michael's behaviors were different over time but his behavior patterns were somewhat stable.

Variables that help determine the stability of a childhood behavior problem involve proximal and distal factors (Mash & Dozois, 2003). Proximal factors are those close to a child that have more direct impact on his behavior, such as

1. development of a disorder early in life, especially one that affects language;
2. major changes in a child's brain or other physical status;

3. early and ingrained learning patterns;

4. strong biological predispositions triggered by early environmental events;

5. ongoing experiences that threaten a child's self-esteem and social and academic competence;

6. obstacles that lead a child to pursue more maladaptive behavior patterns.

Regarding the latter, obstacles such as family conflict or sexual abuse could initiate an adolescent's noncompliance or increased alcohol use.

Michael did not have major stressors or biological problems early in life. He did learn that one of the best ways to get parental attention, however, was to act inappropriately. Michael effectively trained his parents over time to give him attention when he was noncompliant, aggressive toward his sister, or problematic in school. In addition, Michael experienced several obstacles when he tried to build long-term friendships, such as loss of recess at school and discomfort bringing potential friends to his house. Lack of friendships then led to maladaptive behaviors such as social withdrawal and depressed mood.

Other factors that affect the stability of childhood behavior problems are distal ones, or those that indirectly affect a child. Distal factors include

1. poverty and/or homelessness;

2. marital conflict and/or inconsistent or neglectful parenting;

3. loss of a parent early in life;

4. severe family dysfunction;

5. general community disorganization.

Marital conflict was most pertinent to Michael. Some of Michael's tantrums were triggered by his parents' fighting or were done deliberately to get his parents to stop fighting.

Treatment

Treatment for the Rappoport family got off to a rough start. Mr. Rappoport became progressively more withdrawn and, after 3 weeks, stopped attending therapy. He did agree, however, to speak with the psychologist by telephone and to help his wife with therapy procedures. Mrs. Rappoport remained adamant about maintaining the focus of treatment on her son. The psychologist, in response, spent the first four sessions describing the family mechanisms behind many of Michael's behaviors and the necessity of including Mrs. Rappoport and Michael's teacher in therapy. Mrs. Rappoport reluctantly but eventually agreed to participate in therapy. She also agreed to consider the psychologist's recommendation that she and her husband pursue marital therapy.

During this 4-week period when Mrs. Rappoport considered her role in therapy, the psychologist worked with Michael to address his fear of disease and excessive hand washing. Michael was fully educated about the transmission of disease in general and of AIDS in particular. The psychologist focused on external causes and internal effects of illness, much to Michael's fascination. His self-reported anxiety regarding illness and general medical procedures declined somewhat during this time.

The psychologist then focused on Michael's hand washing that occurred when sitting next to someone who "looked sick." The psychologist first had Michael sit next to different people in the clinic's waiting area. He could wash his hands only if someone next to him sneezed. Otherwise, he entered the psychologist's office and did not wash for at least an hour. Michael saw that his anxiety declined without hand washing during this time. Michael was required to wait even longer before washing in subsequent sessions. He practiced waiting before hand washing in real-life settings as well. His response to this approach was immediate and positive. By the end of the 4-week period, he was washing his hands for a normal amount of time each day.

Mrs. Rappoport agreed to play a more active role in treatment but insisted that the first area of focus be on Michael's noncompliance, tantrums, and aggression. The psychologist explained that Michael often reacted to his parents' fighting by acting out, so Mrs. Rappoport and her husband agreed to hold their "discussions" in private as much as possible. Both parents were shown they waited too long to respond to Michael's misbehaviors. Instead, one parent or the other was to place Michael in time-out immediately for 10 minutes if he was noncompliant to a direction. The psychologist felt time-out was a good alternative punishment to spanking as well. Further assessment yielded no evidence of abuse but everyone agreed spanking was not a preferred option. Three weeks of therapy thus focused on using time-outs following noncompliance. Michael did heed his parents more, though he may have been compliant simply because of the extra attention he received.

Michael's tantrums also decreased during this period, suggesting again that reduced parental fighting and increased attention influenced his behavior. His aggression toward his sister worsened in this initial stage of therapy, however. The psychologist therefore recommended that Mr. and Mrs. Rappoport increase their supervision of Michael and his sister when they were together. Much of his aggression could thus be prevented. The psychologist did not recommend spanking for aggression because children often model this aggressive behavior. The psychologist instead advised Mr. and Mrs. Rappoport to ignore Michael after he hit his sister and give their daughter much sympathy and extra attention. This combination worked moderately well during the next 3 weeks.

At this time in therapy, Michael's parents separated and Mr. Rappoport left the house. Mrs. Rappoport continued to participate in Michael's treatment despite her depressed mood. The psychologist decided to provide support to Mrs. Rappoport and fine-tune therapy recommendations from previous sessions. Mrs. Rappoport would thus not be overwhelmed with new treatment responsibilities but would still be able to control Michael's behavior. Fortunately, Michael's response to his father's absence was not too negative because the two spent time together on the weekends. Michael also promised to help his mother with household chores because his father was no longer there to assist.

Given Mrs. Rappoport's emotional state, the psychologist focused more on Michael's school-related problems. This shift of focus let the psychologist spend about half the therapy time with Mrs. Greco, Michael's teacher, who graciously offered to attend. Mrs. Rappoport did not wish Michael medicated for his behavior so the psychologist established a token economy based on a card system. Michael received a warning for acting-out behavior; if he did not stop, he would have to change his card from green to yellow. If he continued to act out, he would receive another warning and then a red card. A red card meant Michael would have to spend the rest of the day doing his schoolwork in the principal's office. A green card for the entire day meant Michael could receive different prizes or classroom privileges.

Michael's acting-out behaviors did not change over a 5-week period. In addition, Mrs. Greco said the token economy was difficult for her to maintain consistently. Part of the problem was defining exactly what acting-out behaviors should be considered. The psychologist thus changed the focus of the token economy to Michael's academic behaviors. Michael was required to stay in the classroom regardless of his behavior; instead, Mrs. Greco rewarded or disciplined Michael primarily for amount of work completed. Unfortunately, Michael's homework performance or grades still did not change.

This lack of change may have been partly due to Michael's family situation, which worsened. Mr. and Mrs. Rappoport decided to divorce and Mr. Rappoport suddenly moved to a job in another state. Within 3 weeks, he was gone and had no face-to-face contact with Michael or other family members for some time. Michael went through a month-long period of sadness and lack of motivation regarding school, friends, and sports. He eventually rebounded to some extent when his father resumed direct contact with him but he remained uninterested in therapy.

Mrs. Rappoport and Michael attended therapy intermittently during the next 6 weeks. Eventually, despite urgings from the psychologist, Michael and his mother no longer visited the clinic. Mrs. Rappoport consulted with the psychologist occasionally by telephone over the next year and said the family situation and Michael's home behavior had stabilized. Michael's academic problems and school-related misbehaviors continued to some extent, however.

DISCUSSION QUESTIONS

1. Which of Michael's behaviors do you think were more "disturbed" and which do you think were more "disturbing" to his parents and teacher? Which of Michael's behavior "problems" might seem normal for a 9-year-old?

2. What were Michael's primary behavior problems? Identify five you consider most important and explain your reasoning. Three DSM-IV-TR diagnoses were assigned to Michael. Which ones do you think were most pertinent? Defend your answer.

3. In a case like Michael's, the family may be as problematic as the child. How would you explain to parents and others that their behavior must change if a child's behavior is to change? How would you convince a family to stay in treatment if you believed they could greatly benefit from doing so? Should you do so if family members say they are no longer interested in therapy? Why or why not?

4. A key goal for developmental psychopathologists is to identify pathways that lead to, and away from, mental disorder. Choose a childhood disorder or behavior problem and develop a causal model for it. Form a theory about why some children develop that particular problem and others do not. Discuss "protective" factors that help children avoid such misbehaviors. Outline factors that might move a child away from maladaptive behavior or improve her prognosis for the future.

5. Outside of Rappoport family members and Michael's teacher, which people might be important for addressing Michael's behavior problems? What would you want to ask or say to these people? Why?

Chapter 2

Social Anxiety and Withdrawal

Symptoms

Bradley Mavin was a 12-year-old European American male referred to a specialized clinic for youths with social anxiety and withdrawal. Bradley was in seventh grade at the time of his initial assessment. His stepfather and mother, Mr. and Mrs. Nelson, referred Bradley to the clinic after reading a newspaper advertisement calling for participants in a group therapy project. The project involved testing an assessment and treatment protocol for youths with social problems. During the telephone screening interview, Mrs. Nelson said Bradley was having trouble adjusting to his new middle school and seemed depressed and withdrawn. He also seemed upset about her recent divorce and remarriage. Bradley was thus missing more school than usual and his grades were suffering.

An advanced doctoral student in clinical child psychology interviewed Bradley during the intake session. Bradley was initially cautious and unsure of himself, avoiding eye contact and speaking softly. The doctoral student, who had experience with shy and socially anxious children, first talked to Bradley about various topics Bradley seemed to enjoy. These topics included his pets, school projects, and sisters. Bradley seemed more relaxed following this development of rapport. The student then questioned Bradley about his recent social problems.

Bradley said his new middle school was quite different from the elementary school he had been in since kindergarten. He said many of his friends from elementary school now went to a different middle school, so he did not know many people at his current location. He wanted to transfer to the other middle school to be with his old friends. Bradley claimed that few of his new classmates spoke to him or invited him for lunch or other activities. The interviewer discovered, however, that Bradley rarely initiated contact with others in school. Bradley said he "hated" physical education class where everyone "made fun of him" for his size; he was slightly smaller than his peers. He generally felt lonely, sad, and "left out."

Bradley also complained about oral presentations in his English class, an assignment he never had before. He said his first oral presentation went badly.

He was supposed to give a presentation on the history of automobiles but became anxious when asked to stand before his classmates. Bradley said he trembled and had trouble breathing, which made his hands and voice shake noticeably. He saw some of his classmates snicker and decided then not to give another presentation. Unfortunately, he was required to give three other presentations; not doing so would result in a failing grade.

Bradley started refusing school because of these experiences. He began by occasionally skipping his physical education class but in the past month missed 1–2 full days of school per week. Bradley would stay home, do homework, and watch television when skipping school. He had already asked his parents to transfer him to a new middle school or place him in home schooling.

The interview then focused on other areas of Bradley's social life. Bradley said he was active with neighborhood friends but avoided anyone new. He had a good relationship as well with his mother and two sisters. His relationship with his stepfather was strained, however. Bradley said his stepfather was strict and was not afraid to spank him for various offenses. His stepfather was livid about his refusal to go to school and his parents often fought about this issue. They immediately called the number in the newspaper when they saw it was for children with social problems.

Mr. and Mrs. Nelson largely confirmed Bradley's report during their interview. Mrs. Nelson said Bradley was a well-behaved son until about 2 years ago when she and her first husband separated (Bradley's biological father was currently out of state and had no contact with the family). Bradley then became withdrawn and unwilling to play with other children in his neighborhood. Contrary to Bradley's report, he still avoided many of his old neighborhood friends and spent much of his free time doing homework or playing video games. He did participate in family dinners and outings but generally preferred to stay close to his mother and sisters.

Mrs. Nelson said Bradley's situation worsened during the past 3 months. She confirmed Bradley's fears about his physical education class and oral presentations and agreed he made few, if any, new friends. She also confirmed that Bradley wanted to be placed in home schooling and she was about to do so when she saw the clinic's advertisement. Mrs. Nelson then decided Bradley might benefit more from therapy than home schooling and she wanted the advice of clinic staff members on this matter.

Mrs. Nelson said Bradley was an excellent student who was generally shy. He enjoyed working on his school projects as much as other kids enjoyed playing baseball. He was a "loner" who rarely interacted with other children his age and who preferred to play with his two younger sisters. Otherwise, he was a normal child who was compliant, polite, and dutiful regarding his household responsibilities.

Mr. Nelson added that his relationship with Bradley was difficult and that the two "just didn't seem to connect." Mr. Nelson was adamant about Bradley's return to school but deferred to his wife when she recommended therapy. He said he wanted to help Bradley with his problems but was not sure he could. Mr. Nelson hoped therapy would help Bradley become more self-confident and improve their relationship.

The therapist secured Mr. and Mrs. Nelson's permission to interview Bradley's teachers at school. All said Bradley was a fine student with excellent potential but was shy and withdrawn. Bradley's English teacher, Mrs. Arnot, said her student did well on all assignments up to the oral reports. His first oral report had not gone badly but Bradley clearly had physical symptoms of anxiety. She said she had a strict class rule that students could not make jokes or laugh when anyone gave an oral report, and no one did during Bradley's report. Bradley approached her after class and cried profusely, however, asking to be relieved of his remaining oral presentations.

Bradley's physical education teacher echoed this report but said Bradley was teased to some extent. The teacher said Bradley needed to "grow up," interact more with other kids, and become more assertive. Conversations with Bradley's other teachers and guidance counselor confirmed that Bradley avoided many social situations, especially those that required meeting new people, working cooperatively with others, and performing before an audience. The therapist preliminarily concluded that Bradley was moderately socially withdrawn and met criteria for social phobia/social anxiety disorder.

Assessment

The essential feature of social phobia or social anxiety disorder is a "marked and persistent fear of social or performance situations in which embarrassment may occur" (American Psychiatric Association, 2000, p. 450). Social functioning with people known to the person, such as family members, is good, but social fear occurs when a person interacts with unknown others or during situations where the person might feel negatively evaluated, humiliated, or embarrassed. The person usually has a panic attack or panic symptoms when exposed to social situations. Children may display "crying, tantrums, freezing, or shrinking from social situations with unfamiliar people" (p. 456). Those with social phobia, though not necessarily children, recognize their fear as unreasonable and endure social situations with great distress if they cannot avoid them. The disorder must significantly interfere with daily functioning, last at least 6 months, and not be due to a medical condition or substance. Social phobia is generalized if most social situations are feared.

Bradley appeared to meet these criteria. He was fearful and anxious when meeting new people and was reportedly "nervous and sick" in large social situations. Bradley was uncomfortable in situations involving close evaluation from others, such as physical education class and oral presentations. Bradley reported nausea and trembling during these situations and was convinced that others could see him become upset. His level of social anxiety and withdrawal thus interfered with his academic functioning. Bradley's social interactions with his family and relatives were appropriate, however.

The assessment of youths with social anxiety typically includes interviews, self-report measures, self-monitoring, parent and teacher measures, and perhaps physiological evaluation. Therapists often use several measures because results from them do not always highly correlate. A child may report no cognitive symptoms of anxiety in stressful situations but still have substantial physiological arousal.

Semistructured interviews for children with anxiety disorders include the Anxiety Disorders Interview Schedule for DSM-IV (see Chapter 1). Clinicians often use this interview in research settings to identify anxiety symptoms and other pertinent problems in children and adolescents. Bradley's therapist worked in a specialized research clinic and used this interview.

The interview has questions regarding concerns about evaluations by others and feelings of embarrassment or shame in social situations. Therapists ask a child about level of fear in social situations such as answering a question in class, taking a test, eating before others, and dating. Fear of these situations is rated on a 0–8 scale, where 8 represents greatest amount of fear. In addition, questions are raised about whether a child's social fear declines when certain (e.g., younger) people are present and how much social anxiety interferes with daily functioning.

Bradley said he was afraid he would do something stupid or clumsy in different social situations, especially when meeting new people or performing before others. He was concerned as well about snickering from others and feeling embarrassed at these times. Bradley identified social situations that made him feel most nervous: oral reports, physical education class, eating in the cafeteria, starting or maintaining conversations, and answering questions in class.

The assessment of youths with social anxiety can include self-report measures such as the Social Anxiety Scale for Children-Revised (La Greca, 1998; Sanna et al., 2009) and Social Phobia and Anxiety Inventory for Children* (Beidel, Turner, & Morris, 2000). Sample items from the latter include,

1. I feel scared when I have to join in a social situation with a large group of boys and girls.
2. I feel scared when I meet new kids.
3. I am too scared to ask questions in class.
4. I leave social situations (parties, school, playing with others) where there are boys or girls my age that I don't know.
5. When I am someplace (a party, school, soccer game, or anyplace where I will be with others), my heart beats fast.

Bradley's self-rated symptoms included worry when doing something before others, worry about being teased, worry about what others thought of him, nervousness when talking to others not well known to him, feelings of shyness, feelings others were making fun of him, and difficulty asking others to play.

Bradley's therapist asked him to self-monitor several behaviors. Bradley was asked to write down social situations during the day that caused him to feel nervous or sick. He rated, on a 0–10 scale, how nervous and sad he felt during these

---

situations. The therapist further described various thoughts Bradley might have during these situations and asked him to record these as well. Bradley also noted other concerns he had during the day.

Over a 2-week period, Bradley's self-monitoring revealed two main findings:

1. His social anxiety was highest when he entered school, went from class to class, and ate lunch in the cafeteria. He did not rate his physical education and English classes as highly anxious *unless* he had to perform individually before others.

2. Bradley's thoughts during unpleasant social situations were somewhat distorted. He believed others often watched him closely and evaluated him negatively. More darkly, Bradley thought others plotted to "gang up on him" and steal his books and other materials.

Therapists commonly use parent and teacher measures to evaluate children with social anxiety, most notably the Child Behavior Checklist and Teacher's Report Form (Achenbach & Rescorla, 2001). Mr. and Mrs. Nelson noted their son's clinging, clumsiness, preference for younger playmates, and teasing by others. Bradley's English teacher, Mrs. Arnot, recorded Bradley's crying and hurt feelings during evaluative situations. Physiological assessments such as heart rate and sweat indices are sometimes used to assess youths with social anxiety but not in Bradley's case.

The assessment of children who are socially withdrawn can include sociometric measurement and direct observation. Sociometric measurement involves soliciting peer ratings of a child suspected of being rejected or neglected (Poulin & Dishion, 2008). Sociometrics may include nominations, as when children simply list names of classmates they would most or least like to work and play with. In addition, teachers or children can give general rankings of each child in a classroom. This is done to identify one particular child's level of popularity and social interaction. Paired rankings, where each child is directly compared to every other child, may also be examined. Sociometric measures are done carefully, though, so children are not singled out for further rejection. Sociometric measures were not solicited in Bradley's case, however.

Bradley's therapist instead conducted a direct observation of her client during selected times at school. Bradley knew the therapist would come to school to observe him but did not know when. The therapist observed Bradley during lunchtime and outside during his physical education class. The therapist noticed that Bradley generally stood alone, rebuffed interactions from others, and seemed emotionally depressed. The therapist confirmed that Bradley was anxious in these situations and lacked some basic social interaction skills.

Risk Factors and Maintaining Variables

Many factors likely lead to anxiety and withdrawal in youth, perhaps involving a combination of biological vulnerability, family factors, stressful life events, and child characteristics (Hayward et al., 2008). Studies indicate a genetic contribution to social anxiety in twins and the risk for social phobia is greater for relatives of someone with the disorder than the general population (Stein & Stein, 2008). Genetic data may partly reflect an environmental factor, however: how anxious parents raise anxious children.

Family factors do seem to have a strong influence on the development of social anxiety and withdrawal in children. Anxious children tend to model perceptions of environmental threat from their parents (Kashdan & Herbert, 2001). They watch the carefulness, caution, and avoidance shown by their parents and imitate the behavior in their social situations. This seemed true for Bradley. His mother was a shy and reserved woman who reportedly enjoyed the traditional role of wife and mother. Much of her social life involved her husband and children and she infrequently associated with others. She appeared anxious when meeting new clinic staff members. Bradley may have adopted many of his mother's withdrawn, anxiety-based social interaction behaviors.

Other family variables related to social anxiety in children include overprotection, lack of parental warmth, and disrupted attachment (Bogels & Brechman-Toussaint, 2006; Knappe et al., 2009). Bradley's mother was clearly overprotective, often demanding to know where her son was at different times of the day and even picking out his clothes in the morning. She kept him physically close to her when shopping or working outside. Bradley's relationship with his mother was affectionate, however, and his early attachment with her was secure. He had more difficulty getting along with his stepfather, as was the case with his biological father, but this did not seem too relevant to his current social anxiety or withdrawal.

Children with anxiety disorders may have parents with anxiety disorders, depression, or substance abuse. Bradley's biological father had alcoholism and possible depression. Bradley's mother said she felt depressed and would retire to her room when "down in the dumps." Bradley perhaps modeled this behavior in addition to that of others noted earlier.

Various stressful life events, especially those related to social trauma, can influence the development of anxiety and withdrawal. Bradley experienced recent trouble during his oral reports and physical education class. Discussions with Bradley and his mother revealed, however, that Bradley's friendships generally declined in number since fourth grade. Events at that time disrupted Bradley's friendships. Many of his early school-age friends moved out of town when its main industry relocated. In addition, others teased Bradley in first and second grade for occasional wetting.

Precursors to child social anxiety and withdrawal include child characteristics such as social apprehension, feelings of uncontrollability, and behavioral inhibition (Kearney, 2005). Many children such as Bradley expect the worst possible outcome in social situations. When faced with social or evaluative situations, Bradley complained that others were out to harm him or did not like him. He was convinced that peers would ridicule his oral presentation even though no evidence supported this belief. Bradley said he did not ask others to play or work with him because they would "probably push me or steal my stuff."

Children with social anxiety often report feelings of uncontrollability as well. This refers to a general sense of learned helplessness whereby children feel their actions will have little impact on their environment. This may help explain why many children with anxiety have symptoms of depression. Bradley displayed uncontrollability when he said it was pointless to start conversations with others or relax when speaking in class. In addition, the therapist saw that Bradley often stayed by himself and walked with his head down. This behavior suggested that Bradley did not think he could make a positive change in his social situations.

Child social anxiety and withdrawal closely relates as well to behavioral inhibition, which is a type of temperament marked by high arousal and withdrawal from new situations, including social ones. Behavioral inhibition affects about 10–15% of children and may relate to various childhood anxiety disorders (Hirshfeld-Becker et al., 2008). This is so because the temperament is associated with escape, avoidant, dependent, and passive behaviors. Bradley clearly showed these behaviors. He was timid and shy in situations involving people outside his family and withdrew quickly from unfamiliar situations. He seemed dependent on his mother for emotional support and was relatively unassertive.

Various factors thus conspire to cause social anxiety and withdrawal in children. The problem often begins with an irritable, withdrawn temperament and a moderate biological vulnerability to high arousal. As the child grows, negative social events may predispose him to develop a sense of learned helplessness or uncontrollability about the surrounding environment. These events may trigger high biological arousal. The person may then become socially apprehensive as he scans his environment for potential threats. The person then avoids more and more social situations (Kearney, 2005).

Several factors can maintain social anxiety or withdrawal. A child may complain to his parents about social mistreatment at school and receive positive attention. Such attention may be in the form of sympathy, verbal praise, or physical affection. Conversely, a child may wish to escape different situations that involve added work or stress, such as helping a parent at a party. Claims of social anxiety and negative physical symptoms such as a stomachache might help get a child out of certain responsibilities (Kearney & Drake, 2002). Attention-seeking and escape-motivated behaviors were evident in Bradley's case.

Developmental Aspects

One of the core aspects of social anxiety and withdrawal – behavioral inhibition – has a moderately stable course (Hirshfeld-Becker et al., 2008). Inhibited or temperamentally difficult infants often show irregular eating and sleeping patterns, withdrawal from novel situations, poor adaptability, irritable mood, and intense reactions to aversive stimuli, such as loud noises. Conversely, less inhibited or temperamentally "easy" infants have more positive mood and good adaptability.

These characteristics – inhibition and adaptability – remain core aspects of an individual's personality with age. Inhibited children tend to become more shy, fearful of others, cautious, and introverted during preschool years. They can become quieter and cling to adults more over time. This is especially so when new social situations arise. Inhibited children may show more adverse physiological arousal such as increased heart rate and emotional reactivity in these situations than adaptable children (Kagan, 2001).

One developmental model of social withdrawal indicates that these early inhibitions make some school-age children more hesitant to explore new social situations outside the home (Rubin, Burgess, Kennedy, & Stewart, 2003). This reluctance negatively affects normal play and prevents a child from acquiring social and cognitive skills necessary for advanced social relationships. A child thus becomes more anxious during social interactions, avoids them, and feels isolated. Recognizing this social failure, a child may develop a sense of insecurity and poor self-esteem. He may be predisposed to develop conditions such as separation or social anxiety disorder.

Mrs. Nelson said Bradley was a somewhat "fussy" baby but not one who was overly difficult to care for. She said Bradley played appropriately with others during preschool and was never aggressive. She did recall that Bradley's preschool teachers said he was shy, however, and waited for others to approach him before he would interact. Exceptions included adults, whom Bradley liked more than peers. This was demonstrated by his excessive politeness, compliance, and sensitivity to adult feedback. Mrs. Nelson admitted that her marital problems sometimes led her to be overprotective and emotionally dependent on her son. She often kept him physically close to her.

Mrs. Nelson reported some separation anxiety on Bradley's part during elementary school but this faded over time. Of greater concern were her marital problems that worsened and caused great disruption in the family. These problems intensified after the arrival of Bradley's two younger sisters. Mrs. Nelson admitted that her husband's failure to help her with the children caused her to rely more on Bradley, who became responsible for some of the feeding, laundry, and housecleaning chores. Time that might have been spent developing friendships was instead put toward fulfilling family responsibilities. These stressful family events reinforced the emotional bond and dependence between Bradley and his mother.

These patterns deepened during Bradley's later elementary school years. Mrs. Nelson divorced her husband and shifted even more household responsibility onto Bradley. Bradley then relied more on his schoolwork as a source of self-esteem, which took time away from church group activities, participation in sports, and other social events. The therapist thought Bradley lost some opportunities to build better social skills during this time and had trouble understanding how to approach others or how to maintain conversations.

The developmental aspects of specific play behaviors may have important ramifications for treating socially anxious and withdrawn children. Very young children are highly egocentric, adult focused, and rule oriented. Cooperation, sharing, and appreciation of others become more evident during the later preschool period, however. A child playing a game learns to wait for another child to take her turn before proceeding. These behaviors are often the foundation of later social skills development, so treatment for socially withdrawn children may be crucial at this time.

The successful development of these early play behaviors may link to later social behaviors such as delaying immediate gratification, listening to others, appreciating the viewpoint of others, understanding the concept of friendship, solving problems without aggression, communicating effectively, and being assertive. Children who lack these skills are likely to become deficient in social relationships and perhaps require treatment. Bradley's self-discipline and conversational skills with adults were well developed but his understanding of peer relationships was not. He was not very knowledgeable about how many friends most people had or even how friendships developed in the first place. He did not link the development of friendships to better quality of life. Bradley's communication skills with peers, especially his articulation, needed improvement as well.

Gender differences appear for play and social behaviors as well. Preschool boys are more likely to play with transportation toys but girls prefer dolls. Girls are more likely to play with toys traditionally thought of as masculine or feminine but boys prefer primarily masculine toys. Boys tend to be more physically active and spend more time outdoors than girls, which leads to competitive but more frequent and durable social contacts (Alexander, 2003; Martin & Ruble, 2004). Bradley often stayed indoors or close to home during his preschool and elementary school years. This may have prevented some peer social contacts. Bradley's social profile was more traditionally feminine as well. He was meeker, more adult oriented, and more attracted to solitary activities than most boys. The therapist thought these characteristics contributed to Bradley's rejection by male peers.

What about the long-term development of a child with social anxiety or withdrawal? Social isolation and poor social skills development relate to various problems in adolescence, such as depression, negative self-esteem, and loneliness (Rubin et al., 2003). Other possible consequences include substance abuse, ongoing academic and occupational difficulties, and increasingly poor interpersonal relationships. However, a warm family environment, academic competence, and perceptions that one is sufficiently involved in social activities can mediate these long-term effects. Bradley showed some of these mediators, which could blunt some ill effects of his early social withdrawal. His academic prowess and family support may allow him to become a late bloomer and develop lasting friendships in high school and college.

Treatment

Therapists who treat a socially anxious or withdrawn child often note whether the problem is due to (1) lack of social skills or (2) social anxiety that blocks the display of already developed social skills. Bradley originally attended group therapy for his social skills. His immediate problem was social phobia and school refusal behavior, however, so Bradley first began individual therapy to address his anxiety in specific situations.

Therapy for youths with social anxiety often involves exposure to anxiety-provoking social situations and building skills to cope with or reduce anxiety. Clinicians may also use cognitive therapy to help youths think more realistically in social situations. A common strategy is to build a "social hierarchy" or list of specific interactive situations a person avoids. These situations are arranged in order from least to most anxiety provoking (Garcia-Lopez et al., 2006). Bradley listed four situations: entering the cafeteria to buy and eat lunch, participating in physical education class, meeting new people, and giving an oral presentation (the last being the most aversive).

A child then addresses each item on the social hierarchy in the therapeutic setting, beginning with the lowest anxiety-provoking item. Bradley's first item involved his cafeteria behaviors. Bradley discussed his fears about this setting, including dropping food, going too slowly in line, not having enough money to pay the cashier, and being stared at while eating. The therapist first helped Bradley identify thoughts that had no basis. The therapist asked Bradley if any of the "in-line" behaviors he mentioned happened before. They had not. The therapist thus demonstrated that Bradley did not have enough evidence for his thought and should develop a more realistic one. Bradley then said he might drop some food or fail to have enough money but agreed this was unlikely. The therapist pointed out that Bradley rarely looked at anyone while eating and therefore should not expect others to look at him. To confirm this, the therapist took Bradley to a local cafeteria to show him that no one else watched him eat.

The therapist then addressed more difficult items on Bradley's hierarchy. Bradley discussed his fears of physical education class and oral reports, which were remarkably similar: he believed others unfairly dismissed him or made rude comments about his performance. Regarding physical education class, Bradley complained about not being picked for a team even though he was good athletically. Regarding English class, he complained his classmates ignored him or belittled his oral report. The therapist pointed out Bradley's tendency to overestimate others' harsh evaluations and criticism, as he did in the cafeteria setting. She pointed out as well that Bradley's self-imposed withdrawal perhaps made other children wary or avoidant of him.

The therapist asked Bradley to approach more classmates in his physical education class and ask to be picked for a team before class. The therapist helped Bradley practice different lines of conversation to introduce himself and tell people of his skill in a particular area, such as basketball. With Bradley's permission, the therapist contacted the physical education teacher to ask whether Bradley could make team selections more often and assume a leadership role when possible. Bradley adapted well to this new situation and his anxiety during physical education class diminished sharply.

A greater concern was Bradley's refusal to do another oral report. The therapist instructed Bradley to give a series of oral reports to her in the office. This first consisted of reading newspaper and magazine articles. The therapist later assigned brief reports on a topic Bradley had to research. The therapist gave Bradley extensive feedback on his presentation skills during these reports, especially his voice projection, eye contact with the audience, enunciation of syllables, and control of physical anxiety symptoms. Bradley learned to tense and release different muscle groups that were most problematic during his talks. These included tense facial and jaw muscles as well as trembling legs.

Bradley's oral presentation skills in the office were good after frequent therapy sessions in a 1-month period. His therapist then subjected Bradley to a greater audience of unknown people, some of whom were told beforehand to engage in distractions such as sighing, not paying attention, and snickering. Bradley found these distractions upsetting at first but subsequently worked through them and gave his reports without much trouble. The therapist used cognitive techniques so Bradley would not "catastrophize" the situation. Bradley eventually acknowledged, after watching his classmates, that not all of them laughed during the oral presentations. He also saw, with the therapist and teacher's help, that when people did laugh the consequences were not dreadful. Bradley then gave his oral reports in class (the teacher had graciously delayed his remaining reports until last). Bradley gave three reports in a 3-day period and, though his performance was just fair, his anxiety did decline with each presentation. Bradley was able to resume full-time school attendance.

Bradley later participated in group therapy with other children with social skill deficits and social withdrawal. The main purpose was to build Bradley's skills for meeting new people. Group therapy members learned to approach someone and introduce themselves. Group members turned to the one on their left, looked that person in the eye, said hello and their name, and offered a handshake. Many group members found this anxiety provoking but all did at least a fair job. They developed other skills over time, such as the ability to maintain a conversation, compliment others, exit a social situation with grace, and control physical anxiety symptoms. The group also engaged in social outings to practice their skills in real-life settings. Each group member was further assigned the task of joining two social activities in their church, school, or neighborhood.

Group therapy for people with social anxiety and withdrawal has two primary advantages: (1) discovering others have a similar problem and (2) social support. Both advantages were comforting to Bradley, and two members of his group became his good friends. Following a 6-month therapy program, Bradley improved substantially in specific areas of concern, such as speaking before others and maintaining a conversation. He remained somewhat shy overall and still avoided some social situations when anxious. He thus attended several booster sessions over the next 2 years. Bradley's overall social functioning was determined to be fair to good by the end of this time.

DISCUSSION QUESTIONS

1. What differentiates children who are (a) naturally shy, (b) socially anxious, (c) socially withdrawn, (d) neglected, or (e) rejected? Explore family and peer factors as well as child characteristics.

2. What characteristics make one child more "popular" than others?

3. Was Bradley's social anxiety and withdrawal due primarily to personal or family factors? How could a parent encourage more appropriate social

behaviors in a child? What activities would be most effective to help a child develop positive social skills? What social skills are most important for a child to have?

4. What gender expectations do we generally have regarding child social behavior? Explore activities often considered "off limits" for boys and girls. How might this harm the development of social skills?

5. What aspects of your own social behavior do you wish you could improve? What might be the best way to do so? How would you enlist the help of others? How might you help someone who is shy but wants to be more socially active?

6. How might you respond to a child who has no friends but says she does not care?

7. How might you address a child who decided to join a gang or hang out with the "wrong crowd"? What are advantages and disadvantages of this social behavior?

8. What might you have added to Bradley's treatment program? How might you have included his family members in treatment? How might you improve Bradley's social relationship with his stepfather?

9. What could be done in schools to help children with social anxiety or withdrawal?

Chapter 3

Depression

Symptoms

Anna Thompson was a 16-year-old African American female referred to the adolescent unit of an inpatient psychiatric hospital. Her mother, Mrs. Thompson, referred Anna after discovering her daughter bleeding from her wrists in her bedroom. The amount of blood was not substantial but Mrs. Thompson brought Anna to a hospital emergency room for treatment. The attending physician said Anna was not seriously injured but recommended commitment to an inpatient psychiatric hospital for evaluation. Mrs. Thompson consented to a short-term commitment of her daughter given Anna's recent depressive behaviors. A psychiatrist who specialized in adolescent behavior disorders interviewed Anna the next day.

Anna was initially hesitant about talking and angry with her mother for committing her. She was more forthcoming after some initial discussion, however. Anna said she recently moved to a new school following her mother's divorce and that no one seemed to like her. She was upset about being in the racial minority and having few friends. When asked if a specific recent event upset her, Anna said she felt other teenagers made derogatory remarks about her weight as she ate alone during lunch (Anna was quite overweight). Anna could not be more specific, however, so whether remarks were actually made about her was unclear.

Anna said the past 13 months had been difficult. Her parents separated and eventually divorced following some marital conflict. For reasons Anna did not completely understand, her mother moved out of state with Anna and separated her from her father and 13-year-old brother. This was traumatic for Anna because she was close to her father and brother but could no longer contact them. Anna enrolled in her new school in August and began attending in September. She missed about one-third of school days in the first 2 months, however, and had not attended in the past 2 weeks. Anna said she was lonely because her mother often worked and because she had no new friendships.

Anna's mood had worsened over the past 2 weeks. She greatly missed her entire family and complained she could not spend Thanksgiving with her father and brother (her mother already said this was impossible). She thus became less active, lying around the house, watching television, and chatting online. She had left the house only twice in the past week and was overeating and oversleeping. Her mother worked a lot and had not talked to Anna much in the past 2 weeks. When they did converse, she tried to persuade Anna to go back to school.

The psychiatrist then raised the topic of Anna's injuries from the day before. Anna said she was feeling bad and wondered what it would be like if she committed suicide. She wondered how her family would feel and who would come to her funeral. She said she was not optimistic about the future and that suicide sometimes seemed preferable to living. Anna insisted, however, that her behavior was not an actual suicide attempt. She claimed she made a few scrapes with a butter knife to see what would happen. She did get herself to bleed but did not feel her injuries were serious (the medical report confirmed Anna's statements). Anna said her mother came into her room, saw blood, and "freaked out." Anna's mother told her to get into the car and enter the emergency room. The attending physician asked about her injuries and Anna told him truthfully what happened. She was then transferred to her current unit with a person sitting outside her room to watch her.

The psychiatrist asked Anna if she had current thoughts about harming herself, and Anna said no. She said again she had not wanted to kill herself the day before and that she now wanted to leave the unit. She also asked to see her mother and was told she would see her that evening. Anna promised the psychiatrist not to harm herself and to speak with him immediately if she had suicidal thoughts or impulses. The psychiatrist gave Anna a mild sedative and she slept for the remaining afternoon.

The psychiatrist later interviewed Anna's mother, Mrs. Thompson, who provided more information about the family situation. Mrs. Thompson said she and her husband had many past arguments about several issues, most notably his alcohol use and the family's financial status. The last straw came, however, when Mrs. Thompson caught her husband leaning over Anna as she slept. Mrs. Thompson suspected Anna's father of sexual abuse, though this was unproven. Anna denied this in conversations with her mother, but Mrs. Thompson felt she and Anna should leave the state. Mrs. Thompson said she parted company with her son as well because he was unruly and because they had a poor relationship.

Mrs. Thompson confirmed some of Anna's reports with respect to recent events. She confirmed she was busy at work and unable to devote the kind of attention to Anna her daughter was used to. The two did share time together on the weekends, however, though not in the past 3 weeks, and had good rapport. Mrs. Thompson confirmed that she and Anna had little contact with Anna's father and brother. This would include, she said, the upcoming holiday season.

Mrs. Thompson verified that Anna missed a lot of school in the past 2 months and did not make new friends. Both women were concerned about Anna's weight, and Mrs. Thompson knew this was a major source of embarrassment and frustration for her daughter. Despite these situations, Mrs. Thompson said she was shocked to find Anna bleeding in her bedroom. Mrs. Thompson never considered the possibility of suicide, but the apparent seriousness of the situation led her to agree to the inpatient commitment.

The psychiatrist spoke with Anna's guidance counselor at school with Mrs. Thompson's permission. The counselor, Mrs. Deetz, was upset about Anna's condition and said Anna commented about suicide 1 month earlier. Anna came to Mrs. Deetz's office and complained that students in her physical education class ridiculed her weight. Anna cried, complained she could not make friends, and said, "I wish I was dead." Mrs. Deetz then changed Anna's schedule so she would not have to attend that particular physical education class. She also made several recommendations regarding extracurricular activities but Anna dismissed them because she would be in the racial minority. Mrs. Deetz insisted, however, that Anna's concerns about social rejection were unfounded. She remained concerned about Anna and offered to assist the psychiatrist in any way possible.

The psychiatrist reinterviewed Anna the next day to confirm she had no current suicidal thoughts or impulses. He placed her on a low dose of antidepressant medication and asked her to attend group therapy sessions that morning and evening. Anna agreed and the psychiatrist noted that her mood improved somewhat from the day before. Given information received so far, however, the psychiatrist suspected Anna just experienced a major depressive episode and should remain on suicide watch.

Assessment

The essential feature of a major depressive episode is "a period of at least two weeks during which there is either depressed mood or loss of interest or pleasure in nearly all activities" (American Psychiatric Association, 2000, p. 349). The mood in children and adolescents may be irritable rather than sad. A person must experience five of the following symptoms during a 2-week period to qualify for the disorder: constant depressed mood, lack of interest in previously enjoyable activities, significant weight loss or gain, difficulty sleeping or oversleeping each day, restlessness or feeling slowed down, daily fatigue, feelings of inappropriate guilt or worthlessness, difficulty concentrating or making decisions, and suicidal thoughts or attempts. The symptoms must cause significant interference in daily functioning and must not be due to substance use, a medical condition, or an understandable reaction to life events, such as death of a family member.

Many of these symptoms applied to Anna. Her mood over the past month was depressed and she rarely initiated activities for fun. She did not show appreciable weight gain but was overeating and oversleeping. This latter activity – hypersomnia – is common in people with depression who want to escape aversive life events. Early-morning awakenings are also common in this population but Anna did not report these. Anna said she felt "very slowed down" and often tired. She felt guilty about her parents' breakup even though this was unwarranted. Anna had no trouble concentrating but this may be because she did not regularly attend school. Each of these depressive symptoms in combination with Anna's suicidal thoughts and gesture led the psychiatrist to his initial diagnosis.

The assessment of depression in adolescents can take many forms, such as laboratory testing, interviews, self-report measures, and direct observation. Anna underwent various medical tests in the inpatient hospital to identify different conditions that might explain her depression. Several neurological and medical conditions can produce symptoms of depression, including brain and hormonal changes, cardiovascular problems, and severe illnesses, among others (Babin, 2003). Various substances can also produce symptoms of depression. Medical conditions and substances did not apply to Anna, however.

A laboratory test for depression is the dexamethasone suppression test (DST). A person is evaluated for her ability to suppress cortisol secretion. People with depression tend to have high levels of cortisol, a stress-induced hormone. A DST test identifies only 40–70% of depressed youth, however (Kaufman, Martin, King, & Charney, 2001). In addition, a positive DST finding does not necessarily mean a person has depression, only that one marker is present. A negative DST result was found for Anna.

An interview is particularly important for assessing people with possible depression. Clinicians use interviews to obtain information and develop rapport with someone initially unwilling to share personal issues. Structured interviews for this population include the Schedule for Affective Disorders and Schizophrenia for School-Aged Children (Kaufman et al., 1997) and Children's Interview for Psychiatric Syndromes (Weller, Weller, Fristad, Rooney, & Schecter, 2000). Most mental health professionals, including the psychiatrist in this case, rely on an unstructured interview to explore characteristics unique to a certain case.

Several topics should be explored when interviewing someone with possible depression. These topics include symptom description; history of symptoms; family history; and associated problems, such as anxiety, substance use, and acting-out behaviors. A youth's perception of his symptoms, family situation, and other issues can be discussed as well. An interviewer should assess whether someone has thoughts about harming herself. Many people who attempt suicide are willing to communicate their intent beforehand and accurately convey their plan for doing so. The more detailed a suicide plan, the more a person may be at risk for harm. Other important signs should be examined as well, including sudden changes in behavior and recent environmental stressors, such as loss of a relationship.

Anna's symptom history was described earlier. Her perceptions of her situation and significant others in her life were discussed during inpatient group therapy sessions. Anna was confused by recent life events, especially her mother's quick departure from Anna's father and brother. She said she missed the rest of her family and former friends. She admitted feeling scared and upset on the psychiatric unit but acknowledged she had more social contact now than in the past 6 weeks.

Self-report measures are commonly used to assess depression in many inpatient and outpatient settings. Primary examples include the Reynolds Adolescent Depression Scale (Reynolds, 2004) and Children's Depression Inventory (CDI)* (Kovacs, 2003). Anna completed the CDI during her inpatient stay and during later outpatient counseling. The CDI is a 27-item measure of recent depressive symptoms, such as feeling sad, crying, self-blame, indecisiveness, fatigue, eating and sleeping problems, and loneliness. Sample sub-items from the CDI include the following:

1. I am sad all the time.
2. I want to kill myself.
3. I feel like crying every day.
4. I feel alone all the time.
5. Nobody really loves me.

Anna's CDI score was in the clinical range (27) following admission to the hospital. She endorsed several items, particularly those related to feeling sad, tired, lonely, and unmotivated. Her score diminished to 15 (in the normal range) by the end of her 3-week stay, however. The psychiatrist also assessed Anna for hopelessness, a construct often associated with depression in general and suicide in particular. The Hopelessness Scale for Children is a 17-item true-false instrument that emphasizes feelings about the future (Thurber, Hollingsworth, & Miller, 1996). Anna did not complete this scale but her answers to the psychiatrist's questions indicated a moderate to high level of hopelessness.

Direct observation of behavior can be helpful for assessing depression. Assessors should look for

1. sad facial expressions;
2. decreased social and motor activity, such as less talking, game playing, or interactions with others;
3. excessive solitary behavior, such as reading or watching television;
4. slow speech;
5. decreased eye contact;
6. arguing;
7. poor affect in the form of frowning, complaining, or lack of smiling.

Hospital staff members initially noted some of these characteristics in Anna. They saw that Anna kept to herself unless someone encouraged her to attend group activities. Anna also looked sad and talked softly to others.

Other forms of assessment for this population include peer and adult ratings (Hintze, Stoner, & Bull, 2000). Peer ratings were not obtained for Anna because her classmates did not know her very well. Mrs. Thompson's ratings on the Child Behavior Checklist (Achenbach & Rescorla, 2001) were obtained, however, during later outpatient treatment. These ratings indicated a moderate to high degree of loneliness, sadness, crying, and guilt on Anna's part.

Risk Factors and Maintaining Variables

Many cases of depression result from a mixture of biological and psychological factors. People with depression may have neuroendocrine changes such as abnormal cortisol regulation or reduced growth hormone secretion. Changes in the neurotransmitters norepinephrine and serotonin influence depression as well. Low levels of each occur in this population and drugs that increase levels of these neurotransmitters are good antidepressants (Kapornai & Vetro, 2008). No major physical abnormalities were present for Anna, but an undetected physiological factor may have caused some of her depressive symptoms. Anna did not respond much to antidepressant medication either, suggesting that her depression was more environmentally based, or exogenous, than biologically based, or endogenous.

Genetic factors can predispose adolescents to depression. Identical twins are about twice more likely to share depressive symptoms than fraternal twins. Youths whose natural parents had depression are more likely than controls to show depression themselves, even when raised by adoptive, nondepressed parents. Immediate family members of depressed adolescents are more likely to be depressed than the general population (Shih, Belmonte, & Zandi, 2004). Genetic factors do not explain all variables associated with adolescent depression, however. Environmental factors often trigger biological predispositions to depression.

Anna's family history regarding depression was spotty. Mrs. Thompson had some depressive symptoms but whether these were simply normal reactions to recent life events was unclear. Anna's father was thought to have a history of depression and alcoholism, but Anna's mother did not know whether he experienced a major depressive episode. Anna herself had never experienced major depression either. Her current state may have been more environmentally based. Anna and her mother, however, knew few additional family members, so a more detailed family history of depression was unavailable.

Psychological theories of depression may have been more pertinent to Anna. Psychodynamic theory holds that depression results from overdependence on others. When an overdependent person loses someone close, either through perceived loss, death, abandonment, or separation, that person engages in introjection. Introjection is a process whereby a person internalizes feelings of anger and hatred toward the lost one. Feelings of self-blame and worthlessness thus occur and depression begins.

A more widely accepted psychological model of mood disorder is a behavioral one. This model holds that depression generally results from decreased reinforcement for active, prosocial behavior and increased reinforcement for depressed behavior. An adolescent may do all the things expected of her, such as going to school, finishing chores, completing homework, and working at a part-time job. If others take these behaviors for granted, however, the youth receives little positive attention. Conversely, if she becomes depressed and her performance in these activities slips, then others may notice, provide sympathy and support, and inadvertently reward depressive symptoms. Suicidal gestures, such as the one displayed by Anna, may be also done for attention.

Anna was not depressed solely for attention but did relish the social contact her situation brought. She said her mother was more interested in her life now than before her inpatient stay. She enjoyed talking to the other adolescents and staff members on her inpatient ward. Some of the nurses grumbled that Anna was a general nuisance as her discharge approached; she constantly asked them personal questions and wondered aloud if she could maintain contact with them. Mrs. Thompson and the psychiatrist noted this as well and agreed that Anna's mother should encourage and reward her daughter's future social behavior with peers.

A related behavioral theory of depression holds that social incompetence is central to the disorder (Eberhart & Hammen, 2006). Anna was capable of talking and making friends when motivated to do so, however, as she was on the inpatient ward. A self-control model stipulates that people with depression selectively attend to negative life events, overpunish and underreward themselves, and focus on unrealistic goals and short-term outcomes (Spence & Reinecke, 2004). This model did apply somewhat to Anna who focused almost exclusively on negative aspects of her family and her social life. When Anna did focus on the future, she did so in the form of "pie-in-the-sky" expectations. Anna thought she and her mother would eventually reconcile with her father and that she could meet her high school obligations after entering college.

A popular psychological model of depression is Beck's cognitive theory, which emphasizes dysfunctional ways of viewing oneself, the world, and the future (Beck, 2005). Some youths with depression have cognitive distortions about surrounding events and believe things are worse than they actually are. An adolescent may believe everyone will laugh at him during an oral presentation despite clear evidence to the contrary – this is catastrophization. Anna displayed personalization, or attributing external events to oneself without cause. She thought classmates whispering in hallways were necessarily talking about her and making rude remarks. No evidence existed to support this thought, however.

A related cognitive theory of depression is learned helplessness, which links sadness to inaccurate attributions about different life events (Abramson et al., 2002). People with depression may attribute causes of negative events to internal, global, and stable factors. Failure on a test might result in negative self-statements regarding the situation's internality (e.g., "It was my fault"), globality ("I am a failure at everything"), and stability ("I will always fail these tests"). Such thinking is often the result of experiences in which a person felt or had little control over environmental events. Anna often blamed negative, uncontrollable life events, such as her parents' divorce, on herself. She was pessimistic about her future social life. Thoughts like these also occur in nondepressed adolescents, however, so assessing cognitive symptoms of depression in adolescents is sometimes difficult.

Other factors relate to onset and maintenance of depression, such as unassertiveness, impulsivity, anxiety, low peer attachment, poor social support, unpopularity, problem-solving deficits, ineffective coping styles, poor school performance, detached parents, disorganized or hostile families, negative reactions to life stressors, and economic disadvantage (Hammen & Rudolph, 2003). Several of these applied to Anna, especially her troublesome family situation, impulsivity, lack of friendships, and a belief that she had little support from others.

Some theorists combine many risk factors into an integrative model of depression (Hyde, Mezulis, & Abramson, 2008). Some people are likely to have a genetic predisposition to depression as well as troublesome family experiences, poor interpersonal skills and coping styles, and feelings of inadequacy. Later stressful life events may trigger these biological and psychological predispositions to produce depression. Stress hormones, attributions, social contacts and support, and degree of hopelessness among other variables can mediate severity of depression, however. Anna's general predisposition to depression may have developed from negative family interactions. A stressful move to a new school, lack of social support, and cognitive distortions may then have conspired to help produce her major depressive episode.

Developmental Aspects

The developmental course of depression is a controversial topic. Some claim only adolescents and adults can experience "true" cognitively based clinical depression. Researchers have looked at symptoms of depression in preschoolers and young children as well, however. The prevalence and symptomatology of depression across different age groups is not dramatically different but some important distinctions, such as cognitive factors, exist.

Depression in preschoolers can involve sadness, irritability, withdrawal, slow movement, crying, and somatic complaints such as stomachaches (Luby et al., 2003). These symptoms could be due to other disorders, however, and symptoms of depression are sometimes manifested by oppositional behavior at this age. A diagnosis of depression is thus often difficult to make in preschoolers.

Children during the school-age period become more able and willing to express themselves when emotionally distraught. Depressive symptoms in 6–12-year-olds may include somatic complaints such as headaches and stomachaches, sadness, poor school performance and concentration, crying, irritability, fatigue, insomnia, increased or decreased motor activity, worry, and low self-esteem. Suicidal thoughts and attempts also become more prevalent as children age (Steele & Doey, 2007). These symptoms sometimes indicate other disorders, however. In addition, some children with depression show no overt symptoms. Mrs. Thompson said Anna never had obvious behavior problems.

Depression in adolescence and adulthood is closer to the "classic" depression represented by DSM-IV-TR criteria. Adolescents and adults tend to show more depressed mood, psychomotor retardation, and sleep problems than preschoolers or school-age children. Other symptoms common to adolescents with depression were evident in Anna. She was socially withdrawn, especially after her move. Those with depression sometimes shy away from new stimuli or lack energy to cope with new interpersonal situations. Anna enjoyed social contact but was inhibited by fears of rejection and humiliation. Symptoms of worry and anxiety are common to adolescents with depression. Anna constantly worried about her life situation, in particular family finances, her social status, and her mother's general welfare. Anna technically met diagnostic criteria for generalized anxiety disorder, which involves pervasive worrying. Anna's cognitive distortions exacerbated these anxiety symptoms as well.

Other symptoms particularly common to adolescents with depression include disruptive behaviors, somatic complaints, low self-esteem regarding body image, and suicidal ideation (Hammen & Rudolph, 2003). Anna did not have acting-out behavior problems but did have somatic complaints, such as headaches and stomachaches. She was also highly concerned and depressed about her weight. Anna gained a substantial amount of weight in the past few months and felt socially rejected as a result. Her continued overeating and lack of participation in group activities were not helping matters, however. Weight management thus became an important part of her outpatient treatment plan. Anna was obviously having thoughts of suicide and her suicidal gesture indicated that she was at greater risk than the general population for harming herself. The psychiatrist believed Anna's gesture was largely the result of a desire for attention and related to Anna's sometimes impulsive behavior.

Many people experience their first major depressive episode in adolescence and the mean duration of an episode is 12 weeks (Eaton et al., 2008). Extended depression may relate to severity of life events, degree of suicidal ideation and impairment, and comorbid disorders such as anxiety or substance abuse. Anna did have substantial anxiety. Risk for depression increases with the presence of family dysfunction, as was the case for Anna. A high level of expressed emotion, or open hostility among family members, aggravates depression in youth. Low self-esteem predicts depression as well (Orth, Robins, & Roberts, 2008; Tompson et al., 2010).

About 50% of those who experience one major depressive episode will eventually experience a second episode within 1 year (Eaton et al., 2008). A large percentage of those with a depressive episode will continue to display dysthymia, or ongoing depressed mood without major interference in daily functioning (Nobile, Cataldo, Marino, & Molteni, 2003). Anna continued to experience occasional depressed mood and social withdrawal even after out-patient therapy.

Adolescents can show persistent depressive symptoms over time. This applies especially to girls and youths with poor health, somatic complaints, suicidal idea-tion, and school suspensions (Rushton, Forcier, & Schectman, 2002). Ongoing access to treatment and family and social support are also key predictors of whether an adolescent will remain depressed. Anna's referral to outpatient ther-apy and development of peer support were critical aspects of her recovery. Peer support was especially pertinent because Mrs. Thompson continued to deny Anna contact with her father or brother.

Treatment

Treatment for adolescents with depression can occur in inpatient and outpatient settings, as was the case for Anna. Inpatient therapy aims to reduce severe depressive symptoms, suicidal ideation, and imminent harm. Treatments to accomplish this, in addition to individual and family therapy, include antidepressant medication, group therapy, and milieu therapy. Milieu therapy involves establishing an environment that encourages a client to take responsibility for his recovery and participate actively in treatment activities. The psychiatrist, nurses, and other staff members encouraged Anna to attend group therapy sessions and maintain good personal hygiene.

Group therapy typically focuses on resolving interpersonal problems, building social support, and developing social, conversational, and problem-solving skills (Mufson et al., 2004). Short-term group therapy is the norm in an inpatient setting such as Anna's. Anna's stay on the unit was 3 weeks, as was the case for many adolescents there, so group therapists emphasized discussion and support. Anna spoke about her recent problems and fears and discovered that her concerns often overlapped with those of other group members. None of Anna's primary problems were completely solved but her mood generally improved during her hospital stay.

Antidepressant medications for adolescents include tricyclic antidepressants, selective serotonin reuptake inhibitors (SSRIs), and monoamine oxidase (MAO) inhibitors. Several tricyclic antidepressants are available, including imipramine, amitriptyline, nortriptyline, and desipramine. Their effectiveness for depressed adolescents is not strong, however. The SSRI studied most in adolescents with depression is fluoxetine (Prozac) and this drug is effective especially in combination with cognitive behavioral procedures (March et al., 2007). Psychiatrists may use MAO inhibitors if tricyclic and SSRI antidepressants do not work but these drugs have potentially dangerous side effects.

Anna received a low dose of fluoxetine while in the hospital. She told the psychiatrist her mood improved during her 3-week stay, but whether this was due to the drug or Anna's increased social contact was unclear. Anna did report, however, a substantial decrease in anxiety, which may have been the result of the fluoxetine.

A clinical psychologist later saw Anna for outpatient therapy. Outpatient therapy for adolescent depression often involves a behavioral approach supplemented by medication. Anna continued to take fluoxetine for 6 months, after which the drug was discontinued. Behavior therapy for clients with depression often includes scheduling additional activities, increasing positive reinforcement from others, building social and problem-solving skills, and practicing social skills in different settings (Lejuez, Hopko, Acierno, Daughters, & Pagoto, 2011).

The psychologist, Anna, and Mrs. Thompson discussed several treatment goals, including resumption of school attendance, improved mood and socialization, and weight loss. The psychologist made a verbal contract with Anna regarding suicide. Anna agreed to contact her mother or the therapist when she had thoughts of suicide or was tempted to hurt herself.

The psychologist helped Anna develop ways to increase her self-esteem and socialization. Using a problem-solving approach, the two decided Anna could join a local weight-loss clinic, resume school attendance part-time, and participate in at least one peer activity. Anna adopted these solutions and within 2 months had lost some weight, received partial academic credit through an after-school program, and started singing in the school choir. The therapist worked with Mrs. Thompson to increase her time with Anna on the weekends and participate in at least one activity with her daughter outside the home. Mrs. Thompson encouraged Anna to ask others to visit the house for dinner.

The therapist then focused on Anna's social skills, which were good but needed "fine-tuning." Anna had difficulty approaching people she did not know well, especially boys. The therapist worked with Anna to help her start and maintain conversations, integrate verbal and nonverbal behaviors, and apply these skills to those she met at school. Anna had little difficulty talking to people once she knew them and was eventually able to connect with members of her choir and after-school class. Anna avoided these situations at times to spend time with her mother but the therapist and Mrs. Thompson continued to encourage Anna to maintain social contacts with her peers.

Anna's psychologist recognized that some deeper problems needed to be addressed as well during therapy. Anna continued to put herself down, complain about her family situation, and suspect others of wrongdoing. The psychologist thought Anna was intelligent and capable of absorbing aspects of cognitive therapy and this became a major focus of her later stages of treatment. Cognitive therapy often involves several steps, such as the following (Friedberg, McClure, & Garcia, 2009):

1. Self-monitor thoughts.
2. Understand the connection between thoughts and behaviors.
3. Evaluate each thought for accuracy.
4. Substitute more realistic thoughts for inaccurate ones.

One of Anna's ongoing cognitive distortions was personalization, or her belief that others were purposely acting against her. The therapist asked Anna to keep a daily log of times she felt others made derogatory statements or were otherwise rude to her. The therapist pointed out how Anna's thoughts sometimes related to her avoidant behavior and depression. Anna might see classmates snickering and looking at her and think they were talking about her. Anna would then overgeneralize the incident to other people she knew and subsequently avoid certain social situations. She would become depressed as her social withdrawal increased. From Anna's log, the therapist identified other examples of how Anna's thoughts could lead to depressive behaviors.

The therapist then asked Anna to challenge negative thoughts directly. He asked Anna to examine evidence for and against each thought. If Anna could not find credible evidence to support her thought, then she was asked to find a more logical and realistic explanation (e.g., the girls are talking about something else). The therapist also helped Anna think about what to do even if someone acted rudely toward her. Anna's suspiciousness and depressive symptoms gradually declined over time.

Anna remained in outpatient therapy for about a year, after which time the therapist thought she was functioning well enough to end treatment. Some issues did remain unresolved, however. Mrs. Thompson remained adamant about the current family situation, continuing to ban Anna from seeing her father and brother. Anna felt occasionally sad about this but adapted well to her new life-style and now had some good friendships. Telephone contact with her 6 months after therapy revealed no recurrence of major depression or suicide attempt.

DISCUSSION QUESTIONS

1. Do you believe depression truly exists in preschoolers and school-age children? Defend your answer. What symptoms do you feel are most indicative of depression at different ages?

2. Why do you think more girls than boys display depression? Be sure to explore issues of socialization. Do you think women report being depressed more than men? If so, why might this be the case?

3. Why do you think males tend to choose more lethal methods for committing suicide than females?

4. What type of person is most likely to commit suicide by making the act seem like an accident? What do you suppose her motivation for doing so would be?

5. What questions would you most want to ask someone who seems depressed? How would you go about discovering whether the person is thinking about suicide and what would you do with this information?

6. Everyone gets depressed at one time or another. What life events cause you to feel sad or "down in the dumps"? What separates "normal" depression from "abnormal" depression? Was Anna's depression normal or abnormal? Why do you think so?

7. What are major ethical issues involved in giving medication to children or adolescents with depression? Given that depression is often a warning sign that something is wrong, explore how medication might prevent one from solving serious life problems.

8. How might you treat an adolescent with depression who does not want to talk with you? How might you change your treatment plan for a teenager with depression if he also used alcohol or other drugs, was the victim of abuse, or had symptoms of conduct disorder?

Chapter 4

Early-Onset Bipolar Disorder

Symptoms

Dustin Lowell was a 14-year-old European American male brought to a child protective services residential facility after his mother's arrest. Police arrested Dustin's mother, Natalie Chapman, on charges of drug possession and distribution and child neglect. She and Dustin lived together in a small home but neighbors said Dustin was alone and acting oddly. The police report indicated that Dustin sat on his front lawn in the middle of the night, blasted music at all hours, and threatened neighbors as they walked by. He had not been to school for at least 4 weeks and neighbors said they saw little of Ms. Chapman.

One of the neighbors contacted police, who found Dustin alone in the home with little food. He did not know where his mother was and could not remember the last time he saw her. Police officers said he looked gaunt and acted irritable and nervous. They eventually brought Dustin to the child protective services unit for care and evaluation. Ms. Chapman was located a day later in a seedy downtown area and was arrested after police found her using and distributing methamphetamine.

Dustin's behavior at the child protective services unit, a campus of several small group homes, was odd during his first few days. He was quite irritable, snapping at various staff members and other residents, though he did not threaten anyone. Dustin was also overactive. He seemed to have great trouble sleeping; staff members reportedly saw Dustin in the middle of the recreation room at 3:00 A.M. Dustin was fidgety, nervous, and had trouble concentrating. He had substantial energy and difficulty calming himself. Dustin's mood often fluctuated as well – he seemed docile one minute but irritable and anxious the next minute.

The staff psychologist, working in concert with two senior doctoral students in clinical psychology from the local university, evaluated Dustin. Dustin was reserved at first and offered little insight into his living situation or behavior. He did complete some self-report measures, however, regarding symptoms of posttraumatic stress disorder as well as related problems of dissociation, trauma-related cognitions, depression, and anger. The doctoral students administered this assessment protocol to adolescents referred to the child protective services (CPS) unit to identify adjustment and other problems from abuse or transfer to the facility. Dustin's scores on these measures, however, were unremarkable.

The staff psychologist observed Dustin over the next few days to better understand his odd behaviors. She considered exposure to drug use, lingering symptoms of trauma-related stress, depression, and adjustment problems to the new facility as possible explanations. She eventually ruled out drug use because Dustin's behavior changed little during his stay on the unit and because a toxicology screen revealed no illicit substance use. She and other staff members regularly tried to speak to Dustin but he remained quiet, nervous, and distracted.

Dustin stayed at the child protective services unit for 5 days, after which a foster family volunteered to house and care for him until CPS workers could find a long-term solution. The foster family consisted of a young couple, Mr. and Mrs. Boswell, and their 7-year-old daughter Emma. The couple recently completed training as foster parents and was eager to provide a stable if temporary home for Dustin.

A CPS social worker brought Dustin to the foster home to meet the Boswells but the initial meeting did not go well. Dustin entered the house and ran about, checking each room and quickly asking where he was to sleep. The Boswells were a bit startled at his energy but politely showed him his bedroom. Dustin entered the bedroom and started bouncing on the bed until the social worker asked him to stop. Dustin did so but appeared anxious and left to use the bathroom.

The social worker explained Dustin's recent history to the Boswells and encouraged them to speak with her should problems arise. That did not take long. At the dinner table that night, Dustin spoke endlessly of his recent experiences, a clear departure from his behavior at the CPS unit. He rocked back and forth in his chair and told of how his mother came and went with different people in the house and how he often feared for his safety. Dustin described one incident where he was in bed and heard voices "coming through the wall," as if they were ghosts. Mr. Boswell saw that his daughter was terrified at this story and asked Dustin to stop.

The Boswells were in bed when the next set of odd behaviors occurred. Mrs. Boswell awoke to the sound of a door slamming and went to Dustin's room to find it empty. She eventually found Dustin sitting in the front yard, rocking back and forth. She approached him but Dustin quickly stood up and yelled at her. Dustin said to leave him alone and began crying. He also said, oddly, that "they were coming to get him" and that Mrs. Boswell should go inside "or you'll get hurt." Mrs. Boswell was unsure if Dustin meant he would hurt her, so she retreated inside and informed her husband. Mr. Boswell was able to convince Dustin to come back inside and go to sleep.

The Boswell family noted other strange behaviors from Dustin over the next 7 days. Dustin's mood changed often, usually fluctuating from calmness to irritability and back again. His irritable moods were of special concern – he often yelled at the 7-year-old and constantly asked everyone to leave him alone. Dustin ate only irregularly, seemed frantic at times, and had great trouble sleeping. He refused to attend school, which meant someone had to stay home during the day to supervise him.

The last straw for the Boswell family came on the eighth day of their foster care. The family was working in the yard when they noticed that Dustin was missing. A frantic search of the house, yard, and neighborhood revealed no sign of him. The family alerted the CPS social worker and police, who eventually found Dustin sitting in the corner of a convenience store 2 miles from the Boswell home. A police officer said Dustin seemed incoherent and highly agitated. He returned Dustin to the Boswell home but Dustin immediately ran down the street. The police officer retrieved Dustin and brought him to the CPS unit. Dustin received a sedative to ease his agitation.

The psychologist delved further into Dustin's background to get a better handle on what might be causing his odd behaviors. She secured permission to access Dustin's school records. Dustin appeared to be a bright student but one who often missed school. His grades in elementary and early middle school were decent but his entry into high school this year involved excessive absenteeism and poor academic performance. The psychologist noted as well that Dustin's records indicated symptoms of possible attention deficit/hyperactivity disorder.

The psychologist then secured an interview with Natalie Chapman, Dustin's mother. This conversation revealed some fascinating information that helped explain some of Dustin's strange behaviors. This information, combined with observations and review of school records, led the psychologist to conclude preliminarily that Dustin displayed symptoms of early-onset bipolar disorder.

Assessment

The essential feature of bipolar disorder involves one or more manic or mixed episodes that often occur with one or more major depressive episodes (American Psychiatric Association, 2000, p. 382). A manic episode is a "distinct period of abnormally and persistently elevated, expansive, or irritable mood, lasting at least one week" (p. 362). Common symptoms during a manic episode include inflated self-esteem, decreased need for sleep, talkativeness, racing thoughts, distractibility, increased goal-directed activity or agitation, and excessive involvement in pleasurable activities that may lead to painful consequences. Examples of the latter include buying sprees, joyriding, or sexual indiscretions (p. 362). A mixed episode involves rapidly alternating moods of mania and depression for at least 1 week. Symptoms of a major depressive episode are in Chapter 3.

Symptoms of bipolar disorder are less clear for adolescents than adults. Adolescents with bipolar disorder differ from the classic DSM-IV-TR criteria in 70% of cases (Ahn & Frazier, 2004). Adolescents with the disorder often do not show clear episodes of mania and depression (manic-depression) seen in adults. Their clinical picture instead usually involves irritable mood, inflated self-esteem, increased energy, distractibility, pressured speech, racing thoughts, and decreased need for sleep. Adolescent bipolar disorder may be closest to DSM-IV-TR criteria for a mixed episode of rapidly alternating mood states (Kowatch, Youngstrom, Danielyan, & Findling, 2005; Weller, Calvert, & Weller, 2003).

Dustin appeared to have many of these symptoms. He was clearly irritable and agitated at many times and often distracted. The Boswells and the staff psychologist noted that Dustin had great trouble staying calm and maintaining conversations. The Boswells in particular felt they were "walking on eggshells around Dustin" and became afraid of "setting him off" by saying or doing the wrong thing. This apparently happened quite often with Emma, the 7-year-old. At other times, however, Dustin's mood seemed calm. Staff members at CPS and the Boswells told the psychologist they never could predict how Dustin would respond to their social gestures.

Dustin showed increased energy and decreased need for sleep. Recall that he often ran about and bounced on the bed, an odd behavior for a 14-year-old. Dustin appeared to have a history of excessive motor behavior as well – his school records indicated that a school psychologist once recommended a diagnosis of attention deficit/hyperactivity disorder (hyperactive-impulsive type). Another key element of Dustin's problems was that he slept very little. Dustin said he slept only 4–5 hours a night and sat on the front lawn because it helped calm him.

Dustin did not show other symptoms of bipolar disorder to a substantial degree, however. He did not report racing thoughts and did not show pressured speech, though he did have odd speech at times. The police officer and the Boswells noted instances where Dustin spoke incoherently or oddly about "voices" or threats. The psychologist suspected that Dustin may have experienced racing thoughts, however, when he was distracted and could not focus on a conversation.

Further complicating the clinical picture for adolescents is that many mental disorders co-occur with bipolar symptoms. Common examples include pre-psychotic conditions as well as substance use, sleep, anxiety, and attention deficit/hyperactivity disorders (Duffy, Alda, Crawford, Milin, & Grof, 2007; Goldstein et al., 2008). Dustin did not have a full-blown psychotic disorder such as schizophrenia but did display possible symptoms characteristic of this condition. His report of "voices" coming through the wall and his unsubstantiated worry that others "were coming to get him" could indicate early signs of a hallucination or delusion. Dustin did not report or show these symptoms on a regular basis, however. He had no substance use disorder.

Dustin certainly had symptoms of sleep and anxiety disorders. The staff psychologist did not formally diagnose Dustin with either type of disorder but the teenager clearly had trouble sleeping as well as worry and physical agitation. These symptoms were likely secondary to a diagnosis of bipolar disorder, however. Further discussion with school officials revealed that Dustin demonstrated classic symptoms of attention deficit/hyperactivity disorder in elementary and middle school. These symptoms included overactivity, impulsivity, distractibility, inattention, fidgeting, and talkativeness.

Bipolar disorder has a strong genetic basis, so assessment should include family history and interview. The CPS staff psychologist who interviewed Dustin's mother discovered that Ms. Chapman had a long history of mood swings and substance use. Ms. Chapman said she grew up in "a smashed house" marked by constant fighting and drama. She began experiencing severe mood swings in her early 20s and eventually drank large amounts of alcohol to cope. Ms. Chapman gave birth to Dustin when she was 23 years old but admitted that caring for her son was difficult. She said Dustin often had problems in school and that she was overwhelmed with having to care for a child. Her substance abuse worsened over the years to the point that she was heavily involved in the local drug culture. She never received a formal diagnosis of bipolar disorder but nodded in agreement when the psychologist listed possible symptoms. No information was available regarding Dustin's biological father.

Assessment of bipolar disorder can include behavior checklists and self-report measures of mood. The Child Behavior Checklist (Achenbach & Rescorla, 2001) is useful for distinguishing those with bipolar disorder from those with attention deficit/hyperactivity disorder. Parent ratings on this checklist are higher on many scales for youths with bipolar disorder, including anxiety/depression, social and thought problems, and aggression (Diler, Uguz, Seydaoglu, Erol, & Avci, 2007). Another, more specific parent report measure is the Child Bipolar Questionnaire that covers symptoms of mood and attention deficit/hyperactivity disorder to derive a clear picture for a particular case (Papolos, Hennen, Cockerham, Thode, & Youngstrom, 2006).

Other important measures include the Parent Young Mania Rating Scale and Parent General Behavior Inventory-Hypomanic/Biphasic (Gracious, Youngstrom, Findling, & Calabrese, 2002; Youngstrom, Findling, Danielson, & Calabrese, 2001). Evaluations of parent-child interactions such as quarreling and poor affection may be instructive as well (Schenkel, West, Harral, Patel, & Pavuluri, 2008). Dustin's mother did not complete these measures, however.

Clinicians should look for several "red flags" that may indicate a particularly serious form of early-onset bipolar disorder. These red flags include early-onset depression, unusual depression, psychotic features, episodic aggressive behavior, and family history of bipolar disorder (Youngstrom, 2007). Dustin had many of these. He was moody and sometimes depressed, though he tended to be more energetic than lethargic. He may have had early psychotic features but the psychologist thought it was too early to know for sure. Dustin did not display physical aggression but did threaten his neighbors, Mrs. Boswell, and other CPS residents at times. Mrs. Chapman's interview also revealed a likely family history of bipolar disorder.

Risk Factors and Maintaining Variables

Genetics are a key basis for bipolar disorder. Family studies reveal that first-degree relatives of those with bipolar disorder have the disorder themselves in 3–15% of cases. This is generally higher than the prevalence of bipolar disorder in the general population for adolescents (1.0%) and adults (3.9%). Risk of developing bipolar disorder is much greater in cases of early-onset bipolar disorder. Twin studies reveal much higher concordance rates for identical than fraternal twins. Early-onset bipolar disorder may relate most closely to changes on chromosomes 9, 12, 14, and 15 (Faraone, Lasky-Su, Glatt, Van Eerdewegh, & Tsuang, 2006; Kessler et al., 2005; Kloos, Weller, & Weller, 2008; Pavuluri, Birmaher, & Naylor, 2005; Shih, Belmonte, & Zandi, 2004).

The CPS psychologist felt the strongest piece of evidence for diagnosing Dustin with bipolar disorder was a family history of mood swings, substance use, and symptoms of attention deficit/hyperactivity disorder. Ms. Chapman later revealed more details that confirmed this diagnosis. Her parents threw her out of her house when she was 17 years old. Ms. Chapman said she and her mother constantly argued and often "set each other off." She further explained that her mother had an explosive temper that triggered her own wild mood swings and aggression. Ms. Chapman said her mood often fluctuated between irritability, elation, and depression. She found the only way to cope with these changes and with parenthood was substance use. Ms. Chapman also agreed that she displayed many symptoms of attention deficit/hyperactivity disorder as a child. She was distraught to learn that Dustin had similar problems now.

Genetic influences likely set the stage for key brain changes in bipolar disorder. Bipolar disorder may relate to deficits in the anterior cingulate, orbitofrontal cortex, and hippocampus (Bearden et al., 2008; Konarski et al., 2008). These areas of the brain, in conjunction with other brain structures, influence inhibition and motor activity and thus the restlessness, movement, and goal-directed activity seen in people with bipolar disorder. These areas are intimately involved in emotion as well, and may help explain sudden mood swings seen in people with bipolar disorder.

People with bipolar disorder have low levels of serotonin but higher than normal levels of norepinephrine. Rapid cycling in bipolar disorder relates to a less active thyroid as well. Youths with bipolar disorder also show many neuro-cognitive deficits in attention, planning, inhibition, and visuospatial memory. Youths with bipolar disorder may show sleep disturbances such as less rapid eye movement sleep, more awakenings, and longer periods of slow-wave sleep than controls. Some sleep deprivation may trigger manic episodes and especially rapid cycling (Kupka, Luckenbaugh, Post, Leverich, & Nolen, 2003; Mehl et al., 2006; Newberg, Catapano, Zarate, & Manji, 2008).

Dustin's specific neurobiology was unknown but he clearly had cognitive and sleep problems. He sometimes faded in and out of conversations or oddly began speaking about another topic. He was impulsive, as when he suddenly left the Boswells for the convenience store, and did not plan well. Dustin obviously had many sleep problems. He rarely slept through the night, slept only a few hours per night, and reported little dreaming, which is associated with less rapid eye movement sleep.

Psychological risk factors contribute to bipolar disorder as well. Youths with the disorder tend to have poor social and problem-solving skills and few friends. They experience teasing from others as well. Dustin's social skills were only fair. He did maintain conversations, albeit oddly, but often showed poor eye contact and kept his head down when speaking. His speech was sometimes muffled and he threatened others as well. Whether these problems caused or resulted from his disorder was unclear, however. Dustin's social problems could have resulted as well from poor parental feedback and poor social contacts from excessive school absenteeism (Pavuluri et al., 2005).

Children of parents with mood disorders such as bipolar disorder often show certain personality characteristics as well. Many show novelty-seeking, a trait involving impulsive, exploratory, and thrill-seeking behaviors (Rogers et al., 2004). Dustin enjoyed exploring his surroundings, as do many adolescents, but he was not a big thrill-seeker. His mother, however, displayed many thrill-seeking behaviors such as drug use and frequent sex. Other youths of parents with mood disorders show increased neuroticism and hostility (Wilson et al., 2007). Dustin's anxiety and nervousness as well as verbal aggression toward others were evidence of these traits.

Youths with bipolar disorder often fight with their parents and siblings and have little warmth in their families. Dustin's relationship with his mother, though sporadic, was warm, however. The two rarely argued or fought, but this could have been due to the fact they did not interact much. Ms. Chapman's relationship with her parents, though, involved intense conflict, poor attachment, and violence. She expressed little warmth for her parents and described them as "cold" and "uncaring." She had not spoken to her parents in years and was unsure they were even alive.

Developmental Aspects

The developmental course of bipolar disorder involves the study of preschoolers, school-aged children, adolescents, and adults. Researchers generally identify preschoolers for study if at least one of their parents demonstrates symptoms of mania or bipolar disorder or severe mood disorder. Preschoolers in these studies generally show symptoms of mania and depression together, as in a mixed state. Many of these young children show frenetic motor activity such as excessive climbing or running about, fidgeting, and restlessness. Much of their motor behavior seems chaotic as well. Many preschoolers are active but goal-directed in some way, such as when playing a sport. Youngsters with symptoms of mania, however, often show motor behavior with little purpose (Dilsaver & Akiskal, 2004; Wilens et al., 2003).

Ms. Chapman said Dustin was a "handful" as a preschooler, a problem that helped prompt her alcohol use. She said Dustin was always "on the go" and difficult to calm. He would climb on the furniture, get up early in the morning even after a late bedtime, "talk nonstop," and pester her constantly. Ms. Chapman noticed as well that Dustin had few friends in daycare and said he had to leave one place because he was "too hard to handle." The psychologist asked Ms. Chapman about sports and games but Ms. Chapman said Dustin was never interested in team play. He preferred solitary activities, though this could have been because other children rejected him.

Preschoolers with symptoms of mania also demonstrate impairment in school and social functioning (Luby & Belden, 2006). They may have difficulty adjusting to the routines and rules of daycare placements and have trouble controlling their emotions. Preschoolers normally develop a process of emotional control, however, so some children take longer than others to mature in this area. The fact that a youngster is emotionally volatile and throws temper tantrums, for example, does not mean he has bipolar disorder. Preschoolers with symptoms of mania may have more difficulty developing social skills and friendships, perhaps because of their poor emotional control and impulsivity. These children are sometimes described as bossy and hostile in their interpersonal relationships (Maia, Boarati, Kleinman, & Fu-I, 2007).

Ms. Chapman said Dustin was "emotional" and cried often during his preschool years. He often threw temper tantrums when he did not get his way and stayed upset for long periods. She said she was always careful "not to set him off" and thus usually gave him what he wanted. Ms. Chapman said she was dealing with her own mood swings and depression at the time, which led to periods where she drank alcohol and let Dustin do what he wanted. She was quite happy when Dustin was eligible for kindergarten because others could watch him during the day. Ms. Chapman said Dustin was not physically aggressive toward other children but did sometimes "get in their face."

Researchers sometimes examine youths with attention deficit/hyperactivity disorder to identify preschoolers with possible manic symptoms because of the substantial overlap between the disorders. Bipolar disorder occurs in 26% of preschoolers and 18% of school-aged children with attention deficit/hyperactivity disorder. Bipolar comorbid with conduct disorder, a problem often associated with aggression, occurs in 10% of preschoolers and 6% of school-aged children with attention deficit/hyperactivity disorder. These children often face a chronic course of mental disorder (Wilens et al., 2002).

Dustin's behavior from preschool to elementary school did involve increased overactivity and impulsivity. Interview and school record data indicated that Dustin was hard to control in the classroom, often leaving his seat, becoming distracted, and failing to heed instructions. A school psychologist evaluated him when he was in second grade. The school psychologist felt Dustin did not quite meet full diagnostic criteria for attention deficit/hyperactivity disorder because his symptoms, though annoying, were manageable. Dustin's teacher implemented an incentive system in the classroom for good behavior and Dustin responded well to this.

School records and Ms. Chapman's report indicated poor communication between school officials and Dustin's mother. Ms. Chapman said her drug use at this time was worsening and she left Dustin alone much of the time. Dustin generally did well in elementary school, however, and was largely self-sufficient at home. She did admit bringing several men to the house over the years and that some interacted with Dustin. She admitted as well to at least two frightening incidents that may explain Dustin's comment that he sometimes feared for his safety, but she did not provide details.

School-aged children with bipolar disorder often demonstrate more irritable mood, hypomania, pre-psychotic symptoms, depression, and rapid cycling than preschoolers. Average age of onset for a first episode of mania is 6.9 years and this episode typically lasts 79 weeks. Rate of relapse to another episode is about 70%; low maternal warmth is a good predictor of relapse in this age group (Geller, Tillman, Craney, & Bolhofner, 2004). Symptoms evident in the preschool years, such as overactivity and problems with friendships, can continue as well. About 90% of children with bipolar disorder have a family history of mood or substance use disorder, as Dustin did (Faedda, Baldessarini, Glovinsky, & Austin, 2004).

Ms. Chapman and Dustin confirmed that Dustin's mood in elementary school was much more irritable than before. Ms. Chapman said Dustin was "grouchy" and often argued with her about chores and other obligations. Again, she typically let Dustin have his way following an argument. Dustin was also sadder during elementary school than preschool but this may have related somewhat to the instability of his living environment. He and his mother became emotionally detached during his school-aged years as well, which clearly worsened the situation. Dustin did not show any pre-psychotic symptoms, however, until he entered puberty.

Adolescents with bipolar disorder show more hospitalizations, psychosis, suicidal behavior, and poor social functioning than school-aged children. Many show more severe depression, longer duration of mania and depression, more frequent cycling of mood, and symptoms closer to the "classic" adult form of bipolar disorder. Adolescents with bipolar disorder may experience more substance use, family and legal problems, and other mental disorders such as oppositional defiant disorder. Trouble concentrating, distractibility, and interrupting others become frequent as well (Birmaher & Axelson, 2006; Birmaher et al., 2006; Masi et al., 2006; Miklowitz & Cicchetti, 2006; Rucklidge, 2008).

Dustin never indulged in illicit substance use and was never hospitalized or suicidal. As he entered puberty, however, he did become more depressed and his moods changed more frequently. He often shifted from irritability to calmness to sadness. He became more oppositional in his behavior as well, as partly demonstrated by his noncompliance with the Boswells. He was obviously experiencing family problems and his mother was in serious legal trouble. Dustin continued to have great difficulty concentrating and already displayed odd, possibly psychotic-like behaviors.

The long-term prognosis for adolescents with bipolar disorder as they enter adulthood is mixed but generally not good. The recovery rate for mania is only about 37% and most people with bipolar disorder show a chronic course. Earlier onset of bipolar disorder is associated with more chronic course as well as higher likelihood for later suicide attempt, violence, and anxiety and substance use disorder (Geller et al., 2001; Judd et al., 2002; Perlis et al., 2004). The prognosis for Dustin at this point remains cloudy and his family history of mood disorder and early onset of symptoms do not bode well for him.

Treatment

Treatment for bipolar disorder in adolescents commonly involves mood-stabilizing medication, cognitive-behavioral intervention, and family therapy. Dustin received medication from a psychiatrist, cognitive-behavioral intervention in the CPS unit from the staff psychologist, and family therapy with the social worker later when he rejoined the Boswell family. Ms. Chapman eventually agreed to a plea deal and, while she intended to remain in contact with Dustin, would not be living with him for quite some time.

Medication is usually the first treatment for people with bipolar disorder. Adolescents with bipolar disorder often receive mood-stabilizing drugs such as lithium, valproate, or lamotrignine. This is especially the case if a teenager shows no psychotic symptoms. Dustin, however, did appear to have psychotic or pre-psychotic behaviors such as delusional thoughts and possible hallucination. Adolescents whose clinical picture resembles Dustin's may receive a mood-stabilizing drug with an atypical antipsychotic drug such as olanzapine or risperidone. Electroconvulsive therapy is sometimes used as well if medication is ineffective but this was not used for Dustin (Leibenluft & Rich, 2008).

Dustin received a prescription of lithium and olanzepine. His response to the medication was fair. Dustin's mood swings improved to some extent and he showed no more evidence of psychotic symptoms. His level of agitation and restlessness remained, however, as did his sleep problems. A sleep medication was eventually prescribed for Dustin as well. CPS staff also said Dustin's interactions with others at the unit were generally positive or at least free of threats or hostility. Dustin did seem depressed at times but he clearly missed his mother.

Medication for adolescent bipolar disorder is not a cure, so psychological approaches may be used to improve symptoms and social and family relationships (Leibenluft & Rich, 2008). Cognitive-behavioral therapy for this population involves several important components (Pavuluri et al., 2005):

- Keep a regular routine including regular sleep.
- Self-monitor mood and have others provide calming feedback.
- Generate positive self-statements to increase motivation and problem-solving.
- Express and process sad and resentful feelings about others.
- Develop supportive friendships and social skills.
- Solve problems during calm and not upset moods.
- Seek support from others when in a difficult situation.

The staff psychologist and social worker at CPS worked closely with Dustin to improve his sleep hygiene. Dustin kept a specific routine at night, calming himself before a set bedtime and refraining from late-night television, caffeine, and exercise. He took his sleep medication when necessary and achieved more hours of sleep per night. Dustin became better at telling others of his bad moods and allowing the psychologist, social worker, and other staff members to give him gentle and private feedback when he was overly boisterous or loud. He developed some friendships during his CPS schooling and sought out teachers and others for support when he felt poorly. Side effects of his medications can be quite severe as well, so Dustin learned to speak to others when these arose.

Family therapy for adolescents with bipolar disorder concentrates heavily on educating family members about symptoms and other characteristics of the disorder. Family members learn about the cause, course, treatment, and long-term course of bipolar disorder. This process, called psychoeducation, emphasizes the fact that bipolar disorder is not the teenager's fault and that she often has little control of her symptoms. This process helps reduce stigma and involves a discussion of how family members, including the youth himself, must assume responsibility for long-term care (Young & Fristad, 2007).

Following several weeks at the CPS unit, Dustin rejoined his foster family. To their credit, the Boswells were enthusiastic and dedicated to helping Dustin manage his symptoms. The social worker met with the family for two extended sessions prior to Dustin's reintegration. She explained the symptoms of bipolar disorder and emphasized that adolescents with the disorder sometimes show different symptoms than adults. She talked about mood swings, irritability, family history, possible psychotic symptoms, and the need to maintain medication and watch for side effects. She answered the family's many questions about the disorder and made sure to include Dustin in the conversation so he did not feel stigmatized or alienated. Dustin was impressed with the Boswells' level of warmth and care and promised to maintain his medication regimen.

Family therapy for adolescents with bipolar disorder concentrates as well on communication and coping skills to reduce conflict and minimize impairment from the disorder (Young & Fristad, 2007). Family members are encouraged to be open about concerns regarding an adolescent's mood and give him feedback when his behavior seems inappropriate or excessive. Dustin and the Boswells agreed that certain behaviors were unacceptable, including running in the house, leaving the house unsupervised, and threatening the 7-year-old. The social worker also asked Dustin to record his mood changes during the day and to be open about how he felt at a given moment. If he felt especially irritable, then the family members would give him some space.

Family therapy may involve how to address stressful life events, especially those that may lead to symptom relapse. Dustin knew that going back to school would be quite stressful for him and might trigger some irritability and anger. The social worker and the Boswells thus arranged a meeting with Dustin's new school psychologist and guidance counselor to educate them of Dustin's condition, monitor his behavior in school, establish an initial part-time class schedule involving subjects Dustin liked most, and introduce him to extracurricular activities where he could develop friendships. The Boswells provided tangible rewards for school attendance as well. Dustin attended school each day for five classes within 4 weeks.

Medication compliance is a key aspect of family therapy. The Boswells and Dustin agreed to a set schedule for his medication that involved close but private supervision to ensure that Dustin took the medication. The social worker stressed compliance very strongly but the Boswells, who had earlier seen Dustin's bizarre behavior when off medication, needed little prodding. The family later reported good success regarding Dustin's medication regimen and regular visits to the psychiatrist.

Dustin and the Boswells received regular visits from the CPS social worker over the next 6 months. Dustin attended school full-time with occasional absences when feeling particularly irritable or ill. He showed no aggression or threats and his sleep patterns were fairly regular. The Boswells did say that Dustin was sometimes noncompliant but they attributed this more to normal adolescence than to bipolar disorder. Dustin was to stay with the Boswells indefinitely and even received opportunities to visit his mother. Dustin's short-term prognosis seemed good but, given the severity of bipolar disorder and his family history, his long-term prognosis will depend heavily on medication use and support from others.

DISCUSSION QUESTIONS

1. What is the difference between bipolar disorder and normal "moody" behaviors of adolescence? How might symptoms of bipolar disorder be misdiagnosed in a rebellious or grumpy teenager?

2. How do you think Dustin's early home life affected him and his disorder? Could Ms. Chapman or anyone else have done anything to prevent some of Dustin's symptoms? How so?

3. Do you believe preschoolers can show symptoms of bipolar disorder, especially the mood swings most characteristic of the disorder? What symptoms of bipolar disorder could apply most and least to a preschooler?

4. A key problem regarding early-onset bipolar disorder is that different assessment devices can yield different results and diagnoses. What competing diagnoses exist for bipolar disorder? What assessment protocol may help distinguish bipolar disorder from another mental disorder?

5. How would you talk to Dustin and what would you say to him when his mood was irritable, angry, manic, or calm?

6. Imagine a teenager with bipolar disorder who has several psychotic symptoms and suicidal behavior. What do mental health professionals do in this kind of case? Be sure to explore safety and crisis issues that could arise.

7. Outline reasons why bipolar disorder in children has suddenly increased in prevalence over the past several years, especially in the United States. What cultural, biological, media, or social reasons might apply?

8. Explore advantages and disadvantages of using medication to control bipolar disorder in children and adolescents. Discuss the issue of why people would want to take medication to control mood when they feel elated.

Chapter 5

Eating Disorders

Symptoms

Andrea Weston was a 17-year-old European American female referred to a clinical psychologist who specialized in anxiety, depressive, and eating disorders. Andrea was a senior in high school at the time of her initial assessment. Her parents, Mr. and Mrs. Weston, referred Andrea for what they described as "very unusual behavior." Mr. Weston had an initial telephone conversation with the psychologist and said Andrea was caught eating a large amount of sweet foods by her sister. The incident was especially worrisome because Andrea then struck her sister in the face, an act she had never done before. Mr. Weston claimed Andrea was becoming more irritable, withdrawn, and argumentative. Her relationship with her boyfriend was tempestuous and a source of tension between Andrea and her parents. Mr. Weston also said Andrea was reluctant to enter therapy and agreed to do so only if the entire family was involved.

The psychologist found Andrea to be somewhat gaunt and diminutive but not seriously underweight during the initial interview. Her major symptoms initially seemed depressive. Andrea said she experienced several stressful events that felt overwhelming during the school year (it was now early February). She said her parents were constantly interfering with her life and giving her advice on how to look, act, and work toward the future. Her mother often "poked her nose" into Andrea's affairs, especially her appearance, schoolwork, social life, and dating. Andrea said she was doing poorly at school, claiming a severe case of "senioritis." In addition, she felt lonely and rejected because many of her friends were joining other social groups.

The psychologist asked Andrea about recent events that triggered her father's call. Andrea said her parents were unhappy with her boyfriend of the past 5 months. Her parents objected to his older age (20 years), rough demeanor, and questionable status, characteristics Andrea seemed to relish. When asked for more details, Andrea simply said this was her first real boyfriend and that her parents "just don't want me to have any independence." Andrea did not openly admit that annoying her parents was a fringe benefit of dating her boyfriend but her tone led the psychologist to this conclusion.

The psychologist asked Andrea about various depressive symptoms and she appeared to have several. She was sad, often felt tired, had low self-esteem, and occasionally thought about suicide. The psychologist developed a contract with Andrea in which she promised to contact the psychologist following suicidal ideation or before any suicide attempt. Andrea was also concerned about her weight and body size, which she described as "chubby" and unappealing to others. The psychologist saw that Andrea was a bit thin but that her weight was appropriate for her age, gender, and height. Andrea said her parents, especially her mother, made frequent comments about her weight as she grew up. They sometimes said she needed to watch her figure if she was going to fit in with her social group. Andrea was thus sensitive about her weight and felt bad whenever she gained a few pounds or "felt fat."

When asked about her recent episode of binge eating, Andrea became tearful and spoke softly. She said she began dieting about 3 months earlier while dating her current boyfriend. He made an offhand comment about her weight that Andrea took immediately as a threat that he would not see her unless she lost weight. She then lost weight by eliminating certain foods from her diet and by eating substantially less than before. Andrea lost about 20 pounds, reaching her current weight of 100 pounds, and said she felt more attractive but still inadequate. She also felt anxious about her relationship with her boyfriend and other friends. Andrea felt they were becoming more distant from her and she tended to blame this on her weight.

As Andrea lost weight, however, her sense of sadness and anxiety did not go away and she often felt hungry. She began to binge secretly about 2 months ago. The binges usually consisted of sweet foods, such as ice cream, cake, candy bars, and soft drinks. Andrea said the binges occurred only once every other week but the psychologist suspected they occurred more frequently. Andrea said the binges made her feel "gross and fat," so she started vomiting afterward. Andrea said she vomited only twice and that she no longer binged or vomited, but again the psychologist found this doubtful.

The psychologist then interviewed Mr. and Mrs. Weston, who confirmed much of Andrea's report but made the situation sound more dire. Mrs. Weston revealed that Andrea was hospitalized for a suicide attempt the previous year and continued to show signs of depression. Further questioning revealed that the "suicide attempt" was actually a car accident involving Andrea as the driver. Andrea said afterward that she wished she had died in the accident, but whether she actually tried to kill herself was unclear. The psychologist noted Mrs. Weston's tendency to make events such as these sound dramatic.

Mr. and Mrs. Weston also described some recently upsetting events regarding Andrea. At the top of their list was her relationship with her boyfriend, whom the parents described as a "bad seed." Andrea's boyfriend had a history of drug use and was arrested for theft twice in the past 4 years. Mr. and Mrs. Weston felt Andrea was now sexually active with her boyfriend and worried about the possible consequences. They said their attempts to dissuade Andrea from dating the man were unsuccessful. Mr. and Mrs. Weston also said Andrea's grades were suffering, her social life was shrinking, and her participation in family activities was declining. Both parents argued vehemently with Andrea about these issues in the past few months, but their concern produced no change in their daughter's behavior. Both, however, described their relationship with Andrea as excellent.

The psychologist asked about Andrea's weight and eating habits. Mrs. Weston repeated the "binge" story given earlier by her husband and said she felt Andrea was too fussy about the way she looked. Mrs. Weston said her daughter always had a weight problem and that she, Mrs. Weston, tried to control Andrea's diet. Mrs. Weston said Andrea's weight "fluctuated like a yo-yo" as her moods changed. (The psychologist noted the paradox in Mrs. Weston's behavior: she claimed Andrea was too fussy about appearances but emphasized such appearances herself.) Both parents became more concerned when Andrea revealed her recent pattern of binge eating and they believed she was vomiting as well. Their primary treatment goal, however, was to "help Andrea overcome feelings of inadequacy."

The psychologist spoke with Andrea's schoolteachers with Mr. and Mrs. Weston's permission. All said Andrea was normally a good student but that her grades slipped recently because of incomplete homework. They also said Andrea seemed preoccupied with other matters and speculated that her home life caused her recent academic problems. Based on this early information from Andrea, her parents, and her teachers, the psychologist preliminarily concluded that Andrea had subclinical anorexia nervosa of the binging/purging subtype as well as subclinical depression.

Assessment

The essential features of anorexia nervosa are [American Psychiatric Association (APA), 2000, p. 583]

1. refusal to maintain a minimally normal body weight;

2. intense fear of gaining weight;

3. significant perceptual disturbance regarding one's body shape or size;

4. amenorrhea in postmenarcheal females.

People with anorexia maintain their body weight at less than 85% of normal weight for age and height. They commonly fear weight gain even when they are underweight, base their self-worth on weight, and/or deny that a problem exists. Female amenorrhea in anorexia refers to the absence of three consecutive menstrual cycles.

Anorexia nervosa may be of (1) the restricting type, in which a person has lost weight but is not binging or purging, or (2) the binge eating/purging type, in which a person engages in binge eating as well as purging through vomiting, laxative abuse, or excessive exercise. A binge refers to "eating in a discrete period of time an amount of food that is definitely larger than most individuals would eat under similar circumstances" (APA, 2000, p. 589).

Andrea's diagnosis was uncertain. The psychologist tentatively refrained from a diagnosis of bulimia nervosa because Andrea's binge eating and purging occurred too infrequently to meet diagnostic criteria. DSM-IV-TR criteria for bulimia nervosa mandate an average of two binge/purge episodes a week for 3 months. This left a possible diagnosis of anorexia nervosa with binge eating/purging features, a common finding in those with eating disorders. Andrea was not amenorrheic or more than 15% underweight but had lost 20 pounds in the past several weeks. If she continued on this path, as she seemed inclined to do, then she would be seriously underweight in a short period.

The psychologist preferred a diagnosis of anorexia nervosa because of Andrea's fear of weight gain and worry about losing her boyfriend. Andrea was convinced her boyfriend and other friends would abandon her if she gained weight and that her parents would comment on her "obesity." She felt she would look "ugly." The psychologist noticed that Andrea was oblivious to negative consequences of losing more weight and judged her self-worth almost solely on the way she looked. People who meet most but not all symptoms of anorexia nervosa, like Andrea, may receive a diagnosis of "eating disorder not otherwise specified." The psychologist also thought Andrea had depressive symptoms that needed treatment, but she did not meet criteria for a major depressive episode.

Assessing people with anorexia nervosa should begin with a medical examination because severe physical complications and even death can result. Anorexia may result in several physical problems: gastrointestinal distress, bloating, dizziness, dehydration, electrolyte imbalances, lethargy, dry skin, edema, anemia, cardiovascular abnormalities, renal dysfunction, and atypical neurological patterns. In addition, erosion of dental enamel may occur in people who induce vomiting (Rosen, 2010). Andrea had no major physical symptoms and received no medical examination, however.

A psychological assessment or interview of those with eating disorders should concentrate on the following (Anderson, Lundgren, Shapiro, & Paulosky, 2004):

1. Attitudes toward weight and body shape
2. Characteristics of binging and purging and current weight
3. Feelings of loss of control, drive for thinness, distress, anxiety, and depression
4. Dieting behaviors
5. Body image disturbance
6. Maladaptive personality traits such as impulsivity
7. Social and family functioning
8. Reasons for seeking treatment and motivation for change

Andrea said she and her mother always paid close attention to weight and that Andrea's self-worth closely matched her weight. Andrea kept daily records of her weight and eating habits and agreed to provide the psychologist with this information. Keeping such a diary is a common form of assessment in this population.

Assessment should focus on what a person eats, length of a binge, related emotions, and conditions that precede and follow a binge. The psychologist found that Andrea's binges usually came after school and before she saw her boyfriend. Andrea would come home from school sometimes feeling isolated, inadequate, or hungry and would occasionally binge on easily bought and quickly eaten items such as cake. No one was usually home at this time. Following this binge and dinner with the family, Andrea worried that the ingested food would cause her to gain weight and look inferior to her boyfriend. She then purged before dates with him. The psychologist instructed Andrea to keep a record of her binges and purges.

Andrea's moods often related to food. She ate and binged when anxious or depressed and purged when feeling guilty, fat, or ugly. Andrea had few moods not tied to eating and often ate impulsively and with little control. The psychologist found no major patterns of borderline personality traits, aggression, or substance abuse, however. No history of physical or sexual abuse was reported either. These findings support the belief that no one pattern of symptoms necessarily fits all those with anorexia nervosa.

The psychologist also focused on the link between Andrea's social and family interactions and her eating. Andrea had distorted thoughts of abandonment by others if she gained weight and of increased popularity if she lost enough weight. An in-depth discussion with Andrea and her parents revealed vacillating enmeshment and conflict. Andrea and her parents would become overinvolved in one another's lives and then fight about this. Andrea and her mother spent hours shopping and talking about Andrea's appearance. Andrea would then complain her mother was "trying to control me." Similar patterns were evident with respect to Andrea's girlfriends but not her boyfriend.

The psychologist also explored the family's reasons for seeking treatment and their motivation for change. An interesting observation was that no one focused much on Andrea's eating habits, preferring to complain instead about each other's role in the family. Mr. and Mrs. Weston did eventually acknowledge their concern about Andrea's weight following a prompt from the psychologist and the issue became a centerpiece of family therapy conducted later.

Interviews for those with eating disorders also focus on social skills, sexual behavior, and menstrual history, but these were not discussed at length in Andrea's case. Assessment in this area may additionally include rating scales such as the Eating Attitudes Test (Garner, 1997; Garner & Keiper, 2010), cognitive and family measures (Cooper, 2005; Treasure et al., 2008), and a consideration of cultural factors that impinge on a case (Alegria et al., 2007). Sample items from the Eating Attitudes Test* include the following:

1. Am terrified about being overweight.

2. Find myself preoccupied with food.

3. Am preoccupied with a desire to be thinner.

---

* Reproduced with permission by Dr. D. Garner (Garner et al., 1982. The eating attitudes test: Psychometric features and clinical correlates. *Psychological Medicine*, 12, 871–878). Further information on the EAT-26 can be obtained from www.river-centre.org.

4. Feel that others pressure me to eat.

5. Have the impulse to vomit after meals.

Risk Factors and Maintaining Variables

Factors that lead to eating disorders in general and anorexia nervosa in particular involve a mixture of physical, psychological, and sociocultural variables. The causes of eating disorders may overlap with those for depression. Anorexia nervosa and depression are associated with changes in cortisol and the neurotransmitters serotonin and norepinephrine (Bailer & Kaye, 2003). A noteworthy finding in Andrea's case was Mrs. Weston's report that several of her relatives were depressed.

Other biological causes of eating disorders include genetics and sensory response. The concordance rate for anorexia nervosa in identical twins is substantially higher than for fraternal twins. Family members of people with eating disorders are more likely to have eating disorders themselves compared to the general population (Bulik, Slof-Op't Landt, van Furth, & Sullivan, 2007). Those who binge also tend to have a greater sensory response such as salivation to food (Legenbauer, Vogele, & Ruddel, 2004). These factors did not seem pertinent to Andrea's case, however.

Several individual psychological characteristics have been associated with anorexia nervosa. People with anorexia tend to be perfectionistic, obsessive, and compliant. Those who binge and purge show depression and anxiety and impulsivity, require approval from others, and like novel stimuli (Anderluh, Tchanturia, Rabe-Hesketh, & Treasure, 2003; Stein et al., 2002; Troisi, Massroni, & Cuzzolaro, 2005; Vervaet, Audenaert, & van Heeringen, 2003). Some of these characteristics were evident in Andrea but others were not. Andrea was dramatic in her behavior, a characteristic not typical of those with anorexia. She was also moderately noncompliant and enjoyed irritating her parents.

On the other hand, Andrea clearly needed approval from others, especially her friends and boyfriend. The opinion of her parents, despite her objections, seemed important to Andrea as well. Andrea had mood swings and impulsive behavior, a fact that greatly concerned her parents. She sometimes said and did things with little thought, such as driving fast and buying clothes impetuously. Andrea was clearly obsessed about her relationships with other people and about her weight. She had perceptual and cognitive distortions regarding her weight, insisting she was "ugly and fat" even as she lost weight and claiming other people were often talking about her weight behind her back.

Cognitive-behavioral models of eating disorders, especially binge eating, focus on cycles of emotions and obsessional thinking (Wilson, Fairburn, Agras, Walsh, & Kraemer, 2002). One possible scenario is that stressful situations, low self-esteem, and worries about body shape and weight lead to feelings of apprehension. Binge eating temporarily reduces this anxiety and tension. Guilt and shame gradually develop after a binge, however, so a person purges to reduce these emotions. Unfortunately, stressful events and a sense of low self-esteem remain in the person's life and the cycle repeats. This scenario applied to some extent to Andrea, who sometimes binged following a stressful day at school. She then felt regret and distress over the binge, including possible weight gain, and purged by vomiting.

Other psychological theories of eating disorders emphasize family variables. A classic developmental/psychodynamic/object relations view holds that anorexia nervosa is a manifestation of internal conflict. Anorexia is a compensatory behavior for satiation or separation problems during the oral stage of psychosexual development. A related view is that anorexia results from a problematic mother-child attachment. A mother may gratify the physiological but not emotional needs of her child. This may derive from the mother's insecurity or hostility toward the child, but the result is a child who feels insecure, rejected, and possibly vulnerable to depression and eating disorders.

Other family theories of eating disorders focus on interactions among all family members. Some families of adolescents with anorexia are enmeshed. This means family members are overinvolved in one another's lives to the point that even minor events, such as daily dress, become a source of great attention. Perhaps an adolescent, feeling dominated by her parents, rebels by overcontrolling a very personal aspect – weight. In addition, an adolescent may draw extra attention from an enmeshed family by exploiting weight loss and related medical complications.

Andrea certainly had a strange and contradictory relationship with her parents:

1. She valued their opinions but then claimed to reject them.
2. She sought advice from her parents but then complained of being overcontrolled.
3. She professed love for her parents but greatly enjoyed needling them.

Mrs. Weston also gave Andrea mixed messages:

1. She dismissed the importance of appearance and weight but then gave Andrea extensive advice in this area.
2. She told Andrea she loved her while avoiding eye contact.
3. She blended criticisms of Andrea with compliments.

Andrea was probably confused about how her parents and others felt about her. She then developed low self-esteem and the mistaken belief that weight loss was a key way to get affection from others.

Some families of adolescents with anorexia nervosa display overprotectiveness, avoidance of conflict, poor problem-solving skills, and negative communication and hostility. These characteristics were present to some degree in Andrea's case. Her family was often sarcastic, critical, and reluctant to discuss certain problems. Some theorists hold that children model a parent's preoccupation with weight reduction (Wilson, Becker, & Heffernan, 2003). Andrea's mother was particular about her own appearance and the psychologist discovered that

Mrs. Weston weighed herself and dieted regularly. Andrea imitated this behavior as she grew up.

Another popular model of eating disorders is a sociocultural one. The glorification of thinness in the media provokes many young women to diet. The image of the "ideal" female body size in popular literature has gradually become thinner in past decades. This could lead to anorexia in a couple of ways. First, as more young women feel pressured to diet, more could trigger a biological predisposition to anorexia nervosa. Second, failure to meet societal demands for thinness could lead to depression, low self-esteem, and unusual eating patterns (Andrist, 2003).

A sociocultural perspective might explain why patterns of bulimia occur more in females from Western countries, such as Andrea. The psychologist in this case also noted that Andrea and her mother subscribed to several women's fashion magazines. Both often matched their appearance to the models in the magazines as well.

Developmental Aspects

Several developmental variables influence the onset, course, and treatment of adolescents with eating disorders. One developmental variable may explain why girls show anorexia nervosa more than boys: physical development. Females tend to increase their amount of fat tissue at a greater rate than males during adolescence, and this obviously moves them away from the "ideal" body size portrayed in the media. This may also explain why anorexia and bulimia nervosa occur more in adolescents than in children. Other physical factors related to onset of eating disorders include early menarche and breast development (Fairburn & Harrison, 2003). Parental reactions to these events are critical as well.

The psychologist found that Andrea was an "early developer" and was teased by her classmates for being so. Andrea found this humiliating and became sensitive about her weight and figure. This attitude, combined with her mother's comments noted earlier, led Andrea to be self-conscious about her appearance. She was nearly obsessed with how others looked at her and catastrophized even minor flaws in her appearance, such as wrinkles and skin blotches. When the psychologist asked Andrea to list her positive aspects, Andrea mentioned her figure, weight, height, and others' reactions to her appearance. She made little mention of her role as student, daughter, or girlfriend.

Dieting is a key developmental aspect of eating disorders. Dieting is a "rigid and unhealthy restriction of overall caloric intake, skipping meals, and excessive avoidance of specific foods in order to influence body weight and shape" (Wilson et al., 2003, p. 703). Chronic dieting actually induces some people to eat more high-calorie foods, which can then trigger binging and other eating disturbances. Eating alone often precedes dieting and may set the stage for the secretive nature of later eating disorder (Martinez-Gonzalez et al., 2003).

As people diet, their metabolic rates are reduced and weight loss becomes more difficult (Wilson et al., 2003). Subsequently, they may diet even more vigorously and become more vulnerable to binge eating. Biological and psychological vulnerabilities to eating disorders are then triggered. The dieters may feel increasingly "out of control" and decide purging is the only way to moderate effects of binging. The cognitive-behavioral cycle described earlier can then serve to maintain the disorder. For those with restrictive anorexia, dieting may start by eliminating certain foods from their daily menu, such as sweets. As the disorder progresses, however, more and more foods such as meat or bread are added to the "forbidden" list and the person's daily caloric intake and weight decline steadily.

Andrea and her mother had a long history of dieting. Andrea was frustrated over the yo-yo effect of dieting, often losing weight to fit into certain clothes or attend social functions, then putting the weight back on in subsequent weeks. The addition of her boyfriend to her life and his comment about her weight, however, gave her dieting a new sense of urgency. Andrea lost 20 pounds in the past several weeks and was now terrified the lost weight would return. This fear caused her to restrict her diet even more than in the past but this aggravated her feelings of social isolation, depression, and hunger. Her binging and purging thus began.

Depression can influence eating disorders over time. The most consistent predictor of poor outcome in those with bulimia nervosa is depression (Berkman, Lohr, & Bulik, 2007). Andrea's level of depression, though not severe, did extend the length of treatment. Her low self-esteem and general feelings of worthlessness led to cognitive distortions about her "ugly" body size and weight. Andrea mused about suicide as well, which required its own intervention. Finally, Andrea's depression prevented her from interacting with girlfriends, which ironically led to Andrea's impression that no one wanted to socialize with her. Her subsequent feelings of rejection later increased her desire to diet, binge, and purge.

What is the long-term future of those with eating disorders? Some people with anorexia have only one episode of weight loss and soon return to normal patterns of eating and weight control. Others experience a gradual and ongoing course of weight loss and gain. About 6.2% of those with anorexia, however, eventually die from the disorder because of medical complications or suicide (Papadopoulos, Ekbom, & Ekselius, 2009).

The long-term pattern of bulimia is slightly different because the disorder usually develops later in life. Symptoms of bulimia alternately improve and worsen over time. The course of the disorder appears to change favorably after treatment but relapse is common. Many people with bulimia continue to show low-level eating disturbances such as extensive dieting, laxative use, and exercise. Outcome for eating disorders is better if a person has less severe depression, good family and social relationships, and improved impulse control (Berkman et al., 2007).

What about Andrea? Her long-term outcome is probably good and almost certainly better than most people with eating disorders. This is largely because she received treatment relatively early in her disorder; many with anorexia or bulimia nervosa hide their behavior for several years before entering therapy. In addition, Andrea's therapist was experienced in treating eating disorders and utilized cognitive-behavioral methods. Andrea's eating disorder was also rather limited in scope and her family, though problematic, was motivated to resolve their difficulties. Finally, Andrea's level of depression was not clinical and generally dissipated during individual and family therapy for her eating problems.

Treatment

Treating people with eating disorders can involve inpatient and outpatient therapy. Inpatient treatment applies usually to severe cases of eating disorders, especially anorexia nervosa. Inpatient treatment is best when medical complications of anorexia are dire or when a person's behavior is life threatening. Major medical complications include substantial loss of ideal body weight (>25%), electrolyte imbalance, cardiac problems, and severe dehydration. Severe symptoms of depression and suicidal behavior must sometimes be addressed as well.

One of the main goals of hospitalization is to stabilize a person's health and increase weight and nutrition. Staff members set a target weight to meet before discharge. Interventions can include (Guarda, 2008)

1. structured eating sessions with staff and family members;
2. education about eating disorders;
3. reconstruction of proper eating and nutritional habits;
4. group and milieu therapy;
5. medication for physical complications or depression.

Hospitalization was not necessary for Andrea given her relatively moderate eating problem.

Outpatient therapy for anorexia nervosa often involves drug, group, individual, and family therapy. Drug therapy includes antidepressants such as amitriptyline or fluoxetine (Prozac). These are sometimes effective because the drugs successfully reduce obsessive-compulsive and depressive behaviors that trigger or aggravate anorexia. Anti-anxiety drugs sometimes reduce tension and the temptation to binge and purge. Relevant family members should be educated about the use of medication and side effects should be monitored. The use of antidepressants was initially discussed but later abandoned for Andrea. An emphasis was placed instead on individual and family therapy.

Treatment within a cognitive-behavioral framework is usually recommended. Important goals of individual therapy for those with anorexia nervosa involve

1. developing rapport with the client;
2. increasing motivation for behavior change;
3. normalizing weight and eliminating binging and purging;
4. modifying cognitive distortions about weight and body size;
5. addressing other conditions such as depression.

The psychologist spent considerable time developing a positive therapeutic relationship with Andrea. Andrea felt isolated and sometimes distrustful of others so the therapist recognized her concerns and did not judge her behavior. The first three sessions concentrated on developing a positive working relationship as well as education about proper eating habits. The psychologist and Andrea designed a daily eating schedule that was largely fat-free but still nutritious. They agreed Andrea's weight could fluctuate between 100 and 110 pounds but no lower. Andrea agreed to weigh herself before the psychologist during each weekly visit. Andrea's response to this treatment was rapid – she rigorously adhered to her new diet and did not lose more weight. Her motivation to address her binging, purging, and social and family problems also seemed to increase.

The tougher part of individual therapy is to eliminate binging and purging and modify cognitive distortions about body size. A reduction in binging and purging may occur if the behavior is out in the open and the person and those around her actively monitor the behavior. This was the case with Andrea, who binged and vomited only three times since her parents became more aware of the problem. A therapeutic method of eliminating binging and purging is to have a person eat high-calorie foods in a therapist's office and then prevent subsequent purging (McIntosh, Carter, Bulik, Frampton, & Joyce, 2011). This approach is similar to one used for obsessive-compulsive symptoms and assumes a person's anxiety will eventually decrease as she refrains from purging. The person realizes the binge/purge cycle is unnecessary to reduce stress.

The psychologist outlined this therapy technique to Andrea, who agreed to try it. Andrea consumed a fair amount of ice cream, candy bars, and cupcakes within a half-hour and then waited. She could not use the bathroom and the psychologist taught Andrea how to relax. The psychologist reminded Andrea that self-induced vomiting is an ineffective way of negating a binge because the body quickly absorbs many of the calories anyway. Andrea reported some anxiety following this process but was able to relax. She said she did not want to try it again, however, out of fear of weight gain. She instead agreed to have her family members closely monitor her behavior for signs of binging and purging. They reported no such incidents over the next several weeks.

Individual therapy for people with eating disorders may also address cognitive distortions. Such distortions may involve food, weight, and body size as well as themes of abandonment, loss of autonomy, and guilt (Cooper, 2005). The psychologist helped Andrea develop more realistic thoughts about consequences of weight gain and loss, her ideal and real body size, and isolation from others.

The psychologist explored the probable consequences of weight loss and gain. Andrea learned that her friends would not notice much or change their opinion of her as her weight fluctuated slightly. Andrea received feedback about the way she perceived her body and the effect her negative thoughts had on her social relationships. Andrea realized that her fears of abandonment by others led to her withdrawal and even greater feelings of isolation. Andrea engaged in several planned outdoor activities with her friends to dispel these beliefs, increase her social interaction, and reduce her depression.

Family therapy is another important treatment component for youths with eating disorders and focuses on developing cohesion, consistency, communication, and conflict resolution (Eisler et al., 2005). Andrea's therapist explored enmeshed family patterns, concentrating especially on Mrs. Weston's tendency to overcontrol her daughter's appearance and social life. Fortunately, Mrs. Weston was responsive to this and allowed Andrea substantial free time with her friends and boyfriend under certain conditions, such as curfew. In addition, Andrea agreed to eat dinner with her family at least five times per week and allow her parents to monitor her weight and possible binging and purging.

The psychologist addressed issues related to Andrea's boyfriend, school performance, and future educational status. Mr. and Mrs. Weston relayed their concerns about Andrea's dating and Andrea admitted she saw her boyfriend in part to annoy her parents. Andrea did start dating other people as therapy progressed. Mr. and Mrs. Weston also encouraged Andrea to put more effort into her classes, which she did, and to develop a plan for attending college.

Andrea and her family participated in therapy for 4 months. Andrea's overall functioning was good following therapy. Some issues remained unresolved, such as Andrea's sexual activity. Her eating problems were no longer evident and her mood greatly improved since the beginning of therapy, however. The psychologist thought the family developed improved insight into their dynamics and their effects on one another. Family members were also more motivated to work together to solve future problems. Informal telephone contact with Andrea 6 months later indicated no recurrence of eating problems or depression.

DISCUSSION QUESTIONS

1. What distinguishes people with anorexia nervosa, the binge eating/purging type, from those with bulimia nervosa? Explore not just diagnostic criteria but also social, family, and other variables.

2. Bulimia appears to be largely specific to Western societies. Why do you think this is so? What societal changes could lead to less anorexia and bulimia nervosa in the general population? What might be done to prevent the disorders?

3. Eating disorders appear to be largely specific to females. Why do you think this is so? Give specific examples of messages from the media, family members, and peers that might promote this disorder in young women.

4. Do you feel your eating behavior is linked to your emotional state? How so? What changes in how you handle stress, if any, could lead to an improvement in your eating habits?

5. Devise a treatment plan for someone who wanted to lose weight responsibly. What foods, shopping and food preparation behaviors, eating times and places, activities during eating, and other variables would you focus on?

6. Would you say anything to someone who appeared dangerously under-weight? If so, what might you say to that person? What prejudgments would you want to avoid?

7. What influence do you think Andrea's boyfriend had on the development and maintenance of her eating problems? Would involving her boyfriend in the therapy process be a good idea? Why or why not? If yes, how might you do so?

8. What is the danger in placing someone treated for anorexia back with family members? What could be done to prevent a relapse in this situation?

9. What could or would you do if a person were in danger of losing her life from anorexia but refused treatment?

Chapter 6

Attention Deficit/Hyperactivity Disorder

Symptoms

Ricky Smith was a 7-year-old African American male referred by his school psychologist, principal, and mother (Mrs. Smith) to an outpatient community mental health clinic. Ricky was in second grade at the time of his initial assessment. During her initial call to the clinic, Mrs. Smith said her son was "out of control." She said Ricky "was all over the place" and "constantly getting into trouble." She was particularly overwhelmed as a single mother by her son's behavior and scheduled an appointment for 7 days later. Following a postponement, Mrs. Smith and Ricky came into the clinic about 3 weeks after the initial call.

A doctoral intern in clinical psychology interviewed Ricky and his mother separately. The intern interviewed Ricky first and found him to be polite, reserved, and a little socially anxious. Ricky said he had difficulty adjusting to his new school and especially to his new teacher. He said his teacher, Mrs. Candler, was always yelling at him and sending notes home to his mother. Ricky initially said he did not know why the teacher yelled at him but then said it was mostly about not paying attention or following class rules. Ricky said he was often "on red" – the classroom had a discipline system in which students had to change their name card from green to yellow to orange to red for each rule infraction. A red card meant an automatic call to the child's parents. Ricky had accumulated five red and seven orange cards in the past month alone.

Ricky shrugged when asked if he liked school and said he liked some of the classroom activities, especially those related to science (the class was currently studying tadpole growth). He said he had a few friends but often had to keep to himself. This was because Mrs. Candler made him spend much of the school day in a corner of the classroom to complete his work. Unfortunately, little of the work was successfully finished. Ricky said he felt bored, sad, tired, and angry in the classroom. He wanted to leave school and stay home but knew this was unlikely.

Ricky said his mother yelled at him a lot. His mother was often working, however, so his 14-year-old sister usually cared for Ricky. Ricky would watch television, play video games, or ride his bicycle outdoors when his sister was in charge. He said he felt happiest when riding his bike because nobody yelled at him and he could "go wherever I want." Other questions revealed that Ricky had no problems with adaptive behaviors such as dressing and eating but did have trouble sleeping through the night. Ricky said he felt bad about "being a pain to my mom" and was confused about why he was doing so poorly in school.

A subsequent interview with Mrs. Smith confirmed most of Ricky's report, with added detail. Mrs. Smith said Ricky was almost intolerable in the classroom, often throwing tantrums, crying when asked to do something, stomping his feet, and being disrespectful to the teacher. Ricky had a habit of saying no and "I don't care" to the teacher, who would make him change his card as a result. Mrs. Smith had already attended four conferences with the teacher at school, including one involving the principal and school psychologist. The teacher wanted Ricky referred to special education classes but Mrs. Smith opposed this. The school psychologist instead recommended Ricky be evaluated by someone outside the school district. This suggestion prompted Mrs. Smith's call to the mental health clinic.

Mrs. Smith said her son was generally "out of control" at home. He would not listen to her commands and often ran around the house until he got what he wanted. She and her son often argued about his homework, chores, misbehavior, extended absences from home, and her work schedule. Mrs. Smith complained that Ricky did not understand what she said some of the time and that he seemed depressed. More detailed questioning revealed that Ricky often fidgeted and lost many of his school materials. He was disorganized and paid little attention to long-term consequences. The child was also difficult to control in public places, such as a supermarket or church.

Mrs. Smith speculated that certain family factors contributed to Ricky's behavior. She and her husband separated about 14 months earlier and Ricky's contact with his father was only sporadic. Mrs. Smith described Ricky as a "fussy" child before the separation but hinted that intense marital conflict may have triggered more severe misbehavior. Following the separation, Ricky started first grade and seemed completely uninterested in school. The principal sent him home once for fighting and disciplined Ricky several times for taunting other children. Mrs. Smith said Ricky's problems worsened over the past 14 months, especially because she was unable to supervise her son as much as before. Mrs. Smith described Ricky's relationship with his sister as positive but said the teenager could do little to influence Ricky's behavior.

Mrs. Smith gave permission for the intern to speak with school officials about Ricky. Ricky's teacher, Mrs. Candler, said her student was less manageable now than at the beginning of school 2 months before. Ricky was initially withdrawn but his behavior became more difficult as he became more familiar with the classroom. He averaged about three severe tantrums per week, which involved a 20- to 30-minute tirade about people picking on him, his inability to understand classroom assignments, and wanting to die. The teacher generally ignored Ricky's tantrums and he was able to compose himself. Ricky's acting-out behaviors on other occasions, however, were severe enough to have him sent to the principal's office.

Mrs. Candler added that Ricky's academic performance was below average but not failing. He understood and completed his reading and math assignments when motivated to do so but his attention was sporadic and insufficient. Ricky paid closer attention when an assignment or teaching method was relatively new but was easily distracted soon afterward. Ricky was getting out of his seat more and more, requiring a constant response. Mrs. Candler was unsure whether this behavior was intentional and attention-seeking or uncontrollable. She said Ricky responded best to individualized attention and structure but that the curriculum did not allow for much one-on-one instruction. Mrs. Candler suggested that Ricky enter special education.

The intern also spoke with the school psychologist, Mrs. Dee, who said Ricky's tested intelligence level was in the normal range. His overall level of tested achievement, though low, was not more than 2 standard deviations from his intelligence test score. She thus deferred a diagnosis of learning disorder. Ricky's greatest problem was paying attention to extended tasks. His inter-personal relationships with classmates were distant but he was not unpopular. He excelled during physical education class and was one of the more popular children there. Mrs. Dee thought Ricky did not belong in special education but did require some behavior modification or medical program to control his disruptive behaviors. The intern preliminarily diagnosed Ricky with atten-tion deficit/hyperactivity disorder (ADHD) of the predominantly inattentive type.

Assessment

The essential feature of ADHD is a "persistent pattern of inattention and/or hyperactivity-impulsivity that is more frequently displayed and more severe than is typically observed in individuals at a comparable level of development" (American Psychiatric Association, 2000, p. 85). Symptoms of ADHD may include

- inattention;
- not following through on instructions;
- avoiding tasks that require sustained mental effort;
- losing things;
- distractibility;
- forgetfulness;
- fidgeting;

- leaving one's seat;
- running or climbing about;
- excessive talking;
- difficulty waiting;
- interrupting others.

These symptoms must be evident much more so than one would normally expect in a child. A diagnosis of ADHD also requires interfering symptoms present before age 7 years, symptoms in two or more settings, and significant impairment in functioning. Subtypes include predominantly inattentive, predominantly hyperactive-impulsive, and combined. The inattentive type accounts for about 25% of ADHD cases (Weiss, Worling, & Wasdell, 2003).

The clinical psychology intern who evaluated Ricky arrived at a preliminary diagnosis of ADHD, predominantly inattentive type. He based this diagnosis on the fact that Ricky failed to pay close attention to his schoolwork, had difficulty sustaining attention to work tasks, was quite disorganized, often lost school items, and was typically distracted and forgetful. Ricky sometimes, though not often, failed to understand what others said to him. This last symptom occurred mostly with his mother, however.

The clinical psychology intern also determined that Ricky's symptoms affected his test scores and grades and that some of his symptoms, such as distraction and poor attention, were present before age 7 years and before his parents separated. Impairment existed in three different settings as well: school, home, and religious education classes at church. Each presenting problem supported a diagnosis of ADHD, inattentive type.

The intern did not diagnose Ricky with ADHD of the hyperactive-impulsive or combined type because his other symptoms did not occur with sufficient frequency or severity. Ricky did fidget and run about but these behaviors were not outside the range of a normal 7-year-old boy. Ricky often left his seat at school and home but the presence of just one symptom does not warrant a diagnosis of ADHD, hyperactive-impulsive type.

Medical conditions should be ruled out first in cases of possible ADHD. Symptoms of ADHD could relate to tic and other neurological disorders (Greimel, Herpertz-Dahlmann, Gunther, Vitt, & Konrad, 2008). Knowledge of these disorders is important when deciding to use stimulant medication. Ricky had none of these medical conditions, though his mother later revealed a history of moderate alcohol use. Mrs. Smith drank alcohol during Ricky's prenatal period of development, so some fetal alcohol effects may have been manifested. Possible effects in Ricky included agitation, moderate impulsivity, and failure to focus or sustain attention. Ricky had no intellectual deficits, however, which are common to those with fetal alcohol effects. Whether fetal alcohol effects were relevant to this case, therefore, was unclear.

Mrs. Smith's alcohol use also helped trigger her marital separation but the intern noted no current impairments in her occupational functioning or parental obligations. The intern did suggest to Mrs. Smith that she pursue individual therapy for her alcohol use but she rebuffed this suggestion.

Following an inconclusive medical examination, the clinical intern focused his assessment on several sources regarding Ricky's behavior in different settings. This is a necessity for a complex disorder such as ADHD and involves interviews, rating scales, and behavioral observations, among other techniques.

During parent interviews regarding a child with possible ADHD, interviewers should focus on marital problems; stressful life events; family functioning; and parent complaints, attitudes, and possible psychopathology. Interviewers should explore a child's developmental history, symptoms, cognitive and social functioning, and the context of a child's behavior (Barkley, 2003). Adult interviews should focus on parent-child and teacher-child interactions. Significant family factors may have exacerbated Ricky's behavior. The intern therefore concentrated on possible negative effects of his parents' conflict, separation, and alcohol use.

Interviewing a child with possible ADHD is important but children with ADHD often do not show their symptoms in a novel environment. This was particularly true for Ricky – he showed self-control and was even reserved during his initial interview. Ricky's teacher said her student paid closer attention to new teaching methods or assignments. Inattention and hyperactivity often surface over time, however, as habituation occurs. Ricky's classroom behavior had worsened since the beginning of the school year and he became more difficult to interact with as therapy progressed.

Initial interviews with a child with possible ADHD should concentrate on the child's perceptions of his behavior, interpersonal relationships, and school performance. Interviews with young children regarding these topics are sometimes unreliable, however. Ricky was confused about the problems he faced and was unsure about the quantity and quality of his interpersonal relationships at school.

Teacher interviews are critical for this population as well and should concentrate on antecedents and consequences of a child's behavior. Such information is important for knowing why certain behaviors continue to occur over time. Mrs. Candler did not have substantial information about what maintained Ricky's behavior but did say he responded best to one-on-one attention.

Rating scales may be helpful to identify ADHD problems. The Child Behavior Checklist (CBCL) and Teacher's Report Form (Achenbach & Rescorla, 2001), Home and School Situations Questionnaires (Barkley, 2000), and Behavior Assessment System for Children (Reynolds & Kamphaus, 2004) are particularly useful in this regard. The Conners ADHD/DSM-IV Scales* (Conners, 1999) may also be used, and sample items include the following:

1. Leaves seat in classroom or in other situations in which remaining seated is expected.

2. Has trouble concentrating in class.

3. Is always "on the go" or acts as if driven by a motor.

4. Runs about or climbs excessively in situations where it is inappropriate.

5. Has difficulty playing or engaging in leisure activities quietly.

Mrs. Smith completed the CBCL and endorsed significant thought and attention problems. Key items included concentration difficulties, trouble sitting still, and confusion. Tests for inattention, such as a continuous performance test (Conners, 2004), are also useful for children with ADHD. Ricky did not take these tests, however.

Direct behavioral observation is indispensable for assessing children with possible ADHD to (1) evaluate behavior in academic and natural settings and (2) confirm that ADHD symptoms are present in two or more settings. The intern's observation of Ricky in class and at home largely confirmed previous teacher and parent reports. The intern found that Ricky initiated and received many social contacts from his peers, more so than reported by anyone during the interviews.

Assessors should rule out other possible disorders when evaluating a child with possible ADHD. ADHD may be misdiagnosed because other conditions may be misinterpreted as ADHD. Other conditions include oppositional defiant or conduct disorder, learning or mild developmental disability, or general disruptive behavior. Many of these conditions are comorbid with ADHD, further complicating assessment and diagnosis. To distinguish these disorders, an evaluator will pay close attention to general intellectual and adaptive behavior functioning, academic performance, aggression and hostility, quality of interpersonal relationships, social and judgment skills, and classic symptoms of ADHD. The intern believed ADHD was the best diagnosis for Ricky given the child's normal intellectual functioning, passing grades, nonaggressive interpersonal functioning, and classic ADHD, inattentive-type symptoms.

Risk Factors and Maintaining Variables

Several variables, especially biological ones, likely work in tandem to produce ADHD in children. Children with ADHD appear to have differences in certain brain areas. Abnormalities of the frontal lobe may occur because this area is associated with inhibition, thinking, reasoning, concentration, attention, expressive language, and motor control. Some have found less activity in the frontal lobe and especially in the prefrontal cortical-striatal network. Children with ADHD may also have changes in the caudate nucleus that is partially responsible for voluntary movement (Kieling, Goncalves, Tannock, & Castellanos, 2008; Schrimsher, Billingsley, Jackson, & Moore, 2002).

Children with ADHD have other unusual neurological patterns. Laboratory tests reveal these children show atypical event-related potentials when responding to tasks requiring sustained attention and response inhibition (Johnstone, Barry, & Clarke, 2007). These children may thus struggle with many school-related tasks. An interesting observation is that stimulant medications such as Ritalin alleviate many ADHD symptoms, perhaps by enhancing certain neurotransmitters or blood flow to particular brain areas that promote behavior inhibition (Pliszka, 2005).

Ricky received no formal neurological testing but did maintain his attention better in situations involving new and possibly more arousing stimuli, such as a new science assignment. The clinical psychology intern also speculated that pre-natal problems created brain changes in Ricky. This was never confirmed, however.

ADHD can be related to physical problems of early childhood, including meningitis, thyroid problems, otitis media (chronic ear infections), and sensory impairments (especially hearing loss). Contrary to popular belief, diet, sugar, and allergies have little if anything to do with ADHD symptoms. Lead toxicity is more pertinent to the onset of ADHD and is especially problematic in urban areas with high concentrations of automobiles, lead in drinking water, and indus-trial pollution. Ricky did live in a poor area but it was rural and these issues did not seem to be a factor in his case.

Evidence for a genetic component to ADHD includes findings that ADHD (1) runs in families, (2) is more prevalent in identical than fraternal twins, and (3) is more prevalent in biological than adoptive parents of children with ADHD (Biederman & Faraone, 2005; Faraone et al., 2005). Many children with ADHD, like Ricky, have no relatives with ADHD, however, so ADHD may have familial and nonfamilial types (Lehn et al., 2007). Genetic factors that lead to brain differences likely influence most types of ADHD but environmental factors may significantly influence other cases.

The intern never established the cause of Ricky's ADHD symptoms, as is the case for most children with ADHD. Mrs. Smith did drink significant amounts of alcohol during Ricky's prenatal period. Ingestion of alcohol and tobacco during pregnancy can lead to symptoms that mirror ADHD, especially inattention. Mrs. Smith also said Ricky's delivery was difficult. Ricky's birth complications and later symptoms of ADHD were perhaps related. Complica-tions at birth include anoxia and hemorrhaging.

Different biological factors likely account for most of the variance in explaining ADHD onset. Whatever the etiological pathway, however, the result is a core deficit in response inhibition or a person's ability to regulate his behav-ior. Deficits in self-control may then lead to other characteristics of children with ADHD such as poor memory, rule-governed behavior, problem solving, persis-tence, and motor and emotional control (Barkley, 2003; Shiels & Hawk, 2010).

Biological factors are thus important in explaining the etiology of ADHD. Environmental variables likely play a substantial role in *maintaining* ADHD symp-toms and influencing eventual outcome. The most significant of these environ-mental variables is parent-child and teacher-child interactions.

Several parent behaviors are important for understanding ADHD. Many children have difficulty paying attention to or comprehending parent commands. Some parents, including Mrs. Smith, consider this behavior to be deliberate non-compliance or vindictiveness. The parents may then give strong physical punish-ment but this often exacerbates the problem. Some parents acquiesce to their child and his ADHD behaviors, administer over-the-counter medication to control the behaviors, or placate the child by letting him watch television or play video games for long periods. These strategies generally fail in the end, however. Parents who provide structure, feedback, and consistent and appropriate discipline for misbehavior or poor schoolwork will achieve better control over their child's ADHD behaviors than those who do not. Treatment plans for children with ADHD must therefore include extensive parental education and involvement in therapy.

Similar conditions apply to teacher behaviors. Teachers must pay close attention to children with ADHD, but some teachers may overattend to a child with ADHD. This may reinforce a child's behavior or deprive a child of social interactions with peers. Teachers who provide structured education, frequent feedback on academic and social behavior, and consistent discipline may influence more positively a child with ADHD. Treatment plans for children with ADHD must thus involve consultation and cooperation with teachers as well as their input about what they can feasibly do in the classroom.

Developmental Aspects

Researchers have charted the developmental aspects of children with ADHD and identified a general course of the disorder. This developmental research has focused on preschool, childhood, adolescence, and adulthood. Very young children may have certain temperamental characteristics related to later ADHD. These characteristics include irritability, anger, poor self-regulation, and impulsivity (Nigg, Goldsmith, & Sachek, 2004). Mrs. Smith said Ricky was "fussy" during his first few years. She said Ricky resisted being held, crawled all over the house, and was overly curious about things potentially dangerous to him (e.g., poisonous cleaners). Whether Ricky's early behaviors were hyperactive or normal for a 2-year-old, however, was unclear.

In the preschool period (3–5 years), children who eventually develop ADHD have symptoms more characteristic of the disorder. The most noticeable symptoms include hyperactivity, impulsivity, and executive functioning problems (Thorell & Wahlstedt, 2006). These children begin to "get into everything," become more difficult to control, and show erratic patterns of behavior. They leave their seats more often than their peers, become excessively vocal and verbal, and disrupt others' activities. Mrs. Smith described Ricky as rambunctious but was unsure whether his behavior exceeded that normally expected from a 3–4-year-old. She did say Ricky was extremely curious about things, in particular things he had never seen before. This seemed consistent with Ricky's current behavior; he paid closest attention to stimuli that were newest to him.

Preschool children who eventually develop ADHD tend to be more noncompliant and aggressive than most children their age. Some symptoms characteristic of oppositional defiant and conduct disorder may begin to appear. These include excessive arguing, sharp and short temper, willfulness, verbal and physical aggression, and negative affect. Mrs. Smith said Ricky was not generally aggressive toward others and was well liked by most children in his neighborhood. She did say her son insisted on having things done his way, however. If Ricky did not get his way, he would often run around the house and scream. Still, none of Ricky's symptoms was severe enough to qualify him for a diagnosis of ADHD, hyperactive-impulsive type.

Preschoolers with eventual ADHD show greater emotional reactivity to surrounding events. These children tend to get more upset than their peers about things that bother them and stay upset for long periods. Ricky was certainly emotionally reactive. Mrs. Smith said her son would get upset "at the drop of a hat" and the family often felt they were "walking on eggshells around Ricky." Ricky would throw a tantrum if something made him nervous, if he did not get his way, or if he could not get something new. Ricky's tantrums would sometimes last 2 hours, even for something as minor as losing television privileges. Mrs. Smith said Ricky's behavior in this regard had not changed much since preschool.

The preschool period for a child who eventually develops ADHD sometimes involves intense parent–child conflict as well. Some of this conflict arises from the child's chronic inattention to parent commands, which the parent often construes as noncompliance. Ricky's behavior seemed more inattentive than noncompliant. His mother reported, when she knew she had Ricky's undivided attention, that he would listen to her and carry out his assigned task. Ricky fought a lot with his mother when he did not understand what she was saying, however. Mrs. Smith said she could not understand why her daughter was such a responsible and compliant person while her son was persistently irresponsible.

During the school-age period (6–12 years), ADHD symptoms become full-blown as school and social demands increase expectations for appropriate behavior and provide more opportunities for failure. In cases where inattention is the primary problem, as with Ricky, goal direction becomes especially problematic. Problems are chronically evident in work completion, organization, concentration, memory, planning, and social commitments. Self-regulation deficits appear as well and may lead to problems in self-care, completion of chores, social skills, and timeliness (Anastopoulos et al., 2011). Ricky himself showed many of these problems though his social skills were not too disturbed.

Less severe symptoms of inattention, hyperactivity, and impulsivity occur in adolescence. These symptoms are still more problematic than those in the general population, however. Adolescents with ADHD show greater risk for academic problems, antisocial behavior, substance abuse, and lower self-esteem than their peers (Willoughby, 2003). Many still qualify for a diagnosis of ADHD. Predictors of persistent ADHD include comorbid oppositional defiant disorder, lower verbal IQ, and medication use (Todd et al., 2008). Ricky did not have oppositional defiant disorder so his prognosis for adolescence may be better than other children with ADHD.

About one-third of those with retrospectively reported ADHD have current ADHD as adults (Kessler et al., 2005). Adults who had ADHD in childhood are more likely to show anxiety disorder, substance abuse, and antisocial behavior. Other adult consequences of ADHD include divorce, academic and employment problems, less education, and low self-esteem (Davidson, 2008). Many adults with child ADHD function well, however, especially those with less severe symptoms.

Treatment

Treating youths with ADHD often involves a multicomponent approach with an emphasis on medication and behavior modification. Children with ADHD may have trouble inhibiting or regulating their behavior because of certain neurotransmitter or brain changes. Stimulant medication is therefore useful in treating some of these children. The most popular stimulant medication, methylphenidate (Ritalin, Concerta), is relatively short acting and can produce dramatic changes in a child's behavior. This is particularly so for symptoms of hyperactivity and impulsivity.

Ritalin may be given once or several times per day. Dosages vary but many children begin a regimen of 5 milligrams (mg) per dose. Dosages may be increased as needed over time but generally do not exceed 60 mg per day. Other stimulants used for this population include lisdexamfetamine (Vyvanse), dextroamphetamine (Dexedrine, Adderall), and pemoline (Cylert). About three-quarters of children with ADHD who take stimulant medication improve to some degree. Children with ADHD with tic disorders or those who do not respond to stimulant medication may take antidepressants or a nonstimulant medication called Strattera (Olfson, 2004; Remschmidt & Global ADHD Working Group, 2005).

Substantial debate occurred in Ricky's case as to whether medication was best. School officials were very much in favor of medication but Mrs. Smith was unsure and the clinical intern was initially unconvinced that medication would remediate Ricky's inattention. Much of the debate surrounded possible side effects. Side effects of stimulant medication include headaches, stomachaches, tics, restlessness, weight loss, reduced appetite, and insomnia (American Academy of Child and Adolescent Psychiatry, 2001; Leonard, McCarten, White, & King, 2004). Other concerns about medication for this population include (1) overmedication from overdiagnosis, (2) use of drugs as a panacea (many children receive medication without concurrent behavior modification programs), (3) stigma and social ostracism (some children take one dose during the school day), and (4) mixed messages concerning drug use to control or modify behavior.

Mrs. Smith eventually decided to try medication. She revealed that she sometimes gave over-the-counter cold medication or caffeine to control Ricky's behavior. She did this about two to three times per month but the intern recommended she stop this practice immediately. The intern made the recommendation to get a better reading of Ricky's "true" behavior, reduce possible harm from frequent use of the cold medication, and eliminate confounding factors in the pediatrician's upcoming evaluation. Mrs. Smith complied at once but Ricky's behavior changed little.

Ricky saw a pediatrician who specialized in ADHD and she confirmed the original diagnosis. She gave Ricky a 5-mg dose of Ritalin twice per day (10 mg total). Ricky was to take the medication in the morning at home and after lunch in the school nurse's office. Ricky complied with the regimen without complaint. The intern and Mrs. Smith explained to Ricky that he was taking the drug to help him pay closer attention to his mother and teachers. The regimen began 2 days later with little effect. The pediatrician then increased Ricky's dosage twice over the next 4 weeks to a final regimen of 30 mg per day.

Others watched Ricky closely at school and home during this 4-week period. His teacher, Mrs. Candler, said Ricky was somewhat more manageable and did pay greater attention and stay in his seat more. His level of daily academic performance, however, did not improve. Mrs. Smith reported a similar effect though her expectations of improvement may have clouded her perception. The clinical intern therefore conducted two observations of Ricky in the classroom. He noted that Ricky sat in his seat more but that his attention improved only slightly from pretreatment.

The intern also developed a behavior modification program for Ricky. The intern designed the program to improve Ricky's attention, organizational and study skills, and completion of daily school assignments. This consisted of an extensive token economy system that supplemented the classroom card system mentioned earlier. The token economy applied first to Ricky's in-seat behavior. He could earn 20 points for every hour he sat appropriately and could leave his seat when asked to do so by a teacher. The teacher allowed Ricky one "mistake" or unexcused absence from his seat. The first unexcused absence resulted in a warning; subsequent absences during the 60-minute period led to a "response cost" of 2 points. The teacher thus gave no points if Ricky left his seat unexcused more than nine times after the warning. Ricky's teachers and the intern chose in-seat behavior first because they believed he could earn these points with relative ease. By earning points, Ricky would receive positive reinforcement for good behavior and would become familiar with the token economy system.

If Ricky accumulated at least 100 points by the end of the 6-hour school day, he earned the right to participate in an interesting classroom activity. Activities included a new game, videotape, or one-on-one conversation with Mrs. Candler. Ricky's in-seat behavior improved somewhat over 4 weeks but the change was not dramatic because the behavior was not overly problematic to start with. The teachers and the intern subsequently linked Ricky's in-seat behavior only to the green-to-red card system, with rewards given for 2 consecutive "green" days.

The next token economy targeted Ricky's attention and completion of school assignments. Ricky was to listen to Mrs. Candler's instructions and repeat them quietly to himself. If Mrs. Candler thought Ricky was not paying attention, she took away 2 points. Not paying attention included behaviors such as talking to others or failing to make eye contact during instructions. In addition, Ricky lost points for incomplete assignments. This token economy initially progressed slowly because each adult had several questions about how to define certain behaviors and how to supervise Ricky. Fortunately, everyone was motivated to help Ricky and his attentive behavior and assignment completion improved an estimated 50% over a 6-month period.

During this 6-month period, the token economy was expanded to include different study and organizational skills. Ricky received rewards for spending time studying, raising his hand appropriately, and not distracting children around him. He also received rewards for keeping his desk neat, telling time appropriately, handing in his homework on time, and telling his mother what supplies he needed at school. Mrs. Candler did not formally measure these skills but noted general improvement in these areas.

The intern implemented parent training to control Ricky's oppositional problems at home, educate Mrs. Smith and her daughter about Ricky's attention problems, and maintain each party's motivation and consistency regarding the token economy. Mrs. Smith learned how to use time-outs at home to control Ricky's tantrums and noncompliance. In addition, Ricky received a daily report card from Mrs. Candler who graded his behavior for that day. If he did well, Mrs. Smith gave him extra rewards at home. If he did not do well, he went to bed early. Other aspects of contingency management, such as appropriate parent commands, were emphasized as well.

Ricky progressed fairly well during 6 months of therapy, becoming less disruptive and showing general improvement in his attention. His weekly test scores or grades did not change, however. Unfortunately, Mrs. Smith ended Ricky's psychological treatment the following summer. She felt, despite the intern's skepticism, that Ricky improved enough to remain simply on medication. This is a common occurrence in this population. Telephone contact with Mrs. Smith the following year revealed that Ricky's misbehavior was still manageable but that his school performance remained mediocre.

DISCUSSION QUESTIONS

1. What is the difference, if any, between a child with ADHD, hyperactive-impulsive type and one who is overly rambunctious for his age? What about a child simply not motivated to pay attention?

2. ADHD, conduct disorder, mild mental retardation, and learning disability are sometimes difficult to distinguish. What signs and symptoms would lead you to conclude a child had one over another?

3. A substantial debate exists as to whether ADHD is overdiagnosed or simply prevalent among children. What do you think? What biases about a child's behavior would you want to avoid when deciding on a diagnosis of ADHD?

4. ADHD is three to four times more common in boys than girls. Do you think this is a real difference or one more easily explained by expectations we have for boys and girls as they grow up? What possible differences in socialization between boys and girls might explain why boys display symptoms of ADHD more often?

5. What is the best way to assess a child with ADHD? What questions would you like to have asked Ricky or others in his life? What would you look for if you were examining a child at school through a one-way mirror?

6. A substantial debate exists as to what role the medical establishment should play in the treatment of ADHD. What do you think of medication for this population? What are the pros and cons? Why do you think so many children with ADHD are placed on medication for extended periods? Is this good policy? Consider the rights of other children to receive an undisturbed education.

7. Develop a treatment plan for a child with ADHD whose teacher does not wish to participate. How might you go about it? Who else would you involve?

Chapter 7

Learning Disability

Symptoms

Gisela Garcia was an 8-year-old Hispanic female referred to a school psychologist for evaluation and recommendations for possible treatment. Gisela was in second grade at the time of her referral. Gisela's parents, Mr. and Mrs. Garcia, dropped their initially strong objections to an evaluation and consented to the referral late in the academic year. Gisela had many difficulties with reading assignments and spelling tests despite the fact that English was her primary language. These difficulties also affected Gisela's math and science performance because many of her assignments in these areas included story problems requiring extensive reading and writing.

The school psychologist, Mrs. Dartil, had been aware of Gisela's academic problems for about 2 months. Gisela's second-grade teacher, Mrs. Martinez, informed the school psychologist that one of her students was having particular trouble in reading and spelling but that the girl's parents resisted additional assessment or intervention. Mrs. Martinez hoped the school psychologist could join her for a meeting with the parents to convince them of the need to evaluate Gisela. Mr. and Mrs. Garcia reluctantly agreed to such a meeting after several weeks of delay.

Mrs. Martinez outlined her student's academic problems at the meeting with Gisela's parents and the school psychologist. Foremost was Gisela's reading and spelling performance, which lagged severely behind the rest of the class. Gisela was currently in Mrs. Martinez's lowest functioning reading group and had trouble paying attention to and understanding the material. Mrs. Martinez would read a story to the group and then present questions about the story. Most of the children readily answered simple questions about the story though many struggled with more complex questions. Gisela, however, often had trouble answering even simpler questions such as "What animal was this story about?" Part of the problem stemmed from Gisela's inattention – she sometimes sat on the floor and twirled herself around as Mrs. Martinez read a story. She usually stopped after redirection but would soon continue again.

Mrs. Martinez said Gisela had trouble identifying new and different words, even those in word groups such as law, paw, and saw. Each member of the reading group read a short passage from a particular book. Gisela was usually able to read the passage if it was covered within the past month. For relatively new book passages, however, Gisela had trouble identifying almost every other word. Gisela had no trouble identifying letters of the alphabet and, if given enough time, could eventually decipher the meaning of a word and resume her reading. Unfortunately, this often required a lot of time and disrupted the reading group.

Mrs. Martinez further explained that Gisela's reading problems related to her spelling problems. Gisela had enormous trouble spelling words presented orally, as on a test. She had little trouble copying a word from a book or rewriting the word several times, however. The teacher required her students to study new words given on a Monday by spending time rewriting the words during the week. The oral test occurred on Friday. Gisela had little problem studying during the week but wrote her words slowly. Her performances on recent oral spelling tests, however, averaged only 30% correct. This supplemented other failures on rote reading and writing assignments.

Mrs. Martinez further explained that Gisela's reading and spelling problems affected her progress in math and science. This was primarily because the teacher often taught math and science using story problems and creative lab projects (e.g., growing plants) involving reports and other written work. These assignments would thus be difficult for someone struggling with reading and writing. Gisela had little trouble with hands-on work or with tasks that captured her interest and attention, however.

Mrs. Martinez thought Gisela was functioning academically at an early first-grade level. The teacher said Gisela seemed "bright" and had several strengths in school, however. Gisela excelled in music and art class, taking a keen interest in activities there and showing strong motivation. Gisela's social skills were strong as well. She was witty, highly interactive, and one of the best-liked children in the class. Gisela's verbal skills were normal. Mrs. Martinez said Gisela seemed of normal intelligence but that she certainly struggled with assigned schoolwork.

Mrs. Martinez then commented on Gisela's classroom behavior. The teacher said Gisela was somewhat fidgety and had trouble paying attention but was not disruptive. Gisela was not aggressive, highly overactive, impulsive, or impolite. Gisela was generally compliant but needed constant reminders to stay on task. Mrs. Martinez also said Gisela's classroom materials and study skills were extremely disorganized. Her desk was stuffed with irrelevant papers and writing instruments. In addition, she had no systematic way to prepare for tests, complete assignments, or tell time.

Gisela's parents, Mr. and Mrs. Garcia, did not receive these reports well. They adamantly refused to believe their daughter had an internal problem, blaming the school instead (and, indirectly, Mrs. Martinez) for "bad teaching practices." They said Gisela performed well the previous year in another state but refused to release those educational records to the school psychologist. They said Gisela concentrated well at home and finished her schoolwork when they supervised her. They claimed Gisela had no trouble paying attention to them and that, overall, she was a normal 8-year-old.

Mrs. Martinez responded by saying Gisela may have completed her homework but that few assignments were turned in (Gisela often claimed they were lost). The teacher recommended that Mr. and Mrs. Garcia observe their daughter in her reading group and closely review her tests and assignments completed in class. Gisela's parents agreed to do so.

A second meeting occurred 2 months later. The school psychologist, Mrs. Dartil, and Gisela's teacher, Mrs. Martinez, reviewed Gisela's progress and repeated their recommendation for an evaluation. Gisela's school performance was essentially unchanged and Mr. and Mrs. Garcia were now more aware of their daughter's daily academic problems. The parents remained reluctant about testing but, following some private discussions over the next 2 weeks, finally relented and gave their consent. Mrs. Dartil immediately scheduled a comprehensive testing session for Gisela with her initial intent to discover whether the child had a learning disorder or disability.

Assessment

A diagnosis of learning disorder is pertinent when one's "achievement on individually administered, standardized tests in reading, mathematics, or written expression is substantially below that expected for age, schooling, and level of intelligence" [American Psychiatric Association (APA), 2000, p. 49]. "Substantially below" often means a discrepancy of more than 2 standard deviations between levels of achievement and intelligence. Learning problems must significantly interfere with academic or daily functioning. Gisela's learning difficulties certainly interfered with her academic functioning: she had grades of F in reading, spelling, and math and a D in science (though she did receive A grades in music and art). The DSM-IV-TR divides learning disorders into those associated with reading, mathematics, and written expression. Gisela seemed to have learning disorders in reading and written expression.

Learning disorders do not apply if a child's academic problems are primarily due to "normal variations in academic attainment … lack of opportunity, poor teaching, or cultural factors" (APA, 2000, p. 51). Learning disorders do not apply if a person has a sensory deficit, such as visual problems, but may apply if learning problems are clearly in excess of that deficit. Mr. and Mrs. Garcia argued that Gisela's "problems" came from poor teaching in particular and a poorly funded school district in general. They did not think Gisela had a learning disorder. This issue is obviously a delicate one when deciding if a diagnosis of learning disorder applies to a child who fails classes.

Those who evaluate children with possible learning disorders must consider some key points. First, a child's learning problems must be examined in detail because the problems can take many forms, such as poor organization, inability to stay on task, and perceptual problems. Mrs. Martinez mentioned several problems that prevented Gisela from doing well in school. Second, specific deficits such as word-decoding problems could have wide-ranging consequences for general reading or academic achievement. Third, an assessor should carefully consider expectations and concerns of parents and teachers. This was especially pertinent to Gisela given her parents' reservations about her school.

Fourth, an assessor must remember that cognitive and behavioral characteristics influence one another. Language deficits may predispose a child to social withdrawal. Gisela's ongoing academic problems may negatively affect her self-esteem. Fifth, environmental variables such as sociocultural factors must be considered. These factors could affect a child's school-based motivation, competitiveness, attitudes, or achievement orientation. Finally, the presence of biological factors should be considered. An initial assessment of learning disorder may include the Dyslexia Screening Instrument* and the following sample items (Coon, Waguespack, & Polk, 1994):

1. Poor sequencing skills.

2. Poor organization of composition (events are not in chronological order or any discernible order of organization).

3. Has trouble with the alphabet (learning and/or saying).

Mrs. Dartil began her assessment of Gisela using the Wechsler Intelligence Scale for Children (Wechsler, 2003). Cognitive functioning is a central focus when assessing a child with a possible learning disability. One should note wide discrepancies between intelligence test scores and achievement test scores. Gisela received an IQ score of 104, which placed her in the normal or average range. Mrs. Dartil also administered the Wide Range Achievement Test-4 (Wilkinson & Robertson, 2006) to identify weaknesses in Gisela's academic math, reading, and spelling skills. Gisela's standard scores were only 88 for math, 68 for reading, and 60 for spelling. Gisela's intelligence and achievement levels were therefore quite different – she was not performing to her potential.

Some consider discrepancies between intelligence test scores and achievement test scores to be invalid indicators of learning disabilities. Some researchers suggest that reading and listening comprehension should be the focus of assessment (Lyon, Fletcher, & Barnes, 2003). Tests for comprehension should center on a child's absorption of information from a particular passage, inferences made from the passage, and the child's use of information from her background knowledge. In addition, many schools now adopt a "response to intervention" model to replace the traditional IQ-achievement score discrepancy approach. A response to intervention model focuses on universal screening of students to identify early learning problems and more individualized instruction and intervention for such students (Fox, Carta, Strain, Dunlap, & Hemmeter, 2010). A response to intervention model thus replaces a "wait-to-fail" approach, sometimes ascribed to traditional testing (Schatschneider, Wagner, & Crawford, 2008).

Another problem with intelligence and achievement tests is that they do not identify a child's specific deficits or problems. Mrs. Dartil thus reinterviewed Gisela's parents and teacher and examined Gisela's schoolwork and classroom behavior in more detail. Mr. and Mrs. Garcia said Gisela was always a normal child, talking and walking at appropriate ages and interested in others. They did admit that Gisela struggled somewhat in first grade but said her teacher claimed nothing was seriously wrong. No one complained of language problems either. These assertions from the first-grade teacher led Mr. and Mrs. Garcia to their current position that nothing was wrong with their daughter. Mrs. Garcia conceded, however, that Gisela was a slow reader who had trouble identifying certain words. Both were surprised that Gisela could not read by the end of first grade but assumed she was a "late bloomer." Both reaffirmed that Gisela was a well-behaved child and both insisted they were highly motivated to help her academically.

Mrs. Dartil collected copies of Gisela's written classroom work and watched her in the classroom. She noticed that Gisela often took a long time to finish reading and writing assignments and lost points as a result. Her performance improved, however, when allowed enough time. Gisela was easily distracted and fidgety and these behaviors interfered with her on-task behavior. Gisela's work performance did improve, however, when she was isolated from the rest of the class. Finally, the school psychologist saw that Gisela's written work had several problems, such as slow, compressed, and unevenly drawn writing. Gisela spent much time copying and recopying her work, a practice that sometimes frustrated her.

The school psychologist then spoke with Gisela's teacher in more depth. Mrs. Martinez thought Gisela had a "processing deficit" or trouble assimilating and integrating incoming information. She based her assumption on Gisela's struggles with words presented visually. Gisela had problems remembering spelling words she studied from a book. However, Gisela did better when the teacher emphasized learning through the auditory sense, such as saying a word, spelling it aloud, and writing the word on paper. Gisela had no visual sensory deficits, so perceptual or linguistic processing problems may have been responsible for her struggles.

The school psychologist found Gisela's motivation to be good despite her academic setbacks. Gisela said she was interested in extra help to improve her grades and especially her reading. When asked about her fidgeting and moving around, Gisela said she "felt nervous" and sometimes bored in class. She did feel she could control herself, however. Mrs. Dartil saw that Gisela concentrated better and moved less when a task was new or particularly interesting. Mrs. Dartil concluded from her assessment that Gisela did have a moderate learning disorder for reading and written expression. She conveyed to the teacher and to Mr. and Mrs. Garcia, however, that she could address the problems with steps described later.

Risk Factors and Maintaining Variables

Cognitive deficits in learning disorders likely relate to different neurological problems. These cognitive deficits may include (1) perceptual problems, such as trouble distinguishing letters and words, and/or (2) linguistic processing problems, such as trouble organizing speech sounds to form words.

Cognitive deficits or specific linguistic processing difficulties in children with reading problems may relate to abnormalities of the cerebellum and temporal lobe (Eckert, 2004; Silani et al., 2005). Disruptions in neural networks may also lead to a learning disability (Ramus, 2004). Twin data indicate that reading disorder has a moderate to strong genetic influence (Hawke, Wadsworth, & DeFries, 2006). Reading difficulties may relate to changes on chromosomes 1, 2, 3, 6, 11, 13, 15, and 18 (Shastry, 2007).

Changes in the brain's left hemisphere and planum temporale may explain core deficits related to reading problems (Paul, Bott, Heim, Eulitz, & Elbert, 2006). These core deficits, which are independent of intelligence, often include trouble decoding and reading single words. Good readers can recognize single words quickly as they read. Children with reading disabilities identify words more slowly and this lack of speed interferes with their integration and comprehension of the overall material (Shaywitz & Shaywitz, 2005). Whole-language learning, in which children figure out a word by looking at the context of the sentence, may thus be ineffective for this population.

Children with reading disabilities have trouble recognizing words as they read. Word recognition deficits may relate to memory problems as well as language or phonological deficiencies. Children with reading problems have trouble putting together various phonemes, or basic sound units, that comprise a word (e.g., phonemes "sp," "ee," and "ch" comprise the word "speech"). This inability may affect spelling as well.

Gisela's reading and spelling problems did involve trouble with single-word identification. Her academic problems might be due to changes in the left hemisphere and her academic strengths in music and art might be due to a more dominant right hemisphere. Gisela was left-handed as well, which suggests right brain dominance. She did not receive medical or neurological tests, however.

Gisela's reading problems may have been due to memory and phonological processing deficits. She clearly had trouble remembering words she supposedly learned before and often failed to connect sound units to make up a word. Gisela became frustrated when Mrs. Martinez asked the class to sound out a word such as "poisonous." Mrs. Martinez thought Gisela's troubles were simply due to inattention from fidgeting and twirling around. Inattention and phonological awareness, or knowing how to use phonemes to recognize words and process information, are largely independent of one another, however (Lyon et al., 2003). Gisela clearly had learning problems beyond minor behavior problems or symptoms of attention deficit/hyperactivity disorder.

What about Gisela's writing problems? Children with learning disabilities tend to (1) write less, (2) have less organized ideas and transitions in their writing, (3) show less goal orientation, and (4) inadequately monitor their work for appropriate spelling and grammar (Berninger, Nielsen, Abbott, Wijsman, & Raskind, 2008). In addition, many children with writing and spelling difficulties have trouble producing letters, organizing finger movements, mapping out written words phonologically, and integrating visual-motor stimuli.

Gisela certainly had trouble integrating the phonological structure of words. She often became frustrated and did not check her work properly for mistakes.

Her teacher also questioned Gisela's ability to coordinate visual and motor movements. Gisela did show some characteristics of good readers and spellers, however. She was goal-oriented, had no obvious trouble with finger movements, and produced letters without difficulty (albeit slowly and in a compressed manner). Patterns such as Gisela's are not unusual in children with learning disabilities and attest to the enormous heterogeneity or variety of symptoms often seen in this population.

Gisela did not have many problems with math (dyscalculia), but the etiology of this learning disorder is briefly presented here. Children with dyscalculia often have trouble enumerating, manipulating amounts, understanding mathematical concepts, doing computations, and reading, writing, or naming mathematical symbols. These children may have problems with visual-spatial and visual-perceptual functioning, intelligence, verbal ability, and anxiety. Dyscalculia could result from changes in the brain's left parietotemporal area (Shalev, 2004). Some have linked dyscalculia to the structure of elementary textbooks in arithmetic. These textbooks may lack attention to mastery of basic mathematical processes (Lyon et al., 2003).

Learning disorders overlap in many cases (46%) with attention deficit/hyperactivity disorder (ADHD) (Larson, Russ, Kahn, & Halfon, 2011). The causes of ADHD and learning disabilities may therefore overlap. Gisela was often distracted and sometimes overactive when she fidgeted and twirled. In addition, children with learning disabilities may have social, emotional, depressive, and conduct disorder-related problems. These problems are more variable – they did not apply to Gisela – and may relate to the frustration and social rejection that sometimes comes with academic failure.

Developmental Aspects

Children with reading disabilities (dyslexia) often have language or phonological processing deficits. These deficits can occur as early as the first year of life. Delays may occur in vocalizations such as babbling or cooing. Toddlers may show speech or language delay (Nelson, Nygren, Walker, & Panoscha, 2006). Comprehension problems can occur at this time as well and may be present in children with trouble understanding what others say. Behavior problems associated with language difficulties also become more apparent at this time. Common behavior problems include overactivity, impulsivity, inattention, aggression, and social withdrawal.

Mr. and Mrs. Garcia said Gisela was normal during her preschool years. This is not unusual and shows the difficulty in identifying children with learning disabilities before they begin formal schooling. Mr. and Mrs. Garcia did say Gisela was sometimes "scattered" and inattentive but they assumed this was part of her general personality or normal for a preschooler. They noticed Gisela's fidgeting but did not see this or her other behaviors as seriously problematic.

Learning disabilities become more apparent during the initial school-age period as children try to meet academic requirements. Kindergartners must listen to instructions, verbally express their desires, sit still, engage in basic writing, and identify letters, among other tasks. Children with learning disabilities sometimes have trouble with these areas and may act out or withdraw from others. Extra practice and behavior modification programs can often help curtail these problems. If problems go undetected or if a child gets by, however, then learning disabilities will worsen during first and second grade. Language skills are strong predictors of later reading ability (Bishop & Snowling, 2004).

Kindergarten was largely unremarkable for Gisela. Her teacher at the time said Gisela took longer than most children to start a task and was easily distracted. She had no language problems or trouble identifying letters, however. Gisela was socially appropriate and well behaved but sought a lot of teacher attention regarding class projects. Gisela's learning disabilities came into full bloom during first and second grades, however, as she grappled with formal reading, writing, spelling, and mathematical tasks. Phonological processing problems became more evident at this point, and Gisela had trouble decoding various words.

Reading problems are stable over time, reaching even into adulthood. Reading problems may be stable because many children with learning disabilities are not identified until discrepancies between intelligence and reading achievement become very apparent. A delay in finding a learning disability may therefore delay treatment and add to the intransigence of the disorder. The stability of learning disabilities may also result from various and uncoordinated interventions by educators and others. This practice is harmful to those with severe learning problems, so their troubles remain stable. Many children with learning disabilities continue to experience academic failure, so their motivation for completing schoolwork declines as well (Lyon et al., 2003). Decreased motivation obviously harms their chances for achieving normal academic performance in the future.

Gisela had a mixture of good and bad prognostic signs. She was fortunate her assessment and treatment occurred near the end of second grade. Earlier detection and better parental cooperation might have led to faster treatment, however. In addition, Gisela was fortunate that Mrs. Rankin, the school's special resource teacher, had experience treating children with learning disabilities. Gisela's motivation was of most concern, however. Mrs. Martinez, the second-grade teacher, said Gisela was increasingly frustrated with her assignments. Her frustration may have been linked to the difficulty of her assignments, which were more complex as the end of the year approached. Gisela may have been disappointed as well by having so few passing grades despite several months of effort.

The prognosis for children with learning disabilities depends largely on the severity of their speech and language impairments. Children with reading problems often have continued trouble naming words quickly, recognizing basic speech sounds, spelling, and reading symbols. Many eventually have anxiety and antisocial behavior problems and few enroll in college (Beitchman et al., 2001; Johnson, Beitchman, & Brownlie, 2010). Fortunately, Gisela's speech and language were relatively good. Better outcome for those with learning disorders relates to higher intelligence and socioeconomic status, early diagnosis and intervention, early language stimulation, fewer comorbid diagnoses, and less severe disorder (Pratt & Patel, 2007).

Gisela's long-term prognosis is probably good because her intelligence is normal, her learning difficulties were addressed in second grade, and significant others in her life were motivated to improve her condition. Good outcomes may not always be the case, however, in districts whose school psychologists are over-whelmed by the number of children with learning disabilities. Many children in these schools continue to struggle academically without help and drop out of school prematurely. Long-term prognosis can therefore depend heavily on whether extracurricular resources are available.

Treatment

Treatment for children with learning disabilities usually involves several elements that require a coordinated effort among teachers, parents, and the student (Lyon et al., 2003):

1. Enrolling in academic remedial programs (sometimes in a part-time segre-gated classroom setting).
2. Improving metacognitive skills.
3. Controlling associated behavior problems that interfere with learning.
4. Increasing student motivation.

Academic remedial programs should emphasize many opportunities for success and devote extensive time to presenting information to students. These programs must allow students to demonstrate their abilities in different areas and practice various skills. Teachers should provide frequent feedback and closely follow a child's progress in deficient academic areas (Calhoon, Sandow, & Hunter, 2010).

Remedial programs must also be highly structured and directed. They should emphasize concrete concepts, eliminate distractions, and progress systematically. Programs that offer directed instruction for word-decoding and recognition skills work well for those with reading problems (Edmonds et al., 2009). Remedial programs should emphasize one-on-one teaching, mastery learning, generaliza-tion of learned material, and incentives for academic performance. These programs should target all of the child's learning deficiencies (Snowling & Hulme, 2011).

Mr. and Mrs. Garcia allowed Gisela to attend a special instruction class for 1 hour each school day. They agreed to help their daughter practice what she learned during this class for 30 minutes each night. Mrs. Rankin, the special resource teacher, began working with Gisela immediately because little time remained in the school year. Mrs. Rankin decided to concentrate heavily on Gisela's reading and decoding problems. This first involved a review of basic concepts such as knowledge of different vowel and consonant phonemes, pho-neme combinations (e.g., "ou" and "sp"), and blending of phonics into words. Only the last concept seemed particularly difficult for Gisela.

Following this basic review, which lasted 2 weeks, Mrs. Rankin moved quickly to mastery of reading material. She asked Gisela to review a particular passage from a book and write down words she believed she would find trouble-some. Gisela read the words on index cards and practiced identifying the pho-nemes of each word, blending the phonemes, and learning the definition of the word. Mrs. Rankin then read the passage as Gisela followed along with her fin-ger or a pencil. Gisela then read the passage aloud to Mrs. Rankin and once to herself. She repeated reading the passage until she made few errors (Gersten, Fuchs, Williams, & Baker, 2001; Wong, 2008).

The teacher next addressed Gisela's spelling. Many vocabulary words can be generated from reading exercises so Gisela took a certain number home to study. Some suggest that children in first and second grades take home three words and that those in the third and fourth grades take home four words. The child studies the assigned words and takes a spelling and vocabulary test on the words the next day. The child must spell the word presented orally and write out its definition. Words a child has mastered, both in spelling and in meaning, are prominently displayed to enhance the student's self-esteem and give feedback on her aca-demic progress (Wong, 2004, 2008).

Gisela found helpful the extra attention spent on reading and spelling, espe-cially word decoding and recognition. Mrs. Rankin's rapport with Gisela was good and this helped improve Gisela's mood in the classroom. Gisela initially averaged about 11 errors per page read but this quickly diminished to 2 errors per page by the end of the school year. Unfortunately, the books chosen for Gisela to read were at a late first-grade or early second-grade level. Mrs. Rankin thought continued work over the summer might boost Gisela to a mid-second-grade level by the time she entered third grade.

Another goal of treatment for children with learning disabilities is enhancing general metacognition. Metacognition refers to an awareness of one's thinking or problem-solving processes. Metacognition applies especially to children with dys-calculia who have trouble conceptualizing and solving arithmetic problems abstractly (Garrett, Mazzocco, & Baker, 2006). Children learn to state a math problem in words of their choosing, visualize the problem, predict an answer, and self-monitor their computations.

Several metacognitive targets exist for children with dyslexia (Gersten et al., 2001; Wong, 2008):

1. Increase awareness of the purpose of reading (i.e., for meaning, not simple decoding).

2. Improve knowledge of reading strategies (e.g., reading differently for plea-sure and for mastery of material).

3. Develop sensitivity to important parts of a text (i.e., emphasis on relevant information).

4. Learn to detect inconsistencies in sentences.

5. Develop ability to resolve a comprehension problem (e.g., by using "look back" strategies).

Metacognitive skills for reading also involve understanding the reading pro-cess and why reading is important. Mrs. Rankin focused primarily on teaching

Gisela to monitor her comprehension and refer back to the reading material as quickly and frequently as possible to enhance retention.

Another important goal of treatment for this population is to control behavior problems that interfere with learning. This was not too pertinent to Gisela, whose behaviors were limited to twirling, fidgeting, and minor distraction. Mrs. Martinez gave feedback to Gisela when she was overactive or distracted and praised her appropriate on-task behavior. More extensive procedures may be needed for other children. Some children with learning disabilities have symptoms of hyperactivity, so stimulant medication may help them focus attention and curtail excess motor activity. Token economies with response cost may be useful as well for acting-out and disruptive behaviors.

A key challenge when addressing children with learning disabilities is to maintain their motivation to complete homework and other assignments. Gisela's parents placed her on a reward system that included weekend privileges for completing and turning in a certain number of homework assignments (recall that many of Gisela's earlier assignments were lost). This reward system was later extended to include studying appropriately, organizing materials, and developing typing skills so Gisela did not have to write so much.

Gisela's progress through the following summer was good, but she attained a reading level equivalent only to early second grade. Mrs. Rankin, Mrs. Martinez, and Mrs. Dartil discussed the possibility of retaining Gisela in second grade. Mr. and Mrs. Garcia were strongly opposed to this, however, and agreed instead to increase Gisela's reading instruction time with a resource teacher to 90 minutes per day. Both parents promised to remain active in helping their daughter practice her academic skills at home. This was largely successful and Gisela did reach a mid-third-grade reading level by the end of the next school year.

DISCUSSION QUESTIONS

1. A thorny issue in deciding on a diagnosis of learning disorder is discovering whether the problem is internal to the child or a function of external factors such as poor teaching or inadequate schools. What information would you use to make this distinction? What criteria would you use to conclude that a child does not have a learning disorder or that the surrounding environment is to blame for a child's academic problems? How would you address a case involving the latter situation?

2. Some claim that boys, who often have trouble with reading, receive many tutorial and special resource programs at school. Girls, however, who often have trouble with arithmetic, do not always receive the same type of resources. Do you think this is true? Why or why not?

3. Boys generally receive more attention from classroom teachers than girls. Do you think this relates to gender differences seen in learning disorders? If so, how can it be remedied? Explore possible benefits and disadvantages of gender-specific classrooms.

4. Are tests for intelligence culturally or racially biased? What evaluation process could you use to eliminate all bias? Is this possible?

5. Assume Gisela's family was new to the United States. How would the evaluation and treatment process mentioned here change, if at all?

6. How might use of new technology in computers and computer software affect future education in general and the prevalence and treatment of . learning disorders in particular?

7. Gisela's parents resisted having their daughter evaluated. How might you address parents like these in the case of a child with a possible learning disorder?

8. How might you increase a child's self-confidence about her schoolwork?

Chapter 8

Conduct Disorder and Aggression

Symptoms

Derek Pratt was a 15-year-old European American male referred by his school guidance counselor, juvenile detention officer, and father to an outpatient mental health clinic for youths with disruptive behavior problems. Derek was in tenth grade at the time of his initial assessment. Mr. Pratt, Derek's father, contacted the clinic and insisted on an immediate appointment given his son's recent lawbreaking activities, school absences, and contact with the juvenile criminal justice system.

A clinical psychologist who treated adolescents with externalizing behavior disorders interviewed Derek and his father separately. Derek was belligerent and confrontational at the outset of the interview, insisting that the interviewer address him by his street name ("Tree") and saying he would not answer any questions "I don't feel like answering." The therapist informed Derek in detail about his right to confidentiality but Derek remained dismissive and said, "You'll say anything you want to anyway, so just get this over with so I can get out of here."

Questioning revealed that Derek had been getting into more serious trouble of late and was arrested for shoplifting 4 weeks before. Derek was caught with one other youth when he and a dozen friends swarmed a convenience store and took everything they could before leaving in cars. This event followed similar crimes at a compact disc store and a retail clothing store. Derek blamed his friends for his arrest because they apparently left him behind as he straggled out of the store. He was charged only with shoplifting, however, after police found him holding just three candy bars and a bag of potato chips. Derek expressed no remorse for the theft or any care for the store clerk who was injured when one of the teens pushed her into a glass case. When informed of the clerk's injury, Derek replied, "I didn't do it, so what do I care?"

The psychologist questioned Derek further about other legal violations and discovered a rather extended history of trouble. Derek was arrested for vandalism 10 months earlier for breaking windows and damaging cars on school property. He received probation for 6 months because this was his first offense. Derek also boasted of other exploits for which he was not caught, including several shoplifting episodes, heavy marijuana use on the weekends, joyriding, and missing school. Derek missed 23 days (50%) of school since the beginning of the academic year. In addition, he described break-in attempts of his neighbors' apartments and precocious sexual activity, the latter of which seemed overly boastful to the psychologist. Only rarely during the interview did Derek stray from his bravado. Toward the end, for example, he said he did not like himself much, admitting, "I really don't care what happens to me."

The psychologist asked Derek about his current situation and his goals for the future. Derek said he did not expect to receive serious consequences from the judge for the shoplifting charge and did not care about going back to school. He was indifferent or hostile to suggestions made by the interviewer about attending part-time school programs, stating cryptically instead that he and his friends would "take care of ourselves." Derek said his father often worked and did not spend much time with him. Derek did not mind this, however, seeming content and even insistent about maintaining the status quo.

A subsequent interview with Mr. Pratt confirmed some of Derek's report, though Mr. Pratt was not well informed about his son's behavior. He said the school counselor and juvenile detention officer strongly recommended that he and Derek pursue therapy given the upcoming consequences that were expected. With respect to school, Derek was about to be expelled for extended absences. With respect to criminal charges, Derek's recent shoplifting arrest marked his second charged offense, so a jail or community service sentence was expected. The counselor believed that family therapy, however, could mediate punishments from the school and court.

Mr. Pratt was cooperative during the interview but careful to justify his actions as a parent and not assume too much blame. He complained that being a single parent was difficult, that he often worked, that school officials waited too long before telling him of Derek's absenteeism, and that police officers deliberately chose his son instead of gang leaders for arrest. Mr. Pratt said he wanted to help his son "get on the right track" and was hopeful the psychologist would "do what's needed to get through to Derek." This latter statement implied that Mr. Pratt did not want to expend much personal effort in Derek's treatment.

Mr. Pratt said Derek was usually compliant when home but that his son was often with friends during the day and night. He was unsure what Derek did when away from home but speculated that his son stayed with friends and played video games. He said he had a good relationship with his son and they had talked at length about Derek's recent school and legal problems. Mr. Pratt said Derek was willing to change his behaviors and return to school. He said, however, that Derek usually lied about such things and generally could not be trusted. Mr. Pratt stated as well, rather bluntly, that he planned to leave Derek and the area as soon as his son was 18 years old.

The psychologist contacted Derek's school counselor and juvenile detention officer with Mr. Pratt's permission. Derek's school counselor said she was unfamiliar with Derek because of his many absences but had spoken with several of his teachers. The teachers said Derek withdrew in class, contributed little to in-class projects, and completed few homework assignments. He was failing each class and his prospects of passing the academic year were slim. Derek showed no overt behavior problems, however. The counselor believed that the presence of several strong male authority figures at school prevented antisocial behavior on Derek's part.

The juvenile detention officer said Derek was to appear before a judge in the near future, at which time the teenager might receive a sentence of some kind. The officer believed Derek was at risk of receiving a strong punishment because this was his second arrest in less than a year and because Derek had a disrespectful attitude. He was confident the judge would consider their family counseling and mediate the sentence but was skeptical that Derek and his father would continue to attend therapy. The officer based his remark on their history: Mr. Pratt and Derek had kept only one of three appointments with him in the past 3 weeks.

The psychologist (with permission) called Derek's mother, Mrs. Lander, who had remarried and lived out of state. She said she had little contact with Mr. Pratt but did talk to Derek about once a month. She voiced her concern that Derek was not properly supervised. Mrs. Lander added that she had no plans to visit her son and did not think it was possible for him to live with her. She apparently made this decision based on Derek's behavior over the past 2 years. The psychologist preliminarily concluded that Derek met DSM-IV-TR criteria for conduct disorder.

Assessment

The essential feature of conduct disorder is a "repetitive and persistent pattern of behavior in which the basic rights of others or major age-appropriate societal norms or rules are violated" [American Psychiatric Association (APA), 2000, p. 93]. A youth must show three specific symptoms for at least 12 months and at least one symptom over the past 6 months. These symptoms include

- intimidating others;
- starting fights;
- using a weapon;
- being physically cruel to people or animals;
- stealing;
- committing sexual assault;
- destroying property;
- setting fires;
- breaking into another's property;
- lying;
- staying out at night;
- running away from home;
- refusing to attend school.

Researchers sometimes group disruptive child behaviors into four main types: property violations, aggression, status violations, and oppositional behavior (Frick, Cornell, Barry, Bodin, & Dane, 2003). Symptoms of conduct disorder must cause significant impairment in daily functioning. Childhood onset of the disorder is determined if a symptom was present before age 10 years; adolescent onset is determined if no symptom was present before age 10 years. Severity of the disorder can be mild, moderate, or severe.

The psychologist arrived at a preliminary diagnosis of conduct disorder for Derek based on knowledge that, over the past year, Derek engaged in shoplifting, school refusal behavior, acts of vandalism, and curfew breaking. His troubles with the legal system and poor school performance indicated general impairment in functioning as well. Derek had not physically harmed anyone in recent months, however, so the psychologist initially rated his conduct disorder as moderate.

Clinicians usually obtain information from several sources to assess youths with possible conduct disorder. This is because conduct disorder often involves a negative impact on others or negative interactions with others. Assessment should focus on behaviors (e.g., aggression, noncompliance) that are most problematic, whether the behaviors are overt or covert, severity and scope of the behaviors, variables that maintain the behaviors, parental responses to the behaviors, onset of the behaviors, and comorbid conditions, such as attention deficit/ hyperactivity disorder (Matthys & Lochman, 2010).

The psychologist conducted interviews with Derek and his parents, school counselor, and juvenile detention officer. The psychologist also spoke in later sessions with three of Derek's teachers, two of his friends, and one of his neighbors (all with Derek and Mr. Pratt's permission). These interviews revealed that Derek was peer focused and considered fellow gang members to be his surrogate family. This attachment explained his earlier remark that he and his friends would take care of themselves. Derek had a quick temper, seemed frustrated by recent life events, and was a threat to others. A neighbor reported that several residents of the apartment complex were aware of Derek's behavior and took extra precautions to protect themselves and their belongings when he was around. This was especially true if Derek wanted something specific, such as money, or was under the influence of drugs.

Therapists interview many people but use more than one method to assess youths with possible conduct disorder. Such methods include child self-report measures, parent and teacher rating scales, reviews of academic and legal records, and direct observation. Commonly used child self-report measures for assessing youths with conduct disorder include the Youth Self-Report (Achenbach & Rescorla, 2001), which solicits ratings from adolescents of their internalizing and externalizing behaviors, and the Children's Depression Inventory (Kovacs, 2003), which solicits youths' ratings of recent depressive symptoms and acting-out behaviors such as fighting.

Derek's scores on these measures revealed clinical levels of externalizing behavior, as one might expect, as well as near-clinical levels of internalizing behavior. Derek rated certain items on the Youth Self-Report as particularly relevant to himself, including feelings of sadness, worthlessness, self-consciousness, and suspiciousness. Derek scored just below the clinical range on the Children's Depression Inventory. He endorsed items indicating worries about the future, doubts he was as good as other kids, and depressed mood. The psychologist thus believed his client had some level of subclinical depression.

Ratings from adolescents with conduct disorder are not always reliable so ratings from knowledgeable others are commonly solicited. Parent rating scales for this population include the Child Behavior Checklist (CBCL) (Achenbach & Rescorla, 2001), Revised Behavior Problem Checklist (Quay & Peterson, 1996), Conners Rating Scales (Conners 3) (Conners, 2008), and Eyberg Child Behavior Inventory (Eyberg & Pincus, 1999). Family measures may be useful as well. A common teacher rating scale for this population is the Teacher's Report Form (Achenbach & Rescorla, 2001). Clinicians may derive parent and teacher ratings as well from the Conduct Disorder Scale,* sample items from which include (Gilliam, 2002) the following:

1. The person actively defies or refuses to comply with adults' requests or rules.

2. The person creates disturbances.

3. The person shows little or no shame or guilt after being caught doing something wrong.

4. The person lies to obtain goods or favors or to avoid obligations.

5. The person bullies, threatens, or intimidates others.

Derek's father provided CBCL ratings and endorsed very high levels of externalizing behavior and very low levels of internalizing behavior. This may have been due to Mr. Pratt's overemphasis on Derek's recent lawbreaking events and the father's general ignorance of his son's depressive symptoms. Family assessment revealed high levels of independence and surprisingly low levels of conflict in the two-person family.

Teacher ratings were not helpful because school officials did not know Derek well. A review of Derek's school records indicated a gradual decline in school performance. Derek was an A and B student in elementary school, a C and D student in junior high school, but an F student in high school. Such a decline is not unusual in this population, but enhancing academic competence should be a top priority in treatment because good school performance usually means fewer behavior problems.

Direct observations are useful to assess a youth's interactions with his family. The psychologist watched Derek and his father interact in his office. Their interactions were generally cordial but distant. Neither seemed too interested in the conversation of the other and, contrary to what one might expect, no arguing or major disagreements occurred. Each seemed content to let the other live his life with the implicit assumption that the separate arrangement would eventually be

---

* J. E.Gilliam, Pro Ed, Inc., 2002, Conduct Disorder Scale. Used with permission.

permanent. Neither party was thus particularly willing to change the current situation. Derek's disruptive behavior was simply a source of irritation for Mr. Pratt, who was concerned with devoting time to appointments with school officials, a juvenile detention officer, and a psychologist.

Direct observations of a child in his natural environment can yield more information about family and peer interactions, antecedents and consequences of disruptive behavior, and opportunities for reinforcement. Direct observation may help a therapist (1) decide whether a child's behavior is severe enough to warrant residential treatment or (2) discover child maltreatment. Direct observation may also help a therapist dispel bias regarding a family's willingness and ability to pursue behavior change. A therapist might be assigned a court-referred adolescent with conduct disorder and develop erroneous expectations about the family's motivation to resolve their problems.

Risk Factors and Maintaining Variables

Conduct disorder has a complex and intertwined etiology. Many biological and psychological variables influence the disorder. These variables are difficult to pinpoint in a particular case but researchers often infer a combination of biological predispositions and problematic environmental factors. Many cases of conduct disorder likely involve an interaction of genetic or neurological factors with a highly dysfunctional family environment.

No consistent evidence has linked a particular genotype to conduct disorder or aggression. Family factors are probably better predictors of whether someone with a particular genotype will become antisocial. Genetic factors may instead influence conduct disorder by altering temperament, novelty seeking, or level of the neurotransmitter serotonin. Difficult temperament in young children has been associated with general behavior problems over time (Frick & White, 2008). Serotonin levels tend to be lower in those who commit violent offenses and in those with poor impulse control (Cadoret et al., 2003; Cappadocia, Desrocher, Pepler, & Schroeder, 2009). Lower serotonin levels are also common to people with depression and many adolescents with conduct disorder have depressive symptoms. Derek's symptoms included low self-esteem, feelings of worthlessness, and social withdrawal during school.

Other biological factors may relate to conduct disorder as well, especially for boys. These factors include dopamine and endocrinergic changes such as higher levels of testosterone and androstenedione, unusual brain wave patterns, minor central nervous system dysfunction affecting cognitive abilities, increased physiological responsiveness, and lower than normal levels of autonomic arousal (Raine, 2002). Adolescents with conduct disorder may engage in risk-taking and thrill-seeking activities to increase their level of biological arousal. Derek said many of his illegal activities, such as drug use and shoplifting, made him "feel good." Sensory reinforcement may thus be a key reason why some delinquent acts continue despite severe or ongoing punishment.

Biological factors likely play some causal role in conduct disorder, but familial or psychological variables are probably more dominant. Marital discord, family dysfunction, poor parenting, and parental psychopathology are present in many if not most cases of delinquency (Beauchaine, Webster-Stratton, & Reid, 2005). Parents of children with conduct disorder sometimes have antisocial behavior, alcoholism, or other problems themselves. These behaviors, which also have a hereditary component, can be modeled by a child or produce conditions that lead to acting-out behaviors. Mr. Pratt's lack of supervision of Derek bordered on neglect. This led to more opportunities for Derek to engage in antisocial behavior.

Conduct disorder relates closely to marital discord and divorce, as was true for Derek. The mechanisms of this relationship may seem obvious – stress from a parental breakup may be difficult on children. Children often react to parental fighting and divorce with aggression (McCloskey & Lichter, 2003). Conversely, however, acting-out behaviors in children may develop first and then lead to marital disagreements about discipline and other issues. Either way, a strong association exists between family problems and conduct disorder.

Derek's parents had been divorced for 4 years. During their marriage, Mr. and Mrs. Pratt often disagreed about alleged affairs, finances, and division of labor in the home. Their fights, though never physically violent, contained rather venomous verbal exchanges. Mrs. Pratt retained custody of Derek's two younger sisters, moved out of state, and remarried after 12 years of marriage to Mr. Pratt. Derek said these stressful events (divorce, school withdrawal, moving) and loss of contact with much of his family were difficult to handle but he felt he adjusted well after 1 year. The psychologist disagreed, however. Child maltreatment also relates to development of conduct disorder and later violent behavior (Jaffee, Caspi, Moffitt, & Taylor, 2004).

Child-based psychological factors may contribute to conduct disorder. Youths who are more aggressive, compared to those less aggressive, tend to be more egocentric and have less well-developed problem-solving and moral reasoning abilities. These youths are impulsive, view the actions of others as hostile, get caught for negative behaviors, and show little responsiveness to consequences (James, Blair, Monson, & Frederickson, 2001; Warden & MacKinnon, 2003).

What variables maintain conduct disorder across time? Sensory reinforcement may play a role for youths whose biological arousal is lower than normal. Certain behaviors may be designed to increase arousal, including drug use, speeding, sexual assault, fighting, and overactivity. Some adolescents may engage in antisocial behaviors to escape aversive situations as well. Examples of such behaviors include school refusal, noncompliance, running away from home, and social withdrawal.

Achenbach and Rescorla (2001), in their empirical classification system for childhood behavior problems, found that two major factors define externalizing behavior: aggressive behaviors and rule-breaking behaviors. Aggressive behaviors include arguing, being disobedient, fighting, attacking, screaming, teasing, having temper tantrums, and issuing threats. These behaviors imply that social attention can maintain conduct disorder because most require interactions with, or negative attention from, other people, such as parents, teachers, and peers.

Rule-breaking behaviors include lying, cheating, setting fires, stealing, using alcohol and other drugs, and vandalizing. These behaviors imply that tangible rewards can maintain conduct disorder. A teenager may engage in shoplifting, vandalism, and lying to obtain clothes, food, or other items. This was certainly true for Derek.

Knowing what maintains conduct disorder can help a therapist choose the best treatment option. If an aggressive teenager is primarily motivated by social attention or escape, then treatment may need to focus on the adolescent, parents, and relevant others. If an aggressive teenager is motivated primarily by sensory reinforcement or tangible rewards, then treatment could focus more specifically on the adolescent. Many adolescents also engage in conduct-disordered behavior for a variety of reasons, which would naturally make treatment more complex.

Developmental Aspects

Some level of antisocial behavior is typical in many adolescents, and even severe antisocial behavior often starts and ends in the teenage years (Frick, 2006). Many youths with conduct disorder begin their misbehaviors in childhood and this could lead to long-term effects in adolescence and adulthood. Difficult temperament and social information-processing deficits may damage attachment with parents, conditions of poverty may limit intellectual stimulation or nutrition, family dysfunction may escalate a child's attention-seeking and aggressive behaviors, stressful life events and peer rejection may trigger depressive symptoms, and poor educational opportunities may blunt problem-solving abilities (Brennan, Hall, Bor, Najman, & Williams, 2003). These childhood patterns may not necessarily lead to conduct disorder but, if they do, the disorder will tend to be severe and persistent.

Another childhood behavior pattern that might lead to conduct disorder in adolescence is oppositional defiant disorder. The essential feature of oppositional defiant disorder is a "recurrent pattern of negativistic, defiant, disobedient, and hostile behavior toward authority figures that persists for at least 6 months" (APA, 2000, p. 100). These children lose their temper easily, become angry, argue, annoy others, and blame others for their mistakes. They may also be spiteful and oversensitive. These behaviors often worsen over time and, if combined with aggression and family dysfunction, become excellent predictors of adolescent delinquency.

How might parent/family variables and noncompliance/aggression interact in the development of conduct disorder? Patterson theorized that some parents inadvertently reward children for aggression and noncompliance (Granic & Patterson, 2006). Two scenarios may explain how this happens. In a positive reinforcement trap, a child is initially aggressive or noncompliant and parents give rewards or try to bribe the child to stop. Alternatively, parents may blame others, such as school officials, for their child's behavior problems. In a negative reinforcement trap, a child is initially aggressive or noncompliant (1) to get something he wants or

(2) to get out of something he does not want to do. Some parents eventually give in to the child's misbehavior after intense arguing with the child. In both traps, the child learns to "coerce" family members into giving something the child wants by using aggression or noncompliance. This coercion becomes more severe as the child ages.

A negative reinforcement trap was not present during Derek's younger years. As Mr. and Mrs. Pratt fought more, however, a permissive family environment evolved. Derek's parents became more concerned with their problems and less consistent in their parenting. Derek's moral reasoning and social skills may thus not have developed well. Derek also engaged in problematic behaviors to get his parents' attention, including fights at school and stealing. These attempts to get attention largely failed but Derek did get attention from peers and tangible rewards from criminal behaviors, such as shoplifting. He became more popular with his delinquent peers and felt his true "home" to be his association with them. Derek associated with these peers even more following Mr. Pratt's divorce and increased withdrawal from his son.

Many adolescents with conduct disorder no longer show aggressive or criminal behavior in adulthood (Olsson, Hansson, & Cederblad, 2008). More than a third of those with conduct disorder will later display symptoms of antisocial personality disorder, however (Lahey, Loeber, Burke, & Applegate, 2005). This disorder involves extreme sociopathy, failure to conform, deception, impulsivity, aggression, irresponsibility, and lack of remorse. This is a serious personality disorder that may remit somewhat during middle age but often leads to incarceration or death. Prospective studies indicate that youths with conduct disorder are at risk for later substance use, bipolar disorder, anxiety, depression, homelessness, and violence convictions (Biederman et al., 2008; Odgers et al., 2007).

Derek's childhood aggression did seem to be a good predictor of his later delinquent behavior, though many other variables certainly contributed to his problems. The mere presence of aggression does not guarantee the development of delinquency (Frick et al., 2003). Authoritative parenting styles, appropriate punishment of aggression, reinforcement of prosocial behavior, and social and academic competence may help prevent adolescent conduct disorder. Perhaps more careful parenting could have prevented some of Derek's behaviors.

What about girls with conduct disorder? Conduct problems differ little between boys and girls, though girls come to the attention of authorities more so for status offenses. Girls with conduct problems show more depression and experience aggression more within the context of close family relationships than with peers. Early maltreatment may be more common among girls than boys with conduct problems. Girls also tend to be aggressive toward family members but boys are generally aggressive toward peers. Boys and girls with conduct problems often engage in unprotected sex as well, which generally carries more risk for females (Ehrensaft, 2005). Derek's two younger sisters had no maladaptive behavior problems, however.

Derek's long-term prognosis is likely only fair. His childhood aggression, problem-solving difficulties, school failure, depressive symptoms, and extensive family dysfunction were poor prognostic signs. There were some bright spots, however. Derek's intelligence was above average, he was largely self-sufficient, and he did have some insight into the futility of his current behavior. He did not have long-term plans but wanted a more mainstream life like the one he had during childhood.

Treatment

Preventing delinquency is desirable because treating adolescents with conduct disorder is often difficult and unsuccessful. This is due to the complex nature of the problem, its severity and duration, and frequently extensive family dysfunction. Intervention often consists of parent-familial, social-cognitive, peer- and school-based, and community-oriented or residential treatment (Matthys & Lochman, 2010). Derek's treatment included elements of the first three types. Other common therapies include medication and group interventions. A multisystemic approach applies to extensive cases and focuses on relevant home, school, and community factors (Henggeler, 2011).

Parent-familial interventions for more moderate cases typically focus on contingency management or other ways to train parents to change a child's behavior at home (Eyberg, Nelson, & Boggs, 2008). Parents learn to shift social and tangible rewards away from inappropriate and antisocial behaviors and toward appropriate and prosocial behaviors. Techniques include contracting, restructuring parent commands, setting daily routines, and monitoring a child more closely. Clinicians also use communication skills training for family members as an adjunct treatment.

Much of Derek's therapy concentrated on (1) improving communication between Derek and his father and (2) increasing Mr. Pratt's monitoring of his son. Both goals proved difficult to achieve because Derek and his father missed several appointments and were generally unwilling to talk to one another. More time was thus spent discussing Mr. Pratt's personal issues that led to his emotional distance from Derek. The psychologist discovered that Mr. Pratt's divorce was harder on him than first thought and that he actively tried to forget about his failed marriage. Derek was a constant reminder of this, however, and his problems reinforced Mr. Pratt's sense of personal failure. Mr. Pratt's ability to monitor his son's behavior and his motivation to change the current situation remained inadequate.

Communication skills training between Derek and his father was only partially effective because neither had much interest in talking to the other. The psychologist was able to get both to paraphrase the other's statements accurately but poor motivation was the main problem in developing more extended conversations. The psychologist had to be wary of conducting therapy that was perceived by Derek and his father as too challenging or threatening, lest they leave treatment altogether. Substantial therapy time was thus spent exploring general family issues that seemed to inhibit communication.

The psychologist formed contracts to reduce Derek's drug use and school refusal behavior. Derek and Mr. Pratt did put effort into designing these contracts but made little effort to apply them at home. Poor motivation sabotaged this treatment technique as well and no change occurred in Derek's drug use. The one bright spot was that Derek agreed to attend an after-school program that allowed him to earn partial credits toward his high school diploma. His attendance was spotty but Derek completed the necessary work over a 3-month period.

Treatment also involved social-cognitive techniques with Derek. Much of this treatment focused on Derek's negative self-statements and depressive symptoms and he responded best to this approach. He was shown the link between his mood and behavior, especially how negative thoughts sometimes led to reckless and impulsive behavior. The psychologist then described different types of cognitive distortions, especially minimization; Derek had a tendency to undervalue himself and his interactions with others. Derek learned to examine both sides of a thought and think about alternative and more realistic thoughts. Derek's depression did improve to some extent over the course of therapy.

The psychologist instructed Derek in ways to manage his anger and control his impulses. Emphasis was placed on Derek's problem-solving skills. The psychologist presented the teenager with different problem scenarios and asked him to develop potential solutions. The psychologist modeled various self-statements Derek could use in the process. Both assigned a grade to each solution and Derek implemented the one with the best grade. He then learned to evaluate the usefulness and effectiveness of the solution. The psychologist gave Derek a hypothetical problem, such as a dare from his friends to shoplift a compact disc. Various solutions to this problem were generated, including avoidance of these peers, declining the challenge because of prior arrests, and walking away. The psychologist covered many problem scenarios and potential solutions with Derek, who grasped the concept but never applied the skills to real-life situations.

Treatment also involved, to a lesser extent, management of Derek's wide range of behaviors in his new classroom. Derek often shifted between acting disruptively, appropriately, or withdrawn in the classroom. The psychologist identified cues that led Derek to act in such different ways. Derek was most disruptive when unexpectedly asked to answer a question in class, most appropriate when social interactions in the classroom were under his control, and most withdrawn when left alone. The psychologist met with the teacher to illustrate these patterns and prevent future misbehavior. The teacher started giving Derek a short list of questions that might be asked in class the next day. He could then prepare answers for the questions the night before and answer them the next day in class. The teacher made sure Derek had many opportunities to interact with her and his classmates during breaks. The teacher said Derek's attendance remained uneven but his classroom behavior did improve over several weeks.

Derek and his father remained in therapy for almost 4 months but missed about 40% of the sessions. The continuity of therapy and rapport with the psychologist were thus interrupted. Derek was involved in some level of family therapy, however, so the judge sentenced him to 50 hours of community service, which Derek completed. Following completion of his sentence, however,

Derek refused to attend therapy. The psychologist met alone with Mr. Pratt for 3 weeks afterward but Mr. Pratt also ended therapy eventually, despite recommendations from the psychologist that they continue.

Derek was arrested for a third time 1 year later. The charges this time were shoplifting and assault – Derek punched a security guard following an attempted theft at a department store. He was assigned to a juvenile detention facility. He dropped out of school in the interim and resumed many of his previous antisocial behaviors. The psychologist originally assigned to his case found Derek less depressed but uninterested in returning to school or therapy. Derek's parents transferred custody of Derek to the state and severed contact with their son. The recidivism rate for this population tends to be high and prognosis tends to be fair to poor. Recidivism and poor prognosis are aggravated by lack of family contact, as was now true for Derek, and so he was certainly at high risk for future delinquent behavior.

DISCUSSION QUESTIONS

1. What is the difference, if any, between a teenager diagnosed with conduct disorder and a teenager going through a stressful and stormy adolescence? What about a teenager rebelling against abusive parents or who runs away to avoid marital conflict?

2. Critique the DSM-IV-TR diagnosis for conduct disorder. Are three symptoms too few to justify assigning a diagnosis? Which symptoms overlap? Is the diagnosis biased in any way? Are the subtypes or timeline valid? What symptoms might you add, subtract, or combine? Why would you do so?

3. Conduct disorder is about four times more common in boys than in girls and the rate of serious criminal behavior is about nine times more common in boys than in girls. What biological, psychological, familial, societal, or other factors do you think account most for these differences?

4. The issue of juvenile crime has become a topic of intense political and social debate in the United States. Do you think the problem is serious or overblown? What would be the best way to deal with a 14-year-old who has committed a rape and murder? What are societal advantages and individual disadvantages of incarcerating a teenager in an adult prison?

5. How would you assess a child or an adolescent with symptoms of conduct disorder? What would you want to emphasize during your assessment and why? With whom would you want to spend the most time talking?

6. Would you add anything to Derek's treatment? If an adolescent's parents were uninvolved in treatment, like Derek's, what would be the best way to proceed?

7. Conduct disorder is often comorbid with other problems such as depression and substance abuse. How might these other problems complicate the treatment of an adolescent with delinquent behavior?

8. Critique the diagnosis of oppositional defiant disorder. How might this differ from a child who simply seems unruly? Do you think boys would be more likely to receive a diagnosis of oppositional defiant disorder than girls? Why or why not?

9. What oppositional behaviors might be more disturbing to others (e.g., parents, teachers) and thus more likely lead to a diagnosis of oppositional defiant disorder?

Chapter 9

Substance Abuse

Symptoms

Jennifer McAllister was a 16-year-old multi-ethnic (European American and Hispanic) female referred to an outpatient mental health clinic. The referral was made following Jennifer's second arrest in a 2-year period for drug possession. Jennifer was in tenth grade at an alternative high school for adolescents with a history of school attendance problems. School officials there actively promoted a zero-tolerance policy regarding drug possession and therefore had Jennifer arrested when a random check revealed several ounces of marijuana in her locker. Jennifer was charged with drug possession and later sentenced to perform community service. She and her mother were also required to obtain counseling. The juvenile detention officer to whom Jennifer was assigned made the referral to this clinic.

During the initial screening interview, Jennifer said she enjoyed her drug use and had no intention of stopping. She considered the interview and the counseling process a waste of time and fully planned to continue her life as before. She was remarkably cooperative and open about her life but provided details only after assurances that her information would be kept confidential from her mother, Ms. Ruiz. Jennifer wanted to shield her mother from many of the issues that pertained to Jennifer's life because of the family's substantial upheaval in the past 2 years.

Jennifer explained that her mother had divorced her father 2 years earlier after a 15-year marriage marked by ongoing physical, verbal, and sexual abuse. The divorce was not easy because Mr. McAllister repeatedly threatened his wife with financial and physical ruin if she left. After various interventions by police and social service agencies, Ms. Ruiz was finally able to divorce her husband and obtain a restraining order against him. Mr. McAllister soon moved out of state and severed all contact with Ms. Ruiz (her maiden name), Jennifer, and Samuel, Jennifer's older brother. He first deprived the family of all resources in the bank accounts, however. Ms. Ruiz thus had to start from scratch to support the family and currently worked two jobs to do so.

Violence in the family had occurred since Jennifer was in elementary school. Jennifer would surreptitiously leave the house and stay with friends when the fighting was at its worst. As she entered junior high school, Jennifer's time with her friends relative to her family increased and she started missing more school. Her parents were entangled in their own problems and initially neglected Jennifer, allowing her to come and go as she pleased. When Jennifer entered seventh grade, however, her father insisted she stay home more often. Jennifer complied with her father's request but said he began to sexually assault her. He initially did so by entering her room and fondling her, then kissing and caressing her. Jennifer said the advances made her feel confused, angry, and uncomfortable, but she complied out of fear for her and her mother's safety. No vaginal penetration ensued, however, and her parents divorced shortly thereafter. Jennifer never told her mother of her father's advances but was reportedly depressed and anxious following these episodes.

Jennifer said it was at this time, in seventh grade at age 12 years, that she began using drugs. Jennifer initially drank alcohol with her friends following a sexually abusive episode with her father. The drinking was part of a general "counseling" session with her friends who listened to her problems and provided support and alcohol. The group consisted of six to eight girls, some of whom were sexually abused themselves. Alcohol use continued for 1 year and gradually became more frequent. Despite this, Jennifer was able to hide her drinking from her parents and brother.

Jennifer's situation changed dramatically the following year when her father left, her mother began working two jobs to support the family, and her brother withdrew. Jennifer stayed with her friends more, smoked cigarettes and marijuana, and expanded her social group to include boys. The group would often skip school and have day parties at one of the teens' homes. On one occasion, however, a neighbor called police who arrested Jennifer and five other members of the group for drug possession. Jennifer received 12 months of probation because it was her first offense. Interestingly, her mother showed little interest in her daughter's situation. Jennifer said her mother was still recovering from the trauma of her own abuse and divorce.

Jennifer's behavior improved somewhat after her arrest; she attended school and helped her mother tend the house. This lasted only about 6 months, however, during which time Ms. Ruiz became more distant from her daughter. Jennifer began to hang out with her old group of friends and used alcohol and marijuana more so than before. Jennifer usually became drunk about once or twice a week and used marijuana at least once a week, usually on the weekends. Her school attendance dropped sharply and she was placed in an alternative high school so she could earn academic credits at a more moderate pace.

Jennifer also said she became sexually active with one of the boys in her social group. This was an anxiety-provoking experience for her because the event reminded her of earlier sexual encounters with her father. She thus drank alcohol to reduce her anxiety about sexual intercourse. Amazingly, she did not get pregnant and did not contract a sexually transmitted disease despite using no prophylactic measures. Jennifer said she experimented with other drugs, most notably cocaine and methamphetamine. She tried cocaine just three times but used methamphetamine about four times a month (usually preceding or follow-ing sexual intercourse). Jennifer was missing school most of the time at this point but had foolishly left some marijuana in her locker.

The interviewer spoke briefly to Ms. Ruiz, who provided little information. She was primarily interested in her own legal culpability, wondering aloud if she would be arrested for Jennifer's exploits. Ms. Ruiz was assured she would not face arrest so she said she had little knowledge of her daughter's behavior but believed Jennifer was probably doing what most kids in the neighborhood did. Ms. Ruiz also said she sometimes used marijuana herself to unwind and forget about past events involving her husband. Ms. Ruiz did not feel Jennifer's situation was serious and she expressed little interest in changing her or her daughter's behavior.

The interviewer believed that Jennifer's situation was serious and potentially life threatening. After a further review of Jennifer's legal records, the interviewer preliminarily concluded that Jennifer met DSM-IV-TR criteria for substance *abuse* regarding alcohol, marijuana, and methamphetamine. He did not think a diagnosis of substance *dependence* was justified, however, because no clear signs of tolerance or withdrawal were evident.

Assessment

The essential feature of substance abuse is a "maladaptive pattern of substance use manifested by recurrent and significant adverse consequences related to the repeated use of substances" (American Psychiatric Association, 2000, p. 198). Four criteria over a 12-month period must be met for a diagnosis of substance abuse:

1. Recurrent substance use resulting in a failure to fulfill major role obligations at work, school, or home.
2. Recurrent substance use in situations in which it is physically hazardous;
3. Recurrent substance-related legal problems.
4. Continued substance use despite having persistent or recurrent social or interpersonal problems caused or exacerbated by the effects of the substance.

A person must not currently meet criteria for substance dependence, which involves tolerance, withdrawal symptoms, and persistent drug-seeking behaviors. Jennifer did not meet criteria for substance dependence but did meet criteria for substance abuse. Her substance use, in particular alcohol, marijuana, and meth-amphetamine, was recurrent and certainly interfered with her ability to attend school and complete schoolwork. Her ongoing drug use was done in settings that placed her at risk for physical harm. She regularly rode with friends who were intoxicated and engaged in unprotected sexual intercourse. Jennifer now had legal problems stemming from her drug use and continued to use drugs at the expense of family relationships and a long-term plan for her future.

A mental health professional with an advanced degree in counseling psychology was assigned to Jennifer's case as part of the court-mandated assessment. The assess-ment of substance abuse can take many forms but should certainly concentrate on dangerous or life-threatening behaviors. A brief mental status examination for orientation, in which a person must identify names, places, times, and current events, may be done to learn whether a person is intoxicated or delirious from substance use. A more detailed assessment should also be conducted to determine risk of harming oneself or others. This possibility did not apply to Jennifer, however.

More pertinent to Jennifer were events that were potentially life threatening. This included riding with friends who were intoxicated and engaging in sexual intercourse without protection. Jennifer said each of these events occurred four to five times a month in the past year. None occurred within the past month, however. This was primarily because Jennifer was arrested and her mother was now closely supervising her.

Assessment in this area may include a toxicology examination in which a youth is screened for past drug use by testing samples of urine, blood, or hair. Urine and blood analyses detect various drug metabolites and include tests such as the Breathalyzer to determine alcohol content of a breath sample (Schweinsburg, Schweinsburg, Nagel, Eyler, & Tapert, 2011). In addition, alcohol use can be detected by examining cell volume of red blood cells and levels of gamma-glutamyl transpeptidase. Urine tests for recent use of opiates (e.g., heroin), cocaine, amphetamines, antianxiety drugs, and marijuana are available as well. These tests include thin layer chromatography, gas-liquid chromatography, high-pressure liquid chromatography, and enzyme-multiplied immunoassay techniques. Hair analysis is useful for checking drug use within the past several months (Warner, Behnke, Eyler, & Szabo, 2011). Jennifer underwent a blood test because drug use within the past 2 weeks was of most concern. Some traces of cannabis (marijuana) were evident but this may have been a residual reading from Jennifer's last reported drug use 3 weeks earlier. Jennifer learned that blood tests would occur regularly during her court-mandated treatment program.

Initial screening methods for adolescents suspected of substance abuse also include questionnaires or interviews. Examples for adolescent alcohol use include the Rutgers Alcohol Problem Index and Adolescent Drinking Inventory. Screening tests and interviews are available for general drug use as well. Examples include the Adolescent Drug Involvement Scale and Personal Experience Screening Questionnaire (Winters, Fahnhorst, & Botzet, 2007). Sample items from another common screening device, the Adolescent Substance Abuse Subtle Screening Inventory,* include the following (Miller, 2001):

1. Taken a drink to help you talk about your feelings and ideas?

2. Gotten into trouble in school, at home, on the job, or with the police because of your drinking?

3. Taken drugs to help forget about feelings of being helpless or worthless?

4. Gotten really stoned or wiped out on drugs (more than just high)?

5. Felt your drug use has kept you from getting what you want out of life?

---

* G.A. Miller, SASSI Institute, 2001, *Adolescent Substance Abuse Subtle Screening Inventory* (SASSI-A2). Used with permission.

Jennifer said she occasionally thought she was drinking too much and even broached the subject with her friends. She was especially concerned about her methamphetamine use that made her feel out of control. Her friends rebuked her for these doubts, however, so she became quiet. Jennifer said no one annoyed her about her drinking or other drug use but this may have been because no one paid much attention. She also said she did not feel guilty about her drug use but was concerned her mother might discover the full extent of it and suffer further mental strain. Jennifer said she rarely used alcohol or other drugs in the morning, usually preferring to do so in the late afternoon, evenings, and weekends, especially when having sex with her boyfriend.

A clinician should concentrate on an adolescent's reasons for initial and continued drug use when interviewing an adolescent suspected of substance abuse. The interviewer should note whether a youth is motivated to move away from drug use. Jennifer's reasons for *starting* drug use were varied and complex but generally involved

1. escaping thoughts about her family's fighting and her father's sexual advances;
2. conforming to a peer group that made her feel welcome and gave her support;
3. satisfying her curiosity about drugs;
4. experiencing a sense of rebellion against authority.

She said her reasons for *continuing* drug use were more specific and included anxiety reduction during sexual intercourse and sensory reinforcement ("feeling good") from the drugs themselves. These reasons were potent, so Jennifer had little interest in moving away from her current pattern of drug use.

Interviews with significant others can also be helpful for knowing more about an adolescent's substance use. This was not the case regarding Jennifer, however. Ms. Ruiz had little knowledge of her daughter's activities, but whether she was truthful was unclear. She did express a desire to help Jennifer move away from drugs and toward regular school attendance and new friends. Ms. Ruiz's motivation for Jennifer to do so seemed questionable, however. Contact with Jennifer's friends and school officials did not prove fruitful either. Her friends did not want to give any information, possibly out of fear of self-incrimination, and her teachers and guidance counselor simply did not have enough information about Jennifer to provide a useful opinion. Jennifer's brother, Samuel, moved away from home and purposely distanced himself from the family. He was unavailable for interview.

Risk Factors and Maintaining Variables

Multiple risk factors relate to substance abuse, including genetic and biochemical variables, environmental and psychosocial stressors, cultural and societal factors, comorbid disorders, and individual personality characteristics. Alcoholism has a moderate hereditary component, especially for males. Family, twin, and other genetic studies of alcohol abuse reveal a heritability range of 20–26% for the general population and 30–36% for males with severe alcohol dependence (Chassin, Ritter, Trim, & King, 2003; Walters, 2002).

Other biological variables linked to adolescent substance abuse include changes in serotonin, the hypothalamic-pituitary-adrenal axis, and immature frontal-limbic connections (Schepis, Adinoff, & Rao, 2008). Neurological problems related to hyperactivity, impulsivity, and cognitive deficits may predict adolescent substance use as well (Elkins, McGue, & Iacono, 2007; Ivanov, Schulz, London, & Newcorn, 2008). Many environmental factors can mediate these biological variables, however.

Jennifer's family history regarding substance abuse was unclear. Her father was reportedly more violent and sexually inappropriate after becoming drunk, but whether he had alcoholism was unclear. Jennifer's mother, Ms. Ruiz, reported some drug use herself but this was relatively new, infrequent, and a reaction to life events of the past few years. A diagnosis of substance abuse or dependence did not seem to apply to her. Jennifer's brother, Samuel, reportedly had no difficulties with alcohol or other drug use. Whether Jennifer had a genetic predisposition to drug use was thus unclear. An interesting observation, however, is that all family members had symptoms of depression, which is sometimes marked by changes in serotonin and which may lead to self-medication by substance use.

Someone's biological predisposition to substance abuse may be triggered by stressful or aversive environmental events. This was clearly true for Jennifer, whose stressful life events included an abusive father, neglectful mother, poor school achievement, sexual anxiety, feelings of isolation when not with her friends, legal problems, and low socioeconomic status. Environmental risk factors for substance abuse also include modeling or instruction about drug use from others, social reinforcement from drug use, and availability of drugs. Jennifer modeled alcohol use for years from her father and, more recently, her friends. Her social group and older boyfriend taught her how to use different drugs and gave her attention when she did so. Jennifer felt she needed to continue taking drugs to be accepted by the group. The group had a steady supply of drugs that were provided freely to Jennifer by her boyfriend.

Family and parental factors may trigger biological predispositions to substance abuse, and many of these applied to Jennifer. Family factors include expressed emotion, detachment, lack of affection, inconsistent discipline, and nontraditional values (Watts, 2007). Parental factors include drug use, permissive attitudes toward drug use, low expectations, and disinterest in their children's lives (Li, Pentz, & Chou, 2002; Simons-Morton, Haynie, Crump, Eitel, & Saylor, 2001). More general environmental factors may have enhanced Jennifer's drug use as well, including local norms favoring drug use and neighborhood disorganization (Wright, Bobashev, & Folsom, 2007).

Comorbid psychiatric disorders can also exacerbate substance-related problems in youth. These include depression and conduct, oppositional defiant, and attention deficit/hyperactivity disorders (Armstrong & Costello, 2002; Wilens, 2007). Jennifer technically met diagnostic criteria for conduct disorder and was somewhat impulsive, depressed, and anxious. The anxiety appeared as symptoms of posttraumatic stress disorder from Jennifer's earlier sexual abuse.

Individual personality characteristics may predispose youths to drug use and include

- desire for independence;
- curiosity;
- rejection of traditional social norms and values;
- rebelliousness;
- novelty and high-sensation seeking;
- poor academic achievement;
- male gender;
- delinquent or criminal activity;
- anger;
- low self-esteem;
- an expectation that drug use will lead to positive social and sensory consequences.

Some of these personality characteristics applied to Jennifer; others did not. No one drug personality or profile marks this population. Jennifer said she felt torn between wanting to have a normal family life and wanting to be completely autonomous with her boyfriend and other friends. She hoped her mother would remarry and that her brother would rejoin the family but realized this was unlikely. Even if it did happen, Jennifer said her first loyalty was to her friends and that they were now her family.

Jennifer was curious and often pursued new and sensational experiences. She was not shy about experimenting with different drugs. She liked trying new drugs and enjoyed the natural and physical high she got from doing so. Other characteristics that applied to Jennifer included poor school performance (which was mostly a function of her absenteeism), internalizing symptoms, moderate self-esteem, and alienation from those not in her immediate social group.

On the other hand, some risk factors clearly did not apply to Jennifer. She was female, not highly rebellious, did not steal or engage in major criminal activity, and did not have a difficult temperament. Jennifer had good verbal and social skills, was still somewhat compliant to her mother's requests, and was generally cooperative with clinic personnel. Jennifer thus had some but not other characteristics commonly ascribed to those with substance-related problems. This again reflects the high degree of variability in this population.

Other factors may protect youths from substance abuse. Examples include poor availability of drugs, positive family interactions and appropriate modeling, religious affiliation, social skills, and prosocial school activities (Beyers, Toumbourou, Catalano, Arthur, & Hawkins, 2004; Vakalahi, 2001). Protective factors do not lower drug use but do reduce the risk of initial drug use and slow the progression of drug use to abuse. Jennifer had good social skills but this was greatly outweighed by her family, sociocultural environment, and thrill-seeking behaviors. Her drug use was therefore problematic.

Developmental Aspects

The developmental progression of drug use has been a subject of intense scrutiny and controversy because adolescent alcohol and other drug use is common. The lifetime prevalence of alcohol use across eighth, tenth, and twelfth graders is 55.1%. Many of these youths have used alcohol in the past year (48.7%), the past month (28.1%), and on a daily basis (1.4%). Substantial rates of other drug use during the past month are evident as well for cigarettes (12.6%), marijuana or hashish (12.5%), amphetamines (2.6%), inhalants (2.6%), tranquilizers (1.9%), hallucinogens (1.4%), and cocaine (1.3%) (Johnston, O'Malley, Bachman, & Schulenberg, 2009).

A popular model for understanding the developmental progression of drug use involves viewing the behavior along a continuum (Zacny et al., 2003). This continuum may involve stages of nonuse of drugs as well as experimental, casual, habitual, and compulsive drug use. A nonuser may be one who has never used drugs inappropriately. An experimental user might be one who has used drugs a few times out of curiosity, peer pressure, or desire for increased stimulation. This person is typically not caught and has no major problems from drug use. The person's emotional state can be described as excited.

A casual or social/situational user might be one who engages in regular drug use, such as two to four times per week, and who makes an ongoing effort to maintain control. Think of an adolescent who drinks alcohol regularly and struggles to hide the behavior from parents and school officials. Common consequences include decreased school performance, atypical behaviors for that adolescent (e.g., increased lying), and loss of interest in previously enjoyable activities. The adolescent's emotional state at this stage can also be described as excited.

A habitual user might be one who engages in daily drug use, usually with a particular group of friends. The person has not necessarily lost control but experiences major problems with school and family. The adolescent's emotional state can be described as impulsive, erratic, guilt ridden, and depressed. A compulsive or obsessive-dependent user might be one who has lost control over her drug use, which occurs several times per day. The person's behavior largely surrounds the procurement, maintenance, and use of a regular drug supply. Life-threatening behaviors are not uncommon and the adolescent's emotional state can be described as disorganized. People in the last three categories – casual, habitual, and compulsive – are most likely to qualify for a diagnosis of substance abuse or dependence.

Jennifer was certainly more than an experimental drug user but perhaps not a casual, habitual, or compulsive user. A key issue here is whether a person can maintain control of surrounding events, and Jennifer was usually able to do so.

There were times, however, especially after methamphetamine use, when Jennifer reportedly felt out of control. Her engagement in potentially life-threatening behaviors was also evidence of lack of control. Still, Jennifer abstained from drug use for days and weeks at a time as she did in the past month. Her life did not completely surround drug acquisition and use. Jennifer might be a moderate user, or someone between a casual and a habitual user.

Another popular way of viewing substance use from a developmental perspective involves a stage model. Certain gateway drugs may lead to use of drugs that prove to be more serious later (Kandel, 2003). There may be several stages in this process:

1. No use of any drug.
2. Moderate drinking of beer and wine.
3. Smoking cigarettes and moderate drinking of hard liquor.
4. Heavier drinking of alcohol.
5. Smoking marijuana.
6. Using pill drugs such as amphetamines and barbiturates.
7. Using harder drugs such as cocaine, hallucinogens, and opiates.

Alcohol and tobacco use often predict marijuana use. Marijuana, in turn, may be a gateway to harder drug use, such as cocaine, though this view remains controversial (Malone, Lamis, Masyn, & Northrup, 2010). In addition, not everyone who begins drug use necessarily progresses through each of these stages, and not everyone necessarily does so in this order.

A stage model of drug use could loosely apply to Jennifer. Jennifer did start drinking beer first and moved to hard liquor the following year. Her alcohol use did not dramatically increase, however, when she began smoking cigarettes and marijuana simultaneously. Her use of cigarettes and marijuana overlapped with her experimentation with cocaine and methamphetamine. This demonstrates that adolescents with substance-related disorders may show similar patterns of drug use but that unique individual differences must always be considered.

Other developmental theories of substance abuse in adolescents focus on the behavior as part of a general lifestyle that depends on biological predispositions, temperament, peer influences, parental and familial factors, school-related problems, distorted cognitions, and stress (Chassin, Beltran, Lee, Haller, & Villalta, 2010). An adolescent can go down a number of different causal paths leading to different forms of drug use or nonuse. A conforming adolescent whose friends occasionally engage in drug use to relax may go that route, whereas an adventurous teenager who experiences family stress and whose friends have a ready supply of drugs may become a heavier substance user. This model may apply well to Jennifer, whose novelty-seeking personality and acute family stress interacted with a supportive peer group that relied on frequent drug use to cope with problems.

What about the long-term prognosis for adolescents with substance abuse? Many adolescents who experiment lightly with alcohol and tobacco do not abuse these drugs and do adjust well later in life. Other adolescents are particularly sensitive even to small amounts of alcohol and other drugs and may eventually become addicted. Several factors predict increased substance use in adulthood, including high school use, unemployment, and children not living with a person. Less substance use relates to female gender, college graduation, marriage, and custodial parenthood (Merline, O'Malley, Schulenberg, Bachman, & Johnston, 2004). Adolescents who use several substances (polydrug use) have several poor outcomes, such as academic problems, criminal activity, and suicide attempt (Reyes et al., 2011; Tims et al., 2002).

What about Jennifer's prognosis? Her long-term outcome is probably poor given her family and socioeconomic background, frequent drug use at an early age, and lack of treatment responsiveness (see next section). Consequences of drug use will themselves place Jennifer at risk for poor outcome. These consequences include social isolation, refusal to attend school, unprotected sexual activity, and failure to seek appropriate medical care.

Treatment

Therapists who treat substance abuse or dependence often help a teenager maintain abstinence and change family and other factors that instigate or prolong the substance-related problem. Many treatment programs share the view that abstinence is the best policy when addressing this population. This philosophy underlies inpatient therapy as well as self-help groups, such as Alcoholics Anonymous or Alateen (White & Savage, 2005).

Inpatient therapy is often used in severe cases of substance abuse where a person (1) has not responded to outpatient therapy, (2) presents an imminent danger to himself or to others, (3) is at risk for withdrawal symptoms that cause physical and emotional damage, and/or (4) has other problems such as depression that seriously exacerbate drug abuse. Many inpatient settings are based on the Minnesota model that emphasizes an abstinence-based and structured approach, education and support for the adolescent and family, short-term stay (usually less than 2 months), and adoption of the medical or disease model to conceptualize substance abuse. A referral to outpatient treatment after discharge is recommended as well, sometimes in the form of a day treatment program. Inpatient therapy is effective in the short term but not the long term (Muck et al., 2001).

Jennifer's substance use was obviously a problem that placed her at risk for serious consequences. She was in no immediate danger, however, had no withdrawal symptoms, and had relatively good social and verbal skills. Inpatient programs tend to emphasize a person's powerlessness over a substance problem as well as complete abstinence, so the psychologist with whom Jennifer met at the outpatient clinic did not think inpatient therapy would be well suited to her personality or current mood. Increasing Jennifer's isolation on an inpatient psychiatric ward would not have helped either. An outpatient therapy program was thus established for her and she attended Alateen.

Outpatient therapy for an adolescent with substance abuse or dependence typically focuses on increasing several attributes:

1. Insight into the adolescent's problem.
2. Motivation for change.
3. Rapport with the therapist.
4. Association with certain peer groups.
5. Problem-solving ability.

Clinicians also employ family therapy, contracting, contingency management, peer refusal skills training, socially appropriate leisure skills, and treating comorbid problems such as depression (Toumbourou et al., 2007).

Perhaps the foremost goal of treatment is helping an adolescent see that a problem exists. Jennifer's therapist seized upon her doubts about her lifestyle and got her to admit she likely had a problem. Part of this "insight" process depends heavily on a client's past experiences, current functioning, and rapport with the therapist. Jennifer had good rapport with the therapist and responded well to his initial suggestions.

Another crucial aspect of outpatient treatment for this population is family therapy. This is necessary to change dysfunctional communication patterns, increase parental monitoring of an adolescent's behavior, address unresolved issues, provide support, educate family members about a child's substance-related problem, and establish activities to divert an adolescent from drug use. This was only partially effective for Jennifer. Ms. Ruiz, who earlier indicated little desire to participate in Jennifer's treatment program, attended the first few sessions but gradually became distant and uninterested. Ms. Ruiz was dismissive and refused to accept Jennifer's accounts of what happened when asked to discuss the sexual abuse issues Jennifer finally raised. Ms. Ruiz constantly targeted her daughter as "the one with the problem" and downplayed her own ability to influence the treatment process. Ms. Ruiz was willing to support her daughter financially, bring her to treatment, and supervise her school attendance more closely.

The therapist also focused on Jennifer's connection with her peer group, which was a main trigger of her drug use. He tried to get Jennifer to distance herself from the group by having her re-enroll in school, participate in extra-curricular activities that took up much of her time, develop new friendships, and speak with her original peer group only over the telephone. Jennifer showed some initial enthusiasm for these ideas and attended school more regularly. Her boyfriend effectively sabotaged this treatment plan, however, by encouraging Jennifer to resume her drug use and sexual activity. The therapist's attempts to get Jennifer's boyfriend to join the therapy process, or at least support early initiatives of therapy, failed. A major reason why many people with substance-related problems experience relapse is re-exposure to cues that triggered substance use in the first place. Jennifer's renewed contact with her boyfriend seriously damaged any treatment progress. In addition, she stopped attending Alateen meetings.

As treatment seemed to deteriorate, the therapist tried to bolster Jennifer's self-esteem, peer refusal skills, and problem-solving ability. Jennifer had several cognitive distortions about herself and her drug use, including her perceived need to use drugs to cope with stressful events and to keep her boyfriend. This is a form of psychological addiction to drugs. The therapist pointed to Jennifer's various skills and positive characteristics and suggested ways of dealing with her boyfriend to avoid drug use. Unfortunately, Jennifer felt she had to choose between the therapist and her boyfriend and ultimately chose her boyfriend. Jennifer's therapy attendance became more erratic over several weeks and she and her mother stopped coming to appointments after 5 months. A telephone conversation 2 months later with Ms. Ruiz indicated that Jennifer moved out of the house to live with her boyfriend and that their current whereabouts were unknown.

Therapy for adolescents with substance-related problems is fraught with potential obstacles, so prevention may be the best "treatment." Prevention programs include (1) media and law enforcement presentations and other interventions to promote abstinence and antidrug attitudes and (2) specific early interventions for children and adolescents at risk for substance abuse. Early intervention consists of programs to teach youths skills they need to refuse offers of drugs; bolster social skills; establish appropriate recreational options; provide information about harmful drug effects; and reduce risk factors in individuals, parents, families, and communities (Griswold, Aronoff, Kernan, & Kahn, 2008).

Prevention programs can modify children's attitudes about drugs and increase knowledge about drugs, especially peer- and sports team-based training (Elliot et al., 2004). Positive changes in actual drug use have not been consistently demonstrated among most adolescents, however. Prevention programs are more effective for adolescents at risk for substance-related problems. One can only wonder what effect such a program might have had on Jennifer if it was available.

DISCUSSION QUESTIONS

1. How would you make a distinction, if any, between occasional drug use that does not interfere with daily functioning and substance abuse? Would you make a distinction between legal and illegal substances? Why or why not?

2. Many factors appear to explain why youths begin drug use and possibly progress later to drug abuse. Which factors (e.g., individual, family, sociocultural) do you think are most important and why?

3. The assessment of adolescent substance use and abuse now includes home-based tests that let parents submit samples of their child's hair to a laboratory for analysis. Do you think this is a good idea? What are familial, ethical, and clinical ramifications of this technology?

4. The notion that substance abuse is a disease has drawn much controversy in recent years. What are advantages and disadvantages of adopting a medical model to address substance abuse? Explore issues of using drugs to treat substance abuse and the effect on recovery of absolving a person of blame and responsibility.

5. Some believe, for people with alcoholism, that any use of alcohol is a relapse and will lead to dire consequences. Do you think this is true? Can or should a person with alcoholism be taught to use alcohol in moderation? How might you do so?

6. Tobacco and alcohol companies have been accused of directly marketing their products to children and adolescents. Do you think this is true and, if so, how do you think this is done? What steps can or should be taken to prevent such exposure?

7. How would you design an effective prevention program for substance abuse?

Chapter 10

Family Conflict and
Oppositional Defiant Disorder

Symptoms

Jeremy and Joshua Simington were European American males, aged 9 and 11 years, respectively, who were referred to a marriage and family therapist. Mrs. Simington, the children's mother, made the referral because she was having great trouble controlling the boys' behavior. During a telephone screening, Mrs. Simington said both boys were constantly getting into trouble and were increasingly defying her commands. The family was in turmoil over recent events, including the birth of a new baby girl and Mr. Simington's extensive work schedule. The level of fighting in the household was becoming intolerable and Mrs. Simington felt that therapy might be a good way to "reestablish family harmony."

Only Mrs. Simington and her two boys came to the initial assessment session. The therapist interviewed Mrs. Simington first. Mrs. Simington quickly said her husband was working and would not be able to attend that day. She expressed hope, however, that he would attend future sessions. Mrs. Simington then reiterated, nearly in tears, that her boys were "out of control." The therapist thought it best to obtain information about each boy separately and began with the older Joshua. Mrs. Simington said Joshua was getting into more trouble at school. Joshua, who was in sixth grade, was suspended from school a month earlier for 2 days for talking back to his teacher, showing a "poor attitude," and throwing a temper tantrum. The suspension required a meeting with the school principal and Joshua's teacher.

During her meeting with the principal and the teacher, Mrs. Simington discovered that her son had a pattern of misbehavior in the classroom. This included arguing with his teacher and teasing his classmates. The misbehaviors occurred for most of the school year (it was now February) but had become more intense since Christmas. Joshua was refusing to do much of his work at school and the principal asked Mrs. Simington directly if anything was happening at home to cause these problems.

Mrs. Simington told the therapist that she and her husband were under great stress and that her ability to deal with the boys was probably impaired. Their newest child, now about 12 months old, was unexpected and caused some financial strain on the family. Mrs. Simington thus went from working part time to full time, and time and money typically spent on the boys was reduced. Joshua's behavior was particularly bad – he began to argue more with his mother and withdraw from his father. Mrs. Simington explained as well that she and her husband were recently disagreeing about how to discipline the children and this led to inconsistent punishment. Mr. Simington preferred corporal punishment but Mrs. Simington preferred negotiation and positive rewards.

The therapist then asked about Jeremy, the younger child who was in fourth grade. Mrs. Simington noted that Jeremy had no problems in school but did have a history of minor reading difficulties. His behavior at home, however, worsened as Joshua's had. Mrs. Simington suspected that Jeremy was copying his older brother's behavior, especially when he failed to clean his room, sulked, and occasionally refused to go to school. Jeremy did show some behaviors his brother did not, however, such as running away from the house for extended periods, screaming as loudly as possible to wake the baby, and running around the house. Mrs. Simington said that, between her job, caring for the baby, her husband's absence, and the boys' misbehaviors, her ability to maintain control of the household was seriously compromised.

The therapist then asked Mrs. Simington to comment on how each family member (except the baby) got along with the others. Mrs. Simington said, despite their recent misbehaviors, that her relationship with her boys was generally positive. Both sought her advice on problems and homework and both showed better behavior when they saw that their mother was upset. Mrs. Simington's relationship with the younger Jeremy was better than her relationship with Joshua, who she believed was seeking more independence as he neared adolescence. Conversely, Mr. Simington had a better relationship with the older Joshua, with whom he shared interests in sports and other activities. His relationship with Jeremy was more distant and seemed to worsen during the recent family problems.

Jeremy and Joshua's relationship with one another was apparently more complicated. At some level, the boys were friends – they got along most times and helped each other with chores and homework. The boys had separate sets of friends, however, never interacted on the school bus or at school, and argued vehemently over who was getting "more of something," such as food, video game time, and playthings. Mrs. Simington said the boys rarely worked in tandem to get something they wanted from her or her husband. Furthermore, the boys were sometimes aggressive with one another. Jeremy would usually pick a fight with Joshua, who was about his same size. On two such occasions, one the previous summer and one on New Year's Day, the fights were severe enough to warrant minor medical attention. Over the past 3 weeks, no physical aggression occurred but the boys were arguing and screaming at one another almost every day.

To Mrs. Simington's considerable surprise, the therapist asked about her relationship with her husband. Mrs. Simington seemed guarded about this issue and explained tentatively that she had a good relationship with her spouse. She was apologetic about her husband's absence and needlessly explained further about his work schedule. She said she missed him, though the therapist wondered whether she missed more her husband's ability to deal with the boys than his affection and attention. Mrs. Simington also said, after gentle prodding by the therapist, that she and her husband did have heated arguments about whether to abort the third pregnancy (she was adamantly opposed) and how to handle the boys' misbehavior. She did not feel her marriage was in trouble but admitted this was the first time the relationship had been this strained.

Mrs. Simington agreed to encourage her husband to attend the next session and he did so. Mr. Simington was withdrawn about the family situation but did say the "problems" indicated by his wife were not as bad as she believed. He acknowledged some financial strain that added to his skepticism about the need for therapy. He described his relationships with his boys as good and with his wife as fair. When asked about the arrival of the baby and his feelings about the family since then, Mr. Simington acknowledged he felt pressure to support the family and provide quality time to his children. His manner, however, indicated he was aware of his wife's discomfort with the family situation and that he wanted to avoid blame from her and the therapist.

The therapist spoke with school officials with the parents' permission. The teachers and principal confirmed Mrs. Simington's account and said each child was developing serious behavior problems. The principal added that she thought, "something was going on with Mr. and Mrs. Simington" that helped produce the boys' classroom problems. The therapist preliminarily concluded that the Simington family had extensive conflict, perhaps more so than reported in the sessions, and that the boys, especially Joshua, met DSM-IV-TR criteria for oppositional defiant disorder.

Assessment

The essential feature of oppositional defiant disorder is a "recurrent pattern of negativistic, defiant, disobedient, and hostile behavior toward authority figures" that lasts for at least 6 months (American Psychiatric Association, 2000, p. 100). The child must show four of eight symptoms to meet criteria for the diagnosis. These symptoms include frequent loss of temper, anger, vindictiveness, arguing with adults, noncompliance, annoying others, blaming others for mistakes or misbehavior, and oversensitivity to the behavior of others. "Frequent" means much more than for most children that age. The behaviors must cause impairment in areas of functioning such as interpersonal relationships or schoolwork.

These criteria seemed to apply to Jeremy and Joshua. Mrs. Simington said the boys were constantly arguing with her and were noncompliant. The boys, especially Jeremy, often lost their tempers as well. Conversations with school officials confirmed the boys' tendency to blame others for troublesome events and noted that Joshua in particular was vengeful. The therapist's interview with both boys revealed a pattern of anger toward their parents as well as beliefs that others were out to do them harm. Joshua insisted that two of his classmates wanted to get him into trouble and both boys expressed anger toward their parents regarding recent events at home.

When assessing a family with conflict and children with oppositional defiant disorder, family members should be interviewed about (1) the *content* of problems within the home and (2) the *process* by which family members communicate, solve problems, and try to get what they want (content is often thought of as the "what"; process is often thought of as the "how"). Content-related questions can focus on likes and dislikes of different family members, subjects of most arguments, methods of coercing other family members to agree to something, what comes before and after an argument or noncompliant act, and each member's perception of the current family problems (Granic, Hollenstein, Dishion, & Patterson, 2003; Schoppe, Mangelsdorf, & Frosch, 2001).

Different Simington family members were clearly trying to coerce one another into giving what little there was of the family's resources (i.e., money, attention, time). Regarding the boys, attention from their parents sharply declined after the arrival of the baby and after changes in their parents' work schedule. Mr. and Mrs. Simington's attention toward the boys, though negative, increased following troublesome behavior in school and noncompliance at home. The boys were thus actively coercing their parents into giving them more family resources.

This coercion process was not limited to the boys, however. Mrs. Simington complained about her husband's lack of attention to the family because he was not home much to discipline the children. She therefore drew her husband more into the family structure by nagging him and by bringing him to therapy sessions. Few problems were solved and little cooperation was evident because of these coercive family processes, however.

Family interviewers concentrate on process questions as well, which involve actual methods of arguing, effects of communications on others, and hypothetical scenarios. Examples include describing a typical family argument, methods of communicating anger, reactions to anger of others, feelings about family member behaviors, methods of problem solving, possible targets of change, prevention of arguments, family dynamics and rules, and parental discussions about the children.

Few family rules and routines survived the arrival of the baby in the Simington household. The family rarely ate dinner together, chores were done haphazardly, getting the boys to school and to sleep was difficult, curfew was regularly broken, and homework was not always completed. Because of Mrs. Simington's exhaustion and Mr. Simington's withdrawal, problems were not solved with the same efficiency or cordiality as they were before the baby. Both parents were now letting problems slide until they were serious and then administering strong punishment. This practice was becoming less effective over time, however.

Various rating scales are available for assessing family conflict, communication, and dynamics. Examples include the Conflict Behavior Questionnaire

(Robin & Foster, 2002), Parent-Adolescent Communication Scale (Barnes & Olson, 1985), Family Assessment Measure (Skinner, Steinhauer, & Sitarenios, 2000), and Family Adaptability and Cohesion Evaluation Scale (Olson, Portner, & Lavee, 1987). Another commonly used family scale is the Family Environment Scale (FES), a 90-item true-false measure of cohesion, expressiveness, conflict, independence, achievement-orientation, intellectual-cultural orientation, active-recreational orientation, moral-religious emphasis, organization, and control (Moos & Moos, 1986). Mr. and Mrs. Simington completed the FES, which revealed very low scores on cohesion, independence, all three orientation subscales, and organization. A very high score was evident for conflict. These scores indicated that the family did not interact much until problems became severe or until someone wanted something.

Direct observation is also an excellent way to assess family dynamics and communication patterns, especially patterns that seem to contradict one another. Dysfunctional families sometimes engage in "double-bind communications" in which verbal and nonverbal messages conflict. Direct observation may include formal coding systems where a therapist audiotapes or videotapes a family interaction and later dissects the communications into categories such as hostile, neutral, and positive. Examples include the Family Coding System and Rapid Marital Interaction Coding System (Gordis & Margolin, 2001; Heyman et al., 2001).

Many therapists informally observe family members in their office. The therapist for the Simingtons looked for nonverbal behaviors that contradicted positive family interactions. She saw several: Joshua's eye rolling when his mother talked about the "family situation," Jeremy's folded arms and angry looks, and Mr. Simington's sighing. These behaviors indicated that only Mrs. Simington felt a "family problem" existed; indeed, she was the one who initiated therapy and insisted everyone attend. None of the other family members wanted to be in therapy. This gave the therapist some insight into the family's interactions with one another and supported the view that the family was largely disengaged with sporadic episodes of conflict.

The therapist asked the boys and the parents to keep a logbook of arguments, broken rules, and other problems at home. Mrs. Simington kept her logbook with rigor but the males relied on memory when reporting to the therapist. Still, the logbooks and stories indicated an interesting and ongoing pattern: (1) initial confusion about who was responsible for a certain task, (2) subsequent fighting about it, and (3) eventual completion of the task by Mrs. Simington. Mrs. Simington was obviously the one who most wanted therapy and a change in the status quo.

Risk Factors and Maintaining Variables

There are several family patterns that can be dysfunctional and lead to childhood behavior problems. An enmeshed family involves diffuse boundaries between family members such that every member seems overly involved with every other member's life (Sturge-Apple, Davies, & Cummings, 2010). Enmeshed families often display separation anxiety, tension, overcontrol, and hostility. An isolated family eschews contact with those outside the family. Children may spend most of their time with their parents and engage in few extracurricular activities.

Detachment and conflict seemed to be the primary family patterns for the Simingtons. Detachment involves rigid boundaries: each family member keeps to himself or herself until necessary or until he or she wants something from someone else. Communication in this family type is poor and members interact only when the situation absolutely demands it (e.g., a severe behavior problem). Conflictive families display ongoing fighting and animosity. Communication and problem-solving strategies are usually impaired and cognitive distortions among family members (e.g., perceived harmful intent) are common. Families with children with behavior problems may also show more than one dysfunctional pattern, as was evident in the Simingtons' detachment and conflict.

Communication problems can take many forms and may be caused by family members who contradict statements as they say them. Mr. Simington habitually stated his desire for positive family change but sighed and looked unenthusiastic. No one in the family therefore believed his statements and all appeared frustrated as a result. Communication problems may result because family members such as Jeremy are passive and rarely initiate conversations. Problems may result as well from family members who are overly concerned about coalitions among other family members (i.e., people "ganging up" on him or her). This was not the case with the Simingtons, however.

Communication problems may result from a refusal to understand or appreciate another's point of view. One family member may say something to another but the second family member will disavow the statement, ignore it, or think the person meant something else. The last behavior illustrates differences in communication and metacommunication, or differences between the actual message and what underlies the message or what the person is really trying to say. When communications and metacommunications differ greatly, problems develop quickly. This seemed to be the case for Mr. and Mrs. Simington – their level of sarcasm when talking to one another increased dramatically over the past year. They drifted from direct communication and instead used snide remarks to coerce or punish one another.

Other family communication problems are more specific. These problems include accusations, interruptions, communications through a third person, lectures or commands that substitute for simple communications, use of tangents, dwelling on the past, intellectualizing, making threats or jokes, monopolizing a conversation, and silence (Robin & Foster, 2002).

Problem-solving strategies erode in dysfunctional families as well. Problems may relate to everyday situations (e.g., piled garbage) or to family members' feelings of isolation or persecution. The Simington family had both sets of problems that were likely caused by poor communication patterns. Families with problem-solving difficulties define problems poorly, disagree about solutions, fail to negotiate solutions, and implement faulty solutions. The Simington family drifted toward a problem-solving strategy of letting Mrs. Simington carry most of the disciplinary and child-rearing load. This strategy was failing, however, because

Mrs. Simington experienced more stress and could not adequately address all family responsibilities.

Some dysfunctional families focus on past, unsolvable, or overly complicated problems that are not easily fixed. Old hurts, such as a past affair or an incident at school, might be constantly raised not to solve problems but to punish the offending party. Problem-solving strategies may also falter because family members (1) coerce one another to accept their own particular solution, (2) offer solutions that are vague or self-serving, (3) show inflexibility, or (4) become frustrated with the process and give up.

Dysfunctional family patterns can relate to cognitive distortions held by parents and youths (Robin & Foster, 2002). Parental distortions include ruination, obedience, perfectionism, self-blame, and malicious intent. Ruination is the belief that freedom given to a child will result in disastrous consequences. Obedience is the belief a youth should obey every command given by the parent. Perfectionism is the belief a youth should always know and make the right decisions about everyday events. Self-blame is the belief that parents are at fault if a child makes a mistake. Malicious intent is the belief that a youth acts badly only to annoy and anger his parents. This last cognitive distortion did apply to the Simingtons. Mrs. Simington became tearful on several occasions when saying she believed the boys deliberately tried to upset her. Whether her statements were designed to elicit guilt from the boys and her husband, however, was unclear.

Youths also have cognitive distortions such as fairness, ruination, autonomy, and approval (Robin & Foster, 2002). Fairness is the belief that parents are unfair in enforcing rules. Ruination is the belief that family rules will ruin a child's status with his friends or overall life. Autonomy is the belief a child should do as he pleases. Approval is the belief a child should do nothing to upset his parents. All these distortions except approval applied to Joshua, the older child. He believed he should have more independence and that his parents, especially his mother, purposely tried to limit his time with friends. These statements supported Mrs. Simington's earlier assertion that Joshua was entering adolescence and demanding more freedom.

Developmental Aspects

Dysfunctional family patterns often relate to difficulties in communication, problem solving, and cognition, but these difficulties do not develop overnight. A long-term pattern of inadequate parenting, coercion, or other dysfunction is usually present in families with defiant children or extensive conflict. Some families in therapy are reluctant to admit this or to offer information that might cause a family member to "look bad." The Simingtons blamed their current problems on the recent arrival of the baby. Many of the issues raised in therapy were clearly active for years, however.

Child defiance and family conflict may develop through coercive processes of misdirected positive and negative reinforcement (Granic & Patterson, 2006). A parent may issue a command such as "Clean your room" to a child, who says no. The parent may then excuse the child's behavior, blame his noncompliance on someone else, bribe the child to finish the task, or complete the task for the child. The child thus receives positive reinforcement for his noncompliance and the defiant pattern continues and worsens.

Negative reinforcement can apply as well. A parent may issue a command that a child refuses. The child and parent escalate their yelling as the parent tries to force the child to comply. The parent may use physical punishment to force compliance but this is often ineffective. The parent may finally give up trying to get the child to comply. The child thus receives negative reinforcement for noncompliance because the parent gave in and relieved the child of a task, for example, room cleaning. The child learns over time that noncompliance or throwing a tantrum forces parental acquiescence.

These coercive processes applied to the Simingtons. The boys took advantage of their father's absence and their mother's exhaustion by badgering her about something until she gave in. Mrs. Simington herself knew she was too overwhelmed to give the boys much of a challenge, which was why she insisted on getting more help from her husband. Mrs. Simington herself used this negative reinforcement "strategy" by nagging her husband until his behavior improved. Mrs. Simington also used veiled threats of divorce to get her husband to attend therapy.

Family systems therapists sometimes adopt a developmental model of dysfunction. Family systems therapists believe families progress through developmental stages that include the following (Laszloffy, 2002):

1. Marriage

2. Birth of the initial children (beginning family)

3. Children's entry into school and parents' renegotiation of workload and household labor (school-age family)

4. Children's entry into adolescence and changing parental roles (adolescent family)

5. Children leaving home and entering college (launching family)

6. Parental retirement and interactions with grandchildren (postparental family)

Many families progress through these stages with some turmoil but solve problems and move forward. Other families may become stuck at one or more stages and do not resolve key issues. The role of a family systems therapist is to help a family resolve issues that restrict growth.

Three developmental sequences were most problematic for the Simingtons. First, Mrs. Simington complained she had children before fully developing her career. This produced simmering resentment intensified by recent events. A second developmental problem was the unexpected arrival of the baby. This event diminished Mrs. Simington's social life and her ability to raise her sons effectively. A third developmental problem was the boys' growth in general and Joshua's entry into adolescence in particular. Adolescents often have greater desire for autonomy from parents, stronger peer influence, better reasoning skills, increased ability to experience wider and deeper emotions, and intimate relationships. Entry into adolescence can be a turbulent time. This is more likely if a teenager's family is conflictive or if stressful life events occur. Such a situation obviously was true for Joshua.

Family systems therapists also propose that various alliances within families develop over time to cause conflict and childhood behavior problems. Triangulation occurs when two family members consistently disagree about an issue and ask a third family member to intervene and choose sides. Think of a mother and daughter with a strained relationship who constantly ask the father to decide their arguments. A father engaging in triangulation would likely vacillate, moving his support from one party to another to even things out and to avoid suffering rejection himself.

Another problematic alliance is a coalition where two or more family members align themselves against another member. This might involve two children who gang up on another child or, in the case of an extended family, a grandparent and grandchild who assert themselves against a parent (i.e., a cross-generational coalition). In addition, children might align themselves to change parental behavior. Some children act out in school to force their parents to stop fighting and focus instead on their immediate problems.

Some family coalitions are appropriate, of course, as when two parents effectively unite to raise their children. A primary problem for the Simingtons, however, was a weak parental coalition. Parents disagree about discipline or each parent disciplines the children alone or without support. The result may be children who effectively manipulate their parents, establish their own rules, and/or ignore their parents. Jeremy and Joshua Simington were good examples of this – they developed an ability to get what they wanted in a family with parental disarray. A therapist must recognize that a shift in power toward the parents may be necessary to restore balance and help a family progress through its developmental sequences.

Treatment

Family therapists often utilize treatment techniques such as (1) parent training in contingency management, (2) family communication and problem-solving training, and (3) contracting, reframing, and paradoxical interventions (Robin & Foster, 2002). Family therapy may involve separate marital therapy as well. The therapist recommended this approach for Mr. and Mrs. Simington but they declined.

Contingency management involves helping parents provide a united, consistent, and effective front when addressing child misbehavior (Kearney & Vecchio, 2002). Contingency management was highly pertinent to Mr. and Mrs. Simington who needed to agree on house rules, joint enforcement of those rules, and administration of consequences. The therapist initially outlined relevant house rules with the family members. Specific rules were set for curfew, homework, and chores and consequences were set for noncompliance. Family members agreed to the rules and placed a copy on the door of the refrigerator.

Contingency management also involves changing parent behaviors such as commands given to children. The therapist aimed for parent commands that were succinct, clear, and repeated only once. Mr. and Mrs. Simington learned to refrain from lecturing, criticizing, or questioning during commands. The therapist discussed ways Mr. Simington could help his wife address the children. Mr. Simington agreed to alter his work schedule to leave home earlier in the morning and get home earlier at night. He agreed as well to issue more commands to the boys, increase his time with them in recreational activities, and administer more consequences himself. Mrs. Simington had to keep reminding her husband to maintain his effort in these areas, however.

The therapist periodically reviewed house rules with the family and problems that subsequently arose. Some initial confusion occurred about who would take out the garbage and when, so the therapist assigned different days to the males in the household. The therapist helped Mr. and Mrs. Simington establish a regular routine for the morning and evening. The aim here was to smooth the transition to school and bed. This process went well, though the therapist found the family increasingly dependent on her to set up rules and resolve disputes. She thus focused more on communication skills and problem-solving training.

Communication skills training aims to improve ways family members talk to one another and listen appropriately. A therapist may set ground rules for the family, such as no name calling or interrupting. One family member then makes a statement while other family members listen and paraphrase what the first person said. This process helps increase attention and listening skills, allows everyone to hear one person's message, and helps family members absorb everyone's point of view. The therapist handles listening and paraphrasing problems by giving corrective feedback.

The therapist for the Simingtons explained the ground rules and allowed Joshua to speak first. Joshua gave a litany of complaints so the therapist asked Joshua to make only a one-sentence statement about one issue. Joshua then said he wanted to do more things with his friends outside the home. Jeremy tried to paraphrase this statement but made the mistake of starting his own statement. The therapist told Jeremy he could make his statement later, so he correctly paraphrased what his brother said. Mr. and Mrs. Simington were also tempted to respond to Joshua's statement rather than paraphrase but they did so at the therapist's urging.

Communication skills training may focus later on developing short conversations where one person makes two to three statements and the second person listens, paraphrases the statements, and responds in kind as the first speaker listens. A therapist supervises the statements and provides feedback about how the statements are made. In cases where two people do not speak to one another, a therapist may play the role of one and talk to the second as the first one watches. Advanced communication skills training can then focus on more extensive conversations, positive statements such as compliments, and expressions of appreciation for another's point of view.

Communication skills training progressed well in the therapist's office but not at home for the Simingtons. The family said too much chaos there prevented the relaxed atmosphere found in the clinic. The therapist told the family to schedule meeting times during which everyone would sit and practice the communications skills they learned. The family agreed to do so during dinner and did so with moderate success.

The therapist also emphasized problem-solving training for the Simingtons. The therapist raised a specific problem and all family members wrote as many solutions as possible (brainstorming). Even preposterous solutions such as hiring a maid to make the beds are allowed. A therapist will initially address a small problem so a family can practice the procedure with success. An initial problem for the Simingtons was curfew – the boys wanted to be in by 10:00 P.M. and the parents insisted on 8:00 P.M. All possible solutions were described and family members gave a grade to each (i.e., A, B, C, etc.). The therapist and family members then chose the solution with the highest grade. This involved a curfew of 8:30 P.M. on school nights and 10:00 P.M. on weekend nights if all relevant chores were done. The therapist later addressed more intricate problems.

Family therapists may use other techniques to improve family dynamics and solve problems (Barker, 2007). These techniques include contingency contracting, reframing, and paradoxical interventions. Contracting helps address parent-adolescent conflict and requires both parties to agree to a written contract developed by a therapist. The contract contains responsibilities for each party as well as positive and negative consequences for adhering or not adhering to its conditions. An advantage of this method is that it gives an adolescent a say in negotiations and all viewpoints are considered.

Reframing is a process whereby a therapist helps family members transform a seemingly negative statement or problem into a more positive one. Saying a child is missing a lot of school could be reframed as saying he desires more time with his parents. Paradoxical interventions may be used to demonstrate family dynamics. A therapist could encourage a child to tantrum as much as possible to show the parents he is doing so for their attention.

The Simingtons remained in therapy for 7 months, after which the family ended treatment. Each family member reported good progress but whether therapy simply prevented things from getting worse was unclear. Telephone contact with the family 6 months later did reveal some regression to the family's previous level of functioning but nothing severe enough to warrant a return to formal therapy. A particular bright spot was Mrs. Simington's statement that her husband had taken a much greater role in caring for and disciplining Jeremy and Joshua.

DISCUSSION QUESTIONS

1. What is the major difference between children who are regularly noncompliant and children with oppositional defiant disorder? What about the difference between a family that is functional and one that is dysfunctional? Can a family be functional *and* dysfunctional? Give an example.

2. What might happen during socialization to explain why boys are more defiant than girls? Do you think parents and teachers have different expectations for boys and girls? If so, what are they?

3. Would you describe your own family as healthy, enmeshed, isolated, detached, or conflictive? Did different patterns emerge among different subsystems (e.g., parent–parent, parent–child, child–child) in your family?

4. What is the best way to assess a family with many secrets, in which everyone is afraid to tell you what is really going on? What issues do you think families are most reluctant to talk about?

5. A common problem in family therapy is the transfer of skills from the therapist's office to home. What would you recommend or do as a therapist to help a family communicate or solve problems better in a chaotic home environment?

6. Do you think family dynamics are substantially different across cultures? What major differences do you think exist, if any, among Hispanic, African American, Asian American, Native American, and European American families? How might ethnic status influence family therapy?

7. How is the family structure changing in the United States? How might a family therapist modify treatment to meet the needs of a single-parent family, a divorced family, one headed by inexperienced teenagers, or one in which parents cannot spend much time with their children?

Chapter 11

Autism and Mental Retardation

Symptoms

Jennie Hobson was a 7-year-old European American female who attended a school for children with severe developmental disabilities. Ms. D'Angelo was a special education teacher recently hired by the school to supervise the education and training of a small group of children that included Jennie. Ms. D'Angelo's immediate task was to evaluate five children and decide whether their previously assigned diagnoses were still accurate. She was to design and implement an individualized education program that reflected each child's current needs.

Ms. D'Angelo first observed Jennie in a small classroom over a 5-day period. Jennie was often nonresponsive to others, especially her classmates, and rarely made eye contact with anyone. When left alone, Jennie would usually stand, put her hands over her throat, stick out her tongue, and make strange but soft noises. This would last for hours if she were left alone. When seated, Jennie rocked back and forth in her chair but never fell. Her motor skills seemed excellent and she could use crayons and manipulate paper when asked to do so. Her dexterity was also evident in her aggression, however. Jennie often grabbed people's jewelry and eyeglasses and flung them across the room. She moved quickly enough to accomplish this in less than two seconds.

Ms. D'Angelo noticed that Jennie was most aggressive when introduced to something or someone new. A new intern entered the room one day to work with Jennie, who promptly slapped him across his face (Ms. D'Angelo took note not to lean into Jennie when talking to her for the first time). Jennie then sat in a corner facing the wall and pulled her own hair. The intern ignored the behavior and worked with other students in the room. Jennie returned to her seat at the request of the intern after an hour but refused to work on her educational tasks. Her next day with the intern was less problematic, however, as she seemed to adjust to the new situation.

Ms. D'Angelo noticed that Jennie did not speak and vocalized only when making her soft sounds. The volume of her sounds rarely changed but she appeared to make the sounds when bored or anxious. Jennie made no effort to communicate with others and was often oblivious to others. She was sometimes startled when asked to do something. Despite her lack of expressiveness, Jennie did understand and adhere to simple requests from others. She complied readily when told to get her lunch, use the bathroom, or retrieve an item in the classroom. These commands were apparently part of her regular routine and therefore worthy of adherence.

Jennie had a "picture book" with photographs of items she might want or need. Jennie never picked up the book or presented it to anyone but did follow directions to use the book to make requests. When shown the book and asked to point, Jennie either pushed the book onto the desk if she did not want anything or pointed to one of five photographs (i.e., a lunch box, cookie, glass of water, favorite toy, or toilet) if she did want something. Ms. D'Angelo saw that no one currently implemented any *expressive* language programs for Jennie, however.

Jennie's cognitive skills were generally poor and had developed at a very slow pace. She was unable or unwilling to make simple discriminations between colors, understand the concept of yes and no, or follow multistep commands such as "clap your hands and touch your nose." Jennie's former teachers, Mr. Evan and Mrs. Taylor, said Jennie could learn basic discriminations but often did not retain or generalize the information. Jennie would learn the difference between red and blue in the classroom but then became confused by the same distinction in a more natural setting.

Despite her arrested cognitive skills, Jennie's adaptive behaviors were only moderately impaired. Jennie fed herself but never used a knife or fork. This latter skill may have been left undeveloped because of her aggression. Jennie did need some help dressing; Ms. D'Angelo noted that Jennie needed assistance putting on a winter jacket. Jennie used the toilet without difficulty but needed reminders to redress and wash afterward. Ms. D'Angelo later discovered from Jennie's parents, Mr. and Mrs. Hobson, that Jennie needed help bathing. Whether she lacked the skill to wash or was simply being noncompliant was unclear, however. Jennie needed supervision in all public places and most of the time at school and home. She had no history of running away but she often touched things that were potentially harmful, such as a stove.

Following her classroom observations of Jennie, Ms. D'Angelo had an extensive conversation with Mr. and Mrs. Hobson. They said Jennie "had always been like this" and gave examples of her early impairment. Both said Jennie was "different" as a baby when she resisted being held and when she failed to talk by age 3 years. Mr. and Mrs. Hobson initially thought their daughter was deaf but medical tests indicated normal physical functioning and slightly better than normal motor skills. Jennie did acquire basic daily living skills but her behavior problems often prevented full instruction. Mr. and Mrs. Hobson said Jennie would throw tantrums, become aggressive, and stand in the corner for hours when physically prompted to do something, such as hold a spoon.

Mr. and Mrs. Hobson had enrolled their daughter in her current school when she was 4 years old. They said Jennie's behavior problems had improved tremendously over the past 3 years, a fact that was critical to their decision to keep her in their home. The reduced behavior problems allowed others to teach Jennie more adaptive skills but Mr. and Mrs. Hobson said sadly that their daughter "still has a long way to go."

Ms. D'Angelo reviewed Jennie's school file last so as not to bias her initial observations and interviews. Limited psychological testing but extensive observations over the past 3 years largely confirmed Jennie's persistent problems in cognitive and social functioning. Her behavior problems improved to a point that she could be next to other children at the special school. Language remained severely deficient, a fact that distressed Ms. D'Angelo the most. Based on her initial observations, interviews, and review of previous information, Ms. D'Angelo tentatively concluded that Jennie still met criteria for autistic disorder and mental retardation, severity unspecified. The latter designation indicates a suspected presence of mental retardation in someone who cannot be successfully tested using standardized tests or who is unwilling to comply with such tests.

Assessment

The essential feature of autistic disorder is "markedly abnormal or impaired development in social interaction and communication and a markedly restricted repertoire of activity and interests" [American Psychiatric Association (APA), 2000, p. 70]. Children with autism must show delays in normal functioning or show abnormal functioning before age 3 years. The extent of these delays can vary considerably, however. Social, communicative, and behavioral areas of functioning are greatly impaired. Social interaction deficits are the hallmark of autism ("auto" meaning "self") – the child is uninterested in reciprocity, play with others, peer relationships, sharing, or even eye contact. Social and physical contacts are aversive for many children with autism; note Jennie's early response to being held and recent response to the intern who got too close to her.

Most children with autism are mute, like Jennie, or have great difficulty initiating or maintaining a conversation with others. If language is used, it is often odd or difficult to understand. Echolalia, or repeating words one has heard, and pronoun reversal, such as using the word "you" instead of "I," are common. Children with autism sometimes show behavioral problems such as self-injury, aggression, self-stimulation (such as Jennie's sounds and rocking), adherence to routines, and preoccupation with parts of inanimate objects such as shoes on a doll. Jennie's social and language deficits were clear. Her level of problematic behavior, however, fluctuated. She stopped pulling her hair if offered certain foods. Jennie was thus somewhat responsive to external contingencies on her behavior.

The essential feature of mental retardation is "significantly subaverage general intellectual functioning that is accompanied by significant limitations in adaptive functioning in at least two of the following skill areas: communication, self-care, home living, social/interpersonal skills, use of community resources, self-direction, functional academic skills, work, leisure, health, and safety" (APA, 2000, p. 41). Onset of the disorder must be before age 18 years. Mental retardation generally involves deficits in many if not most areas of functioning, whereas autism involves deficits in some areas (e.g., social, communicative) but not others (e.g., physical development, motor skills). Up to 75% of children with autism meet criteria for mental retardation (Bolte & Poustka, 2002). Autism and mental retardation are pervasive developmental disabilities.

Jennie's intellectual functioning was not formally tested because of her unwillingness to participate (hence the proposed diagnosis of mental retardation, unspecified type). Deficits in communication, self-care, social skills, self-direction, academics, and leisure were evident, however. Despite these pervasive, almost psychotic-like deficits, most children with autism do not show symptoms of schizophrenia. Jennie had no history of delusions, hallucinations, or catatonia.

Assessing a child with autism or mental retardation must involve different areas of possibly impaired functioning. This includes an assessment of intellectual functioning when possible. Standardized intelligence tests for evaluating typical children include the Stanford-Binet Intelligence Scale (Roid, 2003), Wechsler Preschool and Primary Scale of Intelligence (Wechsler, 2002), and Wechsler Intelligence Scale for Children (Wechsler, 2003). These tests do not apply to many children with autism or mental retardation, however, because of their heavy reliance on verbal content and language comprehension. An accurate picture of intellectual functioning in this population is often not possible.

Cognitive functioning may be better assessed using tests that do not require verbal instructions. A good example is the Leiter International Performance Scale (Roid & Miller, 1997). For higher functioning children, the Halstead-Reitan Neuropsychological Test Battery (Jarvis & Barth, 1994), Raven's Progressive Matrices (RPM) (Raven, 2000), and Peabody Picture Vocabulary Test (PPVT-4) (Dunn & Dunn, 2006) are useful. The Halstead-Reitan battery is an excellent measure of sensorimotor ability, the RPM is useful for examining perceptual ability, and the PPVT-4 is a good screening device for receptive language problems. Scores from each test correlate well with scores from traditional intelligence tests. Measures more specific to autism include the Autism Screening Instrument for Educational Planning (Krug, Arick, & Almond, 2008) and Childhood Autism Rating Scale* (Mayes et al., 2009; Schopler, Reichler, & Renner, 1988). Sample subitems from the latter include the following:

1. Relating to people: The child is consistently aloof or unaware of what the adult is doing. He or she almost never responds or initiates contact with the adult. Only the most persistent attempts to get the child's attention have any effect.

2. Body use: Behaviors that are clearly strange or unusual for a child of this age may include strange finger movements, peculiar finger or body posturing, staring or picking at the body, self-directed aggression, rocking, spinning, finger-wiggling, or toe-walking.

---

* Material from the CARS copyright © 1988 by Western Psychological Services. Reprinted by permission of the publisher, Western Psychological Services, 12–31 Wilshire Boulevard, Los Angeles, California, 90025, U.S.A., www.wpspublish.com. Not to be reprinted in whole or in part for any additional purpose without the expressed, written permission of the publisher. All rights reserved.

3. Adaptation to change: The child shows severe reactions to change. If a change is forced, he or she may become extremely angry or uncooperative and respond with tantrums.

4. Verbal communication: Meaningful speech is not used. The child may make infantile squeals, weird or animal-like sounds, complex noises approximating speech, or may show persistent, bizarre use of some recognizable words or phrases.

5. Nonverbal communication: The child only uses bizarre or peculiar gestures which have no apparent meaning, and shows no awareness of the meanings associated with the gestures or facial expressions of others.

Developmental scales may be more pertinent for children suspected of very low functioning or who are difficult to test. Jennie had been evaluated previously with the Bayley Scales of Infant and Toddler Development-Third Edition (BSID) (Bayley, 2005). The BSID is a measure of mental, motor, and behavioral functioning that requires a child to perform various tasks and provides a rating scale for emotional and social behavior. Jennie had average to above average motor abilities (e.g., coordination, fine motor skills) but low mental abilities (e.g., discriminations, problem solving, or memory). Such a pattern may characterize children who are deaf or who have autism. Several behavior problems were noted, such as resistance to touch and frequent temper tantrums.

Adaptive behavior is a key assessment target as well, particularly for children with mental retardation and impaired physical and motor development. Too often, diagnoses of mental retardation are based solely on cognitive ability without regard to adaptive behavior. Adaptive behavior scales for people with mental retardation include the AAMR Adaptive Behavior Scale (Nihira, Leland, & Lambert, 1993), Adaptive Behavior Assessment System (Harrison & Oakland, 2003), and Vineland Adaptive Behavior Scales (VABS) (Sparrow, Cicchetti, & Balla, 2005).

The VABS involves caregiver interviews and provides norm-referenced scales for communication, daily living skills, socialization, and motor skills. A maladaptive behavior subscale is included as well. Ms. D'Angelo used the VABS to interview Mr. and Mrs. Hobson, Jennie's babysitter, and Jennie's previous teachers. They rated Jennie's communication and socialization skills very low but rated her motor skills appropriate for her age. Primary maladaptive behaviors included withdrawal and unawareness of immediate surroundings.

Direct behavioral observation is also useful to identify socialization problems and functions of maladaptive behavior. Ms. D'Angelo's observations over several days revealed that Jennie was most responsive to others when she (1) was in situations she considered routine, (2) was not anxious or bored, and (3) did not find her work to be excessive or overly demanding. Ms. D'Angelo noted that Jennie's social responsiveness improved significantly after a break or lunch and the teacher made a note to schedule frequent breaks for Jennie during the day. Ms. D'Angelo noted that Jennie's misbehavior occurred primarily to escape aversive situations. These situations included new stimuli in her environment, tiring tasks, and physical contact. In addition, Ms. D'Angelo found that certain foods attenuated Jennie's misbehavior.

Risk Factors and Maintaining Variables

The etiology of autism is not completely known but, because of the pervasiveness of the disorder and because it occurs at an early age, biological variables are likely suspects. Concordance rates of autism are 60–92% in identical twins but 0–10% in fraternal twins. Siblings of a child with autism have a 2–8% chance of having autism themselves. Autism may be linked to abnormalities on chromosomes 7 and 15 (Muhle, Trentacoste, & Rapin, 2004). Parents do not generally pass autism to their children, however, and parents of children with autism do not show much psychopathology themselves.

No immediate relatives of Jennie displayed overt psychopathology, though Mrs. Hobson said her mother once had a "nervous breakdown." Jennie had two older siblings, a 13-year-old brother and a 9-year-old sister, but neither had social, cognitive, or adaptive functioning problems. Mr. and Mrs. Hobson once considered having a fourth child but were now discouraged given their experience with Jennie and the time needed to take care of her.

Other biological factors influence autism, including brain conditions such as cerebral palsy, meningitis, encephalitis, infections, and accidental injuries. Neurological problems likely account for many cases of autism, however (Vargas, Nascimbene, Krishnan, Zimmerman, & Pardo, 2005). Such problems may involve brain areas most responsible for motor and cognitive functioning, such as the basal ganglia, general limbic system, and frontal lobe. Assessment of these problems may involve brain-imaging techniques such as magnetic resonance imaging. For obvious reasons, however, this is difficult to do with children with autism. Jennie received no such evaluation.

Some children with autism have biochemical changes in the neurotransmitter serotonin, which is involved in mood and motor behavior (Huang & Santangelo, 2008). Drugs that lower serotonin levels, such as fenfluramine, do help control excess motor activity such as self-stimulation. No formal test measured serotonin levels for Jennie. Given her good motor skills and strange motor behaviors, however, an increased serotonin level seems plausible.

Many biological risk factors for autism likely conspire to produce the disorder. This is the "final common pathway" hypothesis – the idea that different factors such as genetics, poor brain development, and high serotonin interact in different ways for different children with autism. These factors all create the same result, or type of brain dysfunction, that leads to autism. Unfortunately, as with Jennie, the factors are often not identified.

The causes of mental retardation involve a greater mixture of biological and environmental variables. Biological variables during the prenatal period often affect brain development. Prenatal changes that lead to mental retardation include (1) malformations, especially problems of neural tube formation, (2) deformations, or abnormal growths of the head or organs, and/or (3) disruptions, or general damage from teratogens such as prenatal alcohol use (Toriello, 2008).

Malformations include genetic disorders or chromosomal aberrations such as fragile X syndrome, Prader-Willi syndrome, and Down syndrome. Down syndrome is typically associated with 3, #21 chromosomes, characteristic physical defects, and moderate mental retardation. Metabolic problems may produce mental retardation as well, including phenylketonuria and Niemann-Pick disease (Levy, 2009). None of these conditions existed in Jennie, however.

Unusual extrinsic factors may lead to mental retardation. These factors include extensive lack of oxygen (e.g., from near drowning), brain trauma (e.g., from head injury), and poisoning (e.g., from excessive lead) (McDermott, Durkin, Schupf, & Stein, 2007). Accidents are a leading cause of harm to infants and children and their consequences regarding cognitive development can be catastrophic.

Mrs. Hobson did say that Jennie's birth was "a very trying experience." Jennie's birth was marked by prematurity (3 weeks), long labor (23 hours), and a complicated delivery. Jennie moved immediately before birth, which made her extraction difficult. Jennie spent a longer period than usual in the birth canal, which placed her at risk for oxygen loss. Following birth, however, Jennie's Apgar test score was normal and she did not appear to have ill effects from the birth process. Whether the natal experience caused her cognitive problems was thus unknown.

Environmental effects also influence mental retardation and may have been prominent for Jennie. These effects involve familial retardation and may include factors like minor neurological impairment, natural placement at a lower intelligence level, and environmental deprivation (Hodapp & Dykens, 2003). Those with familial retardation tend to have mild cognitive deficits, poor educational experiences, low socioeconomic status, and/or parents who are inconsistent in their child-rearing practices.

Jennie's early environmental deprivation was not severe but did occur to some extent. Jennie's early withdrawal often led Mr. and Mrs. Hobson to leave Jennie alone to avoid upsetting her. Jennie thus did not receive much verbal or physical attention from her parents or siblings. In addition, Mr. and Mrs. Hobson made the "mistake" (their word) of waiting to evaluate Jennie until she was 3 years old. They instead hoped Jennie's behaviors were a phase or that she was developing more slowly than most children. Only when Jennie had not yet spoken by age 3 years did Mr. and Mrs. Hobson consent to an evaluation. Even then, both waited another year before enrolling Jennie in her current placement. The loss of educational time during this period, while perhaps not the cause of Jennie's problems, may have contributed to their severity. The window of opportunity for teaching verbal skills was not fully exploited, for example.

Developmental Aspects

People with severe developmental disabilities generally have a poor prognosis. About 78–90% of people with autism continue to have extremely poor social behavior, intellectual functioning, and independence (Billstedt, Gillberg, & Gillberg, 2005). Many continue to need supervised care throughout their lifetime. Other people with developmental disabilities improve more over time and can function independently or with some help. Examples include people with Down syndrome or high-functioning autism (Khouzam, El-Gabalawi, Pirwani, & Priest, 2004).

Good indicators of whether a child with autism will experience favorable outcome over the long run are average intelligence and presence of some language before age 5 years. Neither of these conditions applied to Jennie, however. Early special education services are also associated with a better prognosis for autism (Charman et al., 2005; Rice, Warren, & Betz, 2005). This is especially true if language and interpersonal skills are emphasized. Jennie's enrollment at age 4 years in a school that stressed these skills is a hopeful sign.

The development of comorbid medical and mental disorder symptoms in autism is common. The most prevalent comorbid medical condition is epilepsy, which is seen in about 25% of cases (though not in Jennie) and throughout infancy, childhood, and adolescence. Comorbid mental symptoms include hyperactivity, labile mood swings, inappropriate affect, depression, and oppositional behaviors (Bryson, Corrigan, McDonald, & Holmes, 2008; Hara, 2007).

The developmental course of children with mental retardation relates closely to cognitive functioning levels (Hodapp & Dykens, 2003). These levels remain stable over time, even during childhood and adolescence. Low scores on the BSID (the same test given to Jennie) predict low intelligence scores across childhood and adulthood. This seems to be true even if a child receives special education classes.

Children with moderate, severe, or profound mental retardation tend to have stable and poor cognitive development. Those with mild mental retardation, especially those with good verbal skills, have a much better prognosis. Those with Down syndrome or fragile X syndrome tend to develop intelligence at a much slower rate than those with other types of mental retardation. Greater impairment as one grows older may thus be seen. Many children with mental retardation gradually develop adaptive behavior skills but this depends much on level of intellectual impairment (Bolte & Poustka, 2002).

Jennie's limited language skills are a poor prognostic sign (recall that this worried Ms. D'Angelo the most). Children without good language skills are more apt to withdraw, develop maladaptive behaviors to communicate, and fail to learn appropriate social skills. Ms. D'Angelo strongly suspected Jennie was sometimes aggressive to communicate her desire to withdraw from a taxing situation. Unfortunately, Jennie did not have the means to show her frustration otherwise. The development of some language, perhaps sign language or extensive receptive language skills, was thus made a priority for Jennie.

Jennie did have some good prognostic signs, however. Mr. and Mrs. Hobson expressed a strong desire to help their daughter in whatever way possible. They recognized that Jennie's difficulties were pervasive and that parents have to be active participants for an educational program to succeed. Generalization of language and social skills is a key aspect of treatment for children with autism and mental retardation and leads to better outcome. Mr. and Mrs. Hobson were already engaged in parent training classes at Jennie's school and were now extending the school's educational programs to their home environment.

Another good prognostic sign for Jennie was enrollment in a specialized school that used behavioral strategies to address skills deficits. Jennie's functioning became enhanced by the substantial attention now paid to her behaviors. Early and intensive intervention is crucial and had already helped reduce some of Jennie's overt behavior problems. Her on-task and self-injurious behaviors improved greatly after teachers began using tangible rewards. Jennie's aggression declined when a regular schedule was designed and she became more familiar with her teachers. In addition, her maladaptive behaviors dropped suddenly when she learned to use her picture book to make requests. Despite this progress, however, Jennie still has a long way to go and her long-term prognosis is not generally good.

Treatment

Treatment for children with autism and/or mental retardation focuses on (1) deficits of language, social skills, and adaptive behavior skills and (2) excess maladaptive behaviors such as aggression, self-injury, and self-stimulation. Treatment may follow one of two philosophies. Autism may be treated as a global disorder via medication. Clinicians may also divide autism into separate problems (e.g., language, social) and address them individually with behavior therapy.

Medication for children with autism includes fenfluramine, a drug that reduces serotonin levels in the central nervous system (recall that many children with autism have high levels of serotonin, which relates to motor behavior). Fenfluramine may be most useful for excess motor behaviors. Other drugs to treat autism include amphetamines, antidepressants, antipsychotics, and antiepileptic medications (Leskovec, Rowles, & Findling, 2008). These drugs improve motor and other problem behaviors to some extent but the hallmark symptoms of autism, such as language delays and poor social skills, are unaffected. Medication was never used or considered for Jennie.

Behavior therapy has been a mainstay of treatment for children with autism and can address specific problems. Remediating language problems in this population is a top priority for the reasons mentioned earlier. This may involve shaping or reinforcing successive approximations of a desired response (Newman, Reinecke, & Ramos, 2009). Any sound or vocalization may be reinforced first. After a child vocalizes regularly, a teacher shapes these sounds into phonemes later used to form words. A child could be rewarded with food every time she hums. Humming may then be shaped into a phoneme of "mmmm." Subsequently, a teacher may shape this phoneme into words such as "mama" or "me." Other communication programs for children with autism emphasize reciprocal language interactions, self-initiated questions, and self-management (Vismara & Rogers, 2010).

Ms. D'Angelo started a program whereby Jennie received a reward every time she made her strange sounds. Jennie's vocalizations increased only moderately, however. Jennie found the extra attention to her vocalizations aversive and she often turned away when starting to make her sounds. Ms. D'Angelo further tried to shape Jennie's vocalizations into a short "o" sound but many attempts over a 9-month period proved unfruitful. The teacher concluded that Jennie's language would have to emphasize sign language and receptive skills, including the picture book.

Ms. D'Angelo thus implemented two language programs for Jennie that concentrated on these areas. Jennie had excellent motor skills so she was initially taught some basic signs. Many of Jennie's behaviors were escape motivated so Ms. D'Angelo initially used functional communication training and taught Jennie the sign for "break" (Durand & Merges, 2009). This was a relatively simple sign (two fists placed side by side and then separated) and one reinforced by giving free time. Jennie was allowed a 10-minute break every time she formed the sign. She first needed prompting and reacted aggressively to the necessary physical contact (i.e., a teacher holding Jennie's fists together and "breaking" them apart). Following the prompted response, however, Jennie took a break.

Jennie eventually learned to sign "break" when she wanted to escape a particular task. Jennie was then placed on a schedule where she could ask for a maximum of six breaks per day. This initially created confusion and aggression on Jennie's part but she eventually caught on and used her break times selectively. Ms. D'Angelo noticed that Jennie's escape-motivated aggression in the classroom dropped significantly. Jennie's use of the "break" sign did not generalize well to other areas of school or to home, however.

Ms. D'Angelo tried to teach Jennie other signs, particularly those related to "bathroom" and "drink." Jennie had moderate success with these but her performance was uneven. Jennie formed the signs and received reinforcement on some days but had no desire to use the signs on other days. She never used the signs outside the classroom. Ms. D'Angelo tried other concepts – "yes," "no," "eat," and "hello" – but Jennie never formed signs for these.

Ms. D'Angelo wanted to expand Jennie's use of her picture book in conjunction with the sign language program. This led to much greater success – Jennie could distinguish about a dozen pictures and point to them to request something. In addition to pictures mentioned earlier (i.e., lunch box, cookie, glass of water, one toy, toilet), Jennie's picture book now included articles of clothing, different foods, and certain playthings. A subsequent training program was added so Jennie would carry her picture book and use it in other settings, especially at home. Mr. and Mrs. Hobson learned to prompt Jennie to use the book at home and reward her for appropriate requests.

Jennie successfully used the book and a limited number of signs with prompting over several months. She rarely used her skills without a prompt, however, and seemed unable or unwilling to learn or express new words and concepts. Jennie often showed no motivation to use her current skills and occasionally became aggressive if someone was too avid in prompting her to do so.

Ms. D'Angelo sought to build some basic skills to address Jennie's distaste for social interactions. Jennie essentially had no social behaviors, so establishing eye contact was a top priority. A teacher asked Jennie to look at her. Jennie initially failed to do so and was thus prompted by the teacher who gently raised Jennie's chin and established brief eye contact. Jennie was subsequently rewarded. This process was somewhat aversive to Jennie but she did establish regular eye contact with a teacher on command after 5 months of training.

Ms. D'Angelo then extended Jennie's social skills training to include basic imitation and observation of others. This was done using one-on-one instruction and participation in group activities. Jennie was asked to imitate two-step commands from the teacher such as "stand up and go to the door." She also imitated social behaviors such as waving goodbye, smiling, and raising her hand to signal a desire to point to her picture book. Social programs that required physical contact, however, generally failed. Jennie did participate in simple group activities with other children. She rolled a ball toward others, played basic games, and sang. Jennie interacted with peers somewhat during these group activities but her behaviors were not extensively social.

Ms. D'Angelo concentrated on Jennie's adaptive self-help skills as well. Jennie learned to do several things in a relatively short period:

1. Dress herself fully (though her clothes still needed to be laid out)

2. Eat with a fork

3. Go to the toilet, redress, and wash without prompting afterward

4. Get in and out of a car without assistance

5. Organize school materials

6. Bathe with a prompt to leave the bathtub when finished

Mr. and Mrs. Hobson expressed great satisfaction with Jennie's improved adaptive behavior skills and decreased maladaptive behavior. Jennie's aggression dropped to almost zero by the end of the school year, though she screamed occasionally and tugged at her hair when upset. Ms. D'Angelo worked closely with Mr. and Mrs. Hobson during the school year to help Jennie generalize her new skills to home. Mr. and Mrs. Hobson also received a list of educational programs to practice during the summer so Jennie could retain some of her skills. Fortunately, Mr. and Mrs. Hobson maintained their daughter's overall level of functioning through the beginning of the next school year.

During the following school year, however, Jennie's level of progress remained flat. This applied especially to her language and social skills. Ms. D'Angelo found she had to spend considerable time working with Jennie to retain the skills she had. Given Jennie's level of cognitive functioning, this scenario will likely continue in coming years. This pathway illustrates the difficulty involved in improving the long-term prognosis of children with autism, and the outlook for Jennie in the future remains cloudy.

DISCUSSION QUESTIONS

1. Separating children with autism from children with moderate mental retardation, children with Asperger's disorder, and children with severe learning disabilities can be difficult. What symptoms and behaviors would you rely on most to make these distinctions?

2. Why do you think autism and mental retardation are much more common in boys than girls? Be sure to explore gender stereotypes. Are your proposed reasons preventable? How?

3. What recommendations would you make to Mr. and Mrs. Hobson as they care for Jennie at home? What are the major ramifications of Jennie's condition for the family in general and her siblings in particular?

4. What is the best way to treat people with severe disabilities within the public education system? Examine the pros and cons of segregated education and mainstreamed classrooms for all children involved.

5. A key issue in treating people with disabilities is their (in)ability to give informed consent. Should a person with disabilities be subjected to educational, behavioral, or even aversive treatment without their expressed consent? What if the person engages in life-threatening behaviors?

6. How would you address an adolescent with a severe disability who commits a murder? Should that person be tried like anyone else or be given special considerations? What considerations, if any, would you recommend?

7. Too often, people rely only on intelligence tests to make a diagnosis of mental retardation. What could you do as a professional to ensure that other methods are used to make this determination?

Chapter 12

Pediatric Condition/Pain

Symptoms

Francisco Hernandez was a 12-year-old Hispanic male admitted to a county hospital following a severe car accident. Francisco was in seventh grade at the time of his admission. He entered the hospital after a speeding car struck him in a pedestrian crossing near his school. Francisco was on his bicycle at the time but his clothing became caught on a back part of the car. The car driver unknowingly dragged Francisco along the road for several yards before stopping. Francisco suffered severe lacerations to his right side along his leg, side, and arm. His head and face were unharmed but Francisco bled badly and felt excruciating pain from extensive "road rash."

Francisco was fortunate that many people were around and so an ambulance and police unit arrived on the scene within minutes. Francisco was rushed to the emergency room where doctors controlled the bleeding and made sure no internal organs suffered serious damage. The initial medical report indicated possible internal damage because Francisco, who was in and out of consciousness, said his abdominal area was in great pain. His medical condition eventually stabilized but Francisco was transferred to the pediatric intensive care unit (PICU) so doctors could monitor and address his severe skin damage, vital signs, and pain.

Francisco's parents, Mr. and Mrs. Hernandez, arrived at the hospital while their son was in the emergency trauma center. Neither spoke English so there was some initial confusion about the location and condition of their son. A bilingual nurse explained that Francisco was badly hurt but had no brain injury or sensory damage. She further explained, however, that Francisco did have skin damage akin to a severe burn. He was in considerable pain, heavily sedated, and would not likely respond to his parents when they entered his room.

The hospital's pediatric psychologist visited all children admitted to this hospital for severe medical problems (and their family members). A pediatric psychologist is a mental health professional who studies and addresses areas of functioning that relate to health and illness in children. Pediatric psychologists investigate social, physical, cognitive, and other areas of functioning among youths with pain, asthma, diabetes, cancer, and other medical conditions. The pediatric psychologist for Francisco's case, Dr. Lemos, was responsible for working with family members to enhance treatment outcome and to address obstacles that might prevent full recovery.

Dr. Lemos' first task was to visit Francisco and his parents in the PICU. Mr. and Mrs. Hernandez were understandably distraught and confused about what happened. Francisco was asleep. Dr. Lemos explained in Spanish that she would serve as a primary liaison between the parents and medical staff and assess child and family functioning. She understood that the first order of business, however, was to help the parents stabilize their own emotions and pertinent family issues such as childcare. Mrs. Hernandez was in shock and could barely speak but Mr. Hernandez was quite angry. He swore vengeance on the driver but calmed when Dr. Lemos asked about the quality of care their son received. Mr. Hernandez said the doctors seemed to take good care of Francisco and he was relieved that the ambulance, police, and medical personnel responded so quickly.

Francisco's medical status stabilized more over the next several days but his pain level remained high. He often cried and complained of pain in his gut, a symptom that puzzled doctors because they found no internal damage. Francisco had trouble eating and sleeping and was on sedative medication much of the time. Dr. Lemos checked Francisco and his parents each day; Mrs. Hernandez was usually in her son's room but Mr. Hernandez appeared only intermittently.

Francisco's medical condition improved over the next 3 weeks, so Dr. Lemos spent more time with him to assess various conditions. She was concerned about Francisco's reaction to the accident. Francisco either did not want to speak about the accident or claimed he did not remember what happened. He appeared somewhat "spacey" at times and suddenly stopped talking at other times. Dr. Lemos felt this behavior represented some dissociation, a symptom not uncommon in recently traumatized children. Dissociation is a mental state where a person distances himself emotionally and cognitively from a traumatic event. Dissociation is a key aspect of acute stress disorder, a mental condition following a trauma that may involve detachment, reduced awareness of surroundings, and derealization [American Psychiatric Association (APA), 2000].

Another source of concern for Dr. Lemos was Francisco's pain. Despite heavy medication, Francisco insisted he was in great pain and could not eat or sleep. His comment produced great distress for his mother, who often cried, held Francisco's hand, and brought him toys, special treats, and reading materials. Dr. Lemos noticed that Francisco refused to complete homework sent to him by his teachers. Hospital staff members told Dr. Lemos that Francisco slept fine during the night and had a healthy appetite, especially for foods brought to him by his mother.

Dr. Lemos spoke at length with Mrs. Hernandez about her husband and other family members. Mr. Hernandez worked two jobs and was thus unavailable to sit with Francisco. Extended relatives pitched in to supervise Francisco's two younger sisters and allow Mrs. Hernandez to be at the hospital. Dr. Lemos asked about Francisco's schoolwork but Mrs. Hernandez said her son was too ill to concentrate. Dr. Lemos asked whether Mrs. Hernandez spoke to her son about the accident but the mother simply waved her hands and shook her head. She had no intention of talking to Francisco about the accident and upsetting him further.

With Mrs. Hernandez's permission, Dr. Lemos spoke with several of Francisco's teachers. They said Francisco was a bright child who did well in school. He was well liked though shy. He often preferred to be close to his mother and went home right after school. Mr. and Mrs. Hernandez were not closely involved in their son's education, however. Neither attended parent-teacher conferences or responded to progress notes or report cards, though the language barrier may have been pertinent. A particularly revealing finding, however, was the guidance counselor's note that Francisco sometimes cried at school because he missed his parents, an unusual behavior for a 12-year-old.

Dr. Lemos spoke with Francisco's medical doctors as well. The doctors expressed frustration with Francisco's pain level, saying his wounds were healing but that his reports of pain had not wavered since admission. Francisco insisted he had abdominal pain but no medical cause was found. The doctors noted that Francisco needed less pain medication when his mother was out of the building. They asked Dr. Lemos for an evaluation to determine the psychological nature of Francisco's pain. From initial information gathered from several sources, Dr. Lemos made a preliminary conclusion that Francisco was indeed experiencing intense and recurrent pain. She also thought, however, that significant trauma-related and other psychological factors affected Francisco's pain and could interfere with treatment.

Assessment

According to the DSM-IV-TR, a problem that may be a focus of clinical attention involves psychological or behavioral factors that affect one's medical condition. These factors may aggravate a medical condition, interfere with treatment of the condition, serve as an added health risk, or trigger symptoms of the medical condition from stress (APA, 2000, p. 731). Pediatric psychologists are mental health professionals who typically work in hospital settings to address psychological or behavioral factors that affect children. Pediatric psychologists focus most on helping youths cope with illness, comply with medication and other treatment, manage pain and anxiety, and reduce acting-out behavior problems. In addition, pediatric psychologists may address family issues, such as conflict, confusion about a medical diagnosis, and treatment decisions (Carter et al., 2003; Opipari-Arrigan, Stark, & Drotar, 2006).

Francisco's pediatric psychologist suspected that family and psychological issues influenced his pain. Francisco relished his mother's attention and her doting only increased when Francisco complained of pain. Mrs. Hernandez allowed her son to skip homework and avoid discussions of the car accident. Attention-seeking and escape-motivated behavior thus seemed pertinent to Francisco's case. The pediatric psychologist worried about Mr. Hernandez's general absence from his son and what effect this could have on his marriage. In addition, she was concerned about Francisco's unwillingness to discuss his traumatic experience.

Assessing youths with psychological factors that affect medical conditions usually involves a biopsychosocial perspective. A biopsychosocial perspective assumes that biological, psychological, and social/developmental variables affect a child's medical condition and that a child's medical condition affects these variables (Anthony & Schanberg, 2007; Kroner-Herwig, Morris, & Heinrich, 2008). Biological assessment of pediatric populations focuses on symptoms, cause, and severity of a physical problem to guide medical treatment.

Psychological assessment in pediatric psychology has focused heavily on pain. Assessing pain in children involves different forms of measurement but can be difficult because one child's ability to tolerate and report pain can differ substantially from another child. One common method of pain assessment is facial expression. A child sees different pictures of faces with varying degrees of grimace from pain. The child identifies which face corresponds with his current pain level, a method that may be particularly beneficial for very young children (Schiavenato, 2008). Pain intensity can be evaluated as well on a 1–10 scale where 10 = extreme pain. These methods were not particularly helpful in Francisco's case, however, because he kept endorsing the highest level of pain.

Scales are available to measure pain perception and pain behavior. Pain perception refers to thoughts and feelings regarding pain; pain behavior refers to how a child expresses pain. Techniques for assessing these constructs include self-report measures such as the McGill Pain Questionnaire, Brief Pain Inventory, and Pediatric Pain Questionnaire (Caraceni et al., 2002; Sawyer et al., 2004). In addition, youths may complete pain diaries to record events that precede pain, intensity and duration of pain, and whether medications or other treatments are effective (Gray, 2008).

Behavioral observations are another key assessment technique for children in pain. Observations can include medical variables such as heart rate, blood pressure, and respiration as well as behavioral variables such as facial grimacing, crying, irritability, slow movement, and agitation or restlessness (Chambliss, Heggen, Copelan, & Pettignano, 2002). Dr. Lemos noticed some interesting behaviors when watching Francisco and his mother. Francisco generally showed more grimacing, complaining, and crying when his mother was present but showed more compliance, movement, and emotional control when medical staff spoke to him.

The assessment of youths with psychological factors affecting medical conditions can involve developmental and personality factors. One of the first avenues of developmental assessment is an intellectual evaluation. Psychologists use intelligence tests to see whether a child has major delays in cognitive functioning and whether he can understand a treatment program involving techniques such as cognitive restructuring or pain management. Francisco received no formal intelligence testing but his teachers said he was bright and articulate.

Child personality factors can influence pain and include low self-image, external locus of control, dependency, and ability to handle stress. Instruments useful in this regard include the Personality Inventory for Children (Lachar & Gruber, 2000), interviews, and self-report measures such as the Piers-Harris Children's Self-Concept Scale (Piers, Harris, & Herzberg, 2002). Francisco appeared to have several personality factors important for understanding his pain. He had a low self-image and denigrated his appearance, academic status, and athletic prowess. Francisco was occasionally depressed and socially withdrawn, conditions sometimes associated with somatic complaints. He had been through a deeply traumatic experience, however, so some level of sadness was to be expected.

The pediatric psychologist found Francisco to be dependent and unable to handle stress effectively. He often preferred to be with his mother and sisters and was clearly interested in gaining attention from them. Francisco was not self-sufficient in managing his pain; he often called his mother or the nurse to report pain even after receiving pain medication. Francisco would induce guilt in his mother by saying she did not spend enough time with him or was trying to force schoolwork on him. Francisco's mother usually responded to these statements by giving her son greater attention and excusing him from tasks.

Family and child interviews are the dominant form of assessment for children with pain. Interviews are designed to uncover psychological variables related to a child's pain as well as mental disorders that influence pain management. Key variables covered in an interview include arousal level and emotional states that can increase pain intensity. Examples of the latter include worry, sadness, fear, and anger. Parent reactions to a child's pain and inadvertent reinforcement of pain behaviors are an important focus as well (Kozlowska et al., 2008, Rose, Khan, Kram, Lane, & Collins, 2008).

Dr. Lemos' interviews indicated that Francisco perceived his abdominal pain as a severe symptom that caused him great distress. He seemed to have a low pain tolerance and was often dramatic, even theatrical, when discussing the difficulty of his pain. He had many pained facial expressions, verbal complaints, and requests to see his mother or medical doctor. He was less enthusiastic to see Dr. Lemos, indicating on occasion that the psychologist did not fully appreciate his condition. Dr. Lemos also gauged Mrs. Hernandez's reactions to Francisco's physical symptoms. Mrs. Hernandez was quite emotional regarding her son's symptoms, sometimes crying and asking Francisco detailed questions about his comfort level. She found the family to be somewhat enmeshed with the exception of Mr. Hernandez.

Risk Factors and Maintaining Variables

Many specific variables such as illness, trauma, or accidents cause pediatric conditions in children. Genetic factors are important as well for physical conditions such as asthma and diabetes. The cause of other pediatric conditions is harder to pinpoint; examples include abdominal pain and headache. Different pediatric conditions often have their own set of causal pathways.

Pain is an experience that results from various physiological and psychological factors. Common physiological factors associated with abdominal pain, for example, include autonomic nervous system hypersensitivity, infection, irritable bowel syndrome, lactose intolerance, and lack of dietary fiber. Psychological factors associated with abdominal pain include anxiety, depression, and difficulty regulating attention and thoughts when trying to cope with pain (Scharff & Simons, 2008). Francisco was a generally anxious and shy child who avoided many new social interactions. His teachers described him as sometimes withdrawn as well. Dr. Lemos could not fully determine whether Francisco's anxious and withdrawn temperament aggravated his pain but suspected this was the case.

Some of the most prominent psychosocial factors that affect youths with chronic pediatric conditions involve family variables. Potential family variables that most affect pain include inconsistent parenting, conflict, and enmeshment. Children whose parents inconsistently give attention and discipline may learn to aggravate their physical symptoms for additional sympathy and tangible rewards. Mrs. Hernandez was clearly struggling to raise her children with little help from her husband. Francisco knew, however, that his mother would put aside her busy schedule and tend to his needs when he reported pain or wanted something.

Adherents of a structural family therapy model believe that conflict and enmeshment play key roles in causing and maintaining psychosomatic conditions in children. Poor boundaries between family members can lead to overprotectiveness, overinvolvement in one another's lives, and eventual conflict (Rodenburg, Meijer, Dekovic, & Aldenkamp, 2007). Such conflict increases tension within a family and causes or aggravates a child's illness. Mrs. Hernandez was clearly distressed by many factors, including her ability to address Francisco's pain. She was thus overprotective, which led to conflict with her husband who believed Francisco needed a more disciplined approach. Mrs. Hernandez gave substantial attention to her son but was also frustrated with his ongoing demands.

Other family variables that affect children with chronic pediatric conditions include poor problem-solving skills and support, pessimism, inflexibility, financial burden, isolation, modeling, and family member anxiety regarding the pediatric condition (Kazak, Simms, & Rourke, 2002). Several of these factors applied to Francisco's case. He and his mother did not effectively solve problems, a fact that later delayed Francisco's reintegration to school. The family had little idea how to address Francisco's pain behaviors, for example, crying and refusing to do work. These problems were aggravated by Mrs. Hernandez's own symptoms of depression and pessimism about eventually resolving her son's pain. In addition, Francisco's hospital stay was creating a financial burden on the family and isolation of Mrs. Hernandez from her husband and daughters. Considerable tension was thus building within the family.

Family variables are perhaps the major psychosocial factor that influences pediatric conditions, but other factors include a child's adjustment to the illness, coping methods, and cognitive processes (Casey & Brown, 2003; Key, Brown, Marsh, Spratt, & Recknor, 2001). Francisco's ability to cope with his pain was generally and surprisingly poor. He constantly asked for pain medication, even weeks later when most of his wounds healed. He later asked school officials to send him home because of pain and often sought information about what to do if he experienced pain in a public setting. Francisco also had strange beliefs about his pain. He was convinced he would die from pain despite constant assurance otherwise. He overestimated the importance and severity of daily stressors such as talking to others at school and how these stressors affected his pain.

Recall as well that Dr. Lemos felt concern that Francisco had aspects of dissociation and acute stress disorder. Children perceive injuries and hospitalization as highly stressful events, even more than their parents. Some children view these events with such fear that they develop symptoms of dissociation to detach themselves from the experience. Hospitalized children who engage in such dissociation often have prior psychopathology, severe injury such as brain trauma or disfigurement, and parents with acute stress disorder (Balluffi et al., 2004; Daviss et al., 2000). Francisco was somewhat socially anxious and had extensive though hidden scars after his experience. His refusal to speak about the accident may thus have been due to some dissociation on his part during early phases of his hospitalization. Francisco's mother was clearly horrified by her son's condition and may have had symptoms of acute stress disorder herself.

Developmental Aspects

Children's ideas about illness change as their cognitive abilities develop. Several researchers have outlined major developmental stages that children may progress through when grasping the concept of illness (Koopman, Baars, Chaplin, & Zwinderman, 2004; McQuaid, Howard, Kopel, Rosenblum, & Bibace, 2002). These stages link closely to Piagetian stages of cognitive development. The first stage, incomprehension, refers to very young children (age 0–2 years) who do not understand any concepts related to illness.

The prelogical explanation phase typically occurs at age 2–6 years. Children in this phase advance through two forms of thinking. The initial prelogical explanation phase is phenomenism, which involves poor explanations of illness. A child may think a cold comes from a plant or the sky. These explanations usually represent causes far removed from a child. The latter prelogical explanation phase is contagion, where a child sees the cause of illness as something closer to himself but nothing that produces direct contact. A child may say a cold comes from being outside, standing next to someone who is ill, or by magic.

The concrete-logical explanation phase typically occurs at age 7–10 years. Children in this phase also advance through two forms of thinking and emphasize internal rather than external causes of illness. The initial concrete-logical explanation phase is contamination, where a child distinguishes an external cause, such as low temperature, from an internal effect, such as a stuffy nose. The external cause may be another person or an event that harms a child by direct physical contact, or contamination. The latter concrete-logical explanation phase is internalization. A child develops a clearer understanding of external causes and internal effects and understands more readily that direct physical contact with an external source is not necessary to get sick. A child may realize that one could "breathe in germs" to develop a cold.

Francisco was 12 years old and had clearly developed at least a concrete-logical explanation for his pain. He distinguished the external cause of his suffering (the car accident) from internal effects of his pain. He knew that the more he exerted himself in the hospital the more discomfort he felt. Francisco had a poor understanding of his pain, however. He did not know exactly what caused his pain and sometimes blamed the driver or his pediatric psychologist. When pressed for details, however, Francisco could not say exactly how Dr. Lemos caused more pain. Dr. Lemos found it interesting that Francisco often asked questions about his pain, perhaps to add credibility to his claims of excessive distress.

The final stages of illness understanding involve adolescents who progress through two formal-logical explanation phases. These phases entail even greater internal-external differentiation than before. The first formal-logical explanation phase is physiologic, where a youth realizes that illness specifically affects internal organs or bodily processes. An adolescent may describe a cold in terms of specific symptoms, lowered white blood cell count, or a suppressed immune system. The second formal-logical phase, psychophysiologic, involves an added psychological component to illness. An adolescent may realize that stress precipitates or aggravates a physical condition.

Francisco did not fully grasp these concepts, preferring instead to emphasize the physical aspect of his pain. He readily mentioned the car accident, though not in detail, as an explanation for his wounds and pain. He did occasionally blame other people for his physical condition, however. Francisco complained that Dr. Lemos aggravated him and complained when his mother failed to bring him something he wanted. He shared his father's anger at the reckless driver, though Dr. Lemos felt this was an adaptive response to what happened. Francisco was particularly upset when a physical therapist visited him to tell him he would have to walk soon.

Developmental factors influence children's conceptions of treating illness as well. Younger children are often afraid of medical doctors and procedures because they have not linked illness and treatment. Young children also have cognitive distortions regarding treatment. They may believe they can bleed to death following an injection. Older children and adolescents obviously make a better connection between illness and the benefits of medical treatment. Some take advantage of this; children learn at a young age that a need for treatment is a legitimate way of excusing oneself from something.

Francisco learned quickly in the hospital that one way to get attention and relieve himself of work was to complain about pain. Mr. and Mrs. Hernandez argued often about this and Francisco usually appeared more strong and capable of handling his pain when his father was around. Francisco did understand the benefits of medical treatment and commonly asked for pain medication.

Other variables related to illness can change from childhood to adolescence. Children eventually become more tolerant of pain, more knowledgeable about preventing illness, more attuned to rules of health, and more aware of their bodily sensations and changes in their bodies (especially during puberty). Developmental changes pertain as well to treatment adherence (Matsui, 2007; Rapoff, 2006). Children and adolescents also change rapidly in their physical development, which requires frequent reassessments of their medication and other treatments. Francisco was not highly tolerant of his pain, however, and not attuned well to subtle changes in body sensations other than pain.

Another illness variable that changes over time is a child's ability to cope with health problems. Children learn to cope with pain and other conditions better as they grow older. This is most likely a function of greater experience and a better cognitive understanding of what to do. Different coping methods include distraction, exercise, cognitive activities such as reading, social support, rest, and imagining events incompatible with pain (Sawyer et al., 2004). Francisco's coping skills were not very good. His first response to abdominal pain was to alert an adult and complain about his symptoms in dramatic fashion. Francisco focused on attention and other rewards for his symptoms and not effective treatments.

Treatment

Treatment of pain in children often involves a combination of medical and psychological approaches, including a focus on compliance to medication. Pain medication for children includes non-steroidal anti-inflammatory drugs such as ibuprofen, opiates such as morphine, tricyclics such as imipramine, antineuroleptics such as gabapentin, and adrenergic agonists such as clonidine (Chambliss, Heggen, Copelan, & Pettignano, 2002). If a child's pain extends beyond the hospital setting and becomes chronic, then compliance to medication is important. Compliance to medication involves educating a child and parent about symptoms and the need for medication, establishing regular dose schedules under supervision, simplifying medication dosages, and increasing social support and rewards for proper medication use (Charach, Volpe, Boydell, & Gearing, 2008). Dr. Lemos felt that pain medication compliance would not be a problem for the Hernandez family.

Pain management in children can involve hypnosis, massage therapy, breathing exercises, distraction, and visualization (Kozlowska et al., 2008). Dr. Lemos utilized the latter three with Francisco. Breathing exercises involve teaching a child to inhale slowly through his nose and exhale slowly through his mouth. A child may count as he does so to ensure a slow, regular pace of breathing. Some children imagine they are a hot air balloon filling with air and then deflating. Breathing should be deep and diaphragmatic, meaning a child should push two fingers into his diaphragm to ensure a full and complete breath. Breathing exercises help lower physical arousal that can exacerbate pain.

Dr. Lemos worked with Francisco to distract him when injected with a needle and to visualize his favorite places when feeling the most pain. Francisco thought about his family's recent beach vacation and his bedroom when feeling most uncomfortable. Dr. Lemos encouraged Mrs. Hernandez to use these techniques with her son and she successfully did so. Francisco later reported that he enjoyed the breathing exercises and that they helped ease his pain.

Pain management for children also involves modifying secondary gains or rewards a child may receive for inappropriate expressions of pain. Francisco clearly received substantial attention from his mother for even minor expressions of discomfort. Dr. Lemos spoke privately to Mrs. Hernandez to help her see the connection between her fawning and Francisco's reports of pain. Mrs. Hernandez found it difficult to change her behavior in this regard but did agree to reward Francisco for using his breathing exercises when in pain. She agreed to praise her son for being brave in the face of pain and provided treats and other rewards when he complied with the physical therapist.

Family variables that contribute to a child's pain must be addressed as well. The tension between Mr. and Mrs. Hernandez was obvious and clearly upset Francisco. Dr. Lemos was able to speak to Mr. Hernandez during one of his visits and told him of the efforts his wife was making to reward Francisco's recovery efforts. Mr. Hernandez was receptive to this, so Dr. Lemos encouraged him to use similar tactics with his son. Mr. Hernandez had a long discussion with his son about how proud he was that Francisco started walking. He encouraged his son to begin his homework while in the hospital and Francisco agreed to do so.

Recall as well that symptoms of dissociation and acute stress disorder sometimes occur in hospitalized children following some trauma. Immediate treatment in this situation involves brief education about dissociation, including an explanation that detachment is a common method of adapting to trauma. Clinicians are encouraged during this early, delicate stage not to force children or parents to discuss the traumatic event but to provide support and the opportunity to do so (Winston et al., 2002).

Dr. Lemos visited Francisco and his mother daily in the hospital to build rapport and establish trust. She learned to bring Francisco treats and toys to enhance his opinion of her and offered to play games with him so Mrs. Hernandez could leave to eat or take a break. Dr. Lemos was happy to hear during one of these games that Francisco mentioned the car accident. She did not press him for details but praised him for raising the topic and offered to listen any time he chose to provide more information.

That time came about a week later, again while Mrs. Hernandez was not in the room. Francisco said he was just about to cross the road in the pedestrian walkway when he noticed a blur to his side. He did not remember the impact but had a clear recollection of being dragged and thinking the car would not stop. The time between impact and feeling the car stop seemed like hours to him. Francisco said he did not remember much after that point, just many people screaming and the ambulance siren. He did notice blood and felt scared he might die. Dr. Lemos praised Francisco for divulging this information and did not press him for further details. She did ask him, however, to tell the story again to see if new information came forward. Francisco added more detail about his hospital experience but no more information about the car accident.

Dr. Lemos noticed one important piece of information about the accident that she wanted to cover again with Francisco. He said the time between impact and feeling the car stop seemed like hours to him, almost as if the event happened in slow motion. Dr. Lemos asked Francisco, as they continued to play their game, how long the whole incident likely lasted. Francisco thought for a while and eventually developed the correct answer: only 2–3 seconds at most.

Dr. Lemos praised Francisco for developing this answer and offered her own opinion that, though the event seemed long and hard, it really was short and over quickly. Francisco enjoyed this new perspective and felt it made the trauma less fearful to him. He was able to discuss the car accident several more times with Dr. Lemos and his mother before he left the hospital. Early processing and discussion of traumatic events when a child is in the hospital may help prevent later development of posttraumatic stress disorder (Balluffi et al., 2004).

Francisco remained in the hospital for 5 weeks, during which time his pain and wounds generally improved. His mood improved as well after visits from his classmates and teachers as well as cards and letters from people in the community. He left the hospital on crutches but his medical doctors expected a full recovery, albeit with some scarring. Dr. Lemos contacted the Hernandez family 3 and 6 months later to find that Francisco returned to school and seemed to be adjusting well. She felt that Francisco's long-term prognosis was good.

DISCUSSION QUESTIONS

1. How might you distinguish between real pain and exaggerated pain in children? What might reinforce exaggerated pain?

2. Explore cultural differences with respect to pain expression and treatment. Which cultures might be more stoic and which might be more expressive about pain?

3. Explore how psychological factors affect disorders traditionally thought to be mostly biological in nature. What psychological factors other than stress could trigger pain and other physical responses? How does your own personality and behavior affect your body's functioning?

4. Certainly one issue of great concern in treating children with pediatric conditions is adherence to treatment. How would you go about helping a child keep up with medical doctor appointments, physical therapy assignments, and prescriptive drug regimens?

5. How might treatment differ for Francisco if he had other pediatric conditions? Explore specific issues related to childhood diabetes, visual and auditory handicaps, cancer, and headaches.

6. One of the most serious pediatric conditions involves children with AIDS. As a therapist, what would you need to focus on most when addressing a family with such a child?

7. Many children are terrified of surgical, dental, and other medical procedures that are necessary for their care. How might you reduce a child's fear in these situations? What could hospitals do to ease the treatment of children with pediatric conditions?

8. Explore the issue of social support and its influence on medical problems in a child as well as family members who care for the child.

Chapter 13

Effects from Sexual Abuse and Posttraumatic Stress Disorder

Symptoms

Joline Kennington was a 12-year-old European American female referred to treatment by her mother, Mrs. Kennington, and a social worker from a state family services department. A female clinical psychologist who specializes in youths who have faced traumatic circumstances saw Joline. Joline's circumstances involved alleged sexual abuse by her father who was incarcerated. Mrs. Kennington and the social worker thought Joline should receive therapy to address her current trauma and loss of her father.

The psychologist tried to speak with Joline individually during the initial interview. Joline was reticent and made little eye contact, however. Joline first responded briefly to questions that had nothing to do with the recent abusive situation. She talked about her dog and her favorite television shows and foods. The psychologist tried to develop good rapport with Joline and asked about recent events. Joline cried softly and would not speak. The psychologist comforted Joline and thanked her for coming in. She secured a promise from the girl to meet again the following week.

The psychologist interviewed Mrs. Kennington and found that she had much to say about the current situation. She said Joline's father had sexually abused his daughter 10 months earlier. Mrs. Kennington was apparently suspicious of her husband when he would go into Joline's bedroom, shut the door, and stay there for long periods. Mrs. Kennington insisted she noticed her husband's odd behavior only just before calling the police. She said she asked Joline about the situation and that her daughter started crying and said "Daddy keeps touching me in bad places." Mrs. Kennington said she immediately called the police who in turn contacted the family services department. Following interviews with Mr. and Mrs. Kennington and Joline, the father was arrested on charges of child molestation and was in jail awaiting trial at the time of Joline's referral.

Mrs. Kennington brought Joline for counseling because the girl was upset that her father was to go to trial the next week and that she, Joline, might have to testify. Mr. Kennington vigorously denied the charges but Mrs. Kennington said he was a "pathological liar" who would "say anything to save his skin." The psychologist noticed that Mrs. Kennington was more concerned about Joline's performance on the witness stand than her daughter's emotional state following the performance. Mrs. Kennington was concerned about how Joline would look to the jury, whether she would appear credible, and whether her father would intimidate her.

The psychologist saw that Mrs. Kennington had a detached relationship with her family. She and her husband experienced deep marital problems for several years and often argued about finances, child rearing, and sex. Mrs. Kennington described her husband as abusive, brutish, and coarse. Mrs. Kennington was also unaware of many of Joline's daily activities, such as her schoolwork. She was effusive in her praise for Joline, however, and insisted that she and her daughter had a close, loving relationship. Mrs. Kennington was not close to either of her two sons, both of whom reminded her of her husband. Her sons, 17 and 19 years old, were not living at home when their father was arrested. They had no knowledge about recent family events but "the boys," Mrs. Kennington said, "will be on their father's side."

The psychologist spoke with the family services social worker in charge of Joline's case. The social worker, Mrs. Tracy, provided a more balanced view of the situation. Mrs. Tracy said the entire situation was cloudy and that the police and family services department acted largely on Joline's self-report after her mother called police. Joline said her father was entering her bedroom and fondling her. He was allegedly caressing his daughter's body and asking her to do the same to him. Mrs. Tracy stated that Joline said her father touched her genital area and asked her to fondle his. No kissing, vaginal penetration, or oral sexual contact was initially reported, however.

Mrs. Tracy asked Joline how often and how long the fondling took place but Joline did not give a clear answer. She initially said the abuse lasted since her tenth birthday, about 15 months earlier. When reinterviewed before her mother, however, Joline said the abuse lasted 1 month. Joline reported more thorough abuse during the second interview, adding extensive kissing and oral sexual contact. Exactly what happened was thus unclear. Joline's accounts of events wavered even more during subsequent interviews but she insisted that her father caressed her and asked her to do the same. In recent interviews, she said she could not remember whether kissing and oral contact occurred.

Mrs. Tracy conveyed her suspicions that Mrs. Kennington influenced her daughter's answers. Mrs. Kennington seemed to want to punish her husband for past offenses by encouraging Joline to magnify the seriousness of the alleged abuse. In addition, Mrs. Kennington was minimizing the length of the alleged abuse to avoid blame for reporting delays. What actually happened to Joline, if anything, was now unclear. Mrs. Tracy said her "gut reaction" was that abuse occurred but that the nature of the abuse was unknown. Mrs. Tracy expressed concern that different accounts of what happened might jeopardize the district attorney's chances for a conviction.

Mrs. Tracy said Joline had had other problems in recent months. Her schoolwork suffered dramatically; her B average slipped to D and F grades. Joline had enormous guilt and sadness over the loss of her father as well as anger toward him and her mother. Joline told the social worker that her mother "waited too long" and ignored her complaints about her father. Mrs. Tracy suspected that Mrs. Kennington called police only after a major argument with her husband about another issue. In addition, Joline was quite nervous about the possibility of testifying in court.

The psychologist completed her initial assessment by interviewing Joline's schoolteacher with Mrs. Kennington's permission. The teacher, Mrs. Ecahn, said Joline was a bright child who was having trouble concentrating on her work. The girl appeared agitated and occasionally cried during class. Mrs. Ecahn and other school officials were aware of Joline's situation so they made accommodations to assist her. The teachers gave her substantial emotional support and after-school tutoring. Based on information from all these sources, the psychologist suspected that abuse had occurred and that Joline was suffering from its effects. The psychologist suspected that Joline had symptoms of posttraumatic stress disorder (PTSD).

Assessment

The essential feature of PTSD is characteristic symptoms following exposure to an extreme traumatic stressor involving direct personal experience of an event that comprises actual or threatened death or serious injury, or other threat to one's physical integrity; or witnessing an event that involves death, injury, or threat to the physical integrity of another person; or learning about unexpected or violent death, serious harm, or threat of death or injury experienced by a family member or other close associate [American Psychiatric Association (APA), 2000, p. 463].

A person's response to the trauma must involve intense fear, helplessness, horror, or, in youths, disorganized or agitated behavior (APA, 2000, p. 463). Other PTSD-related symptoms that may occur in those sexually abused include self-destructive and impulsive behavior, somatic complaints, shame, depressive behaviors, social problems, feeling "damaged" or threatened, and personality changes (APA, 2000, p. 465).

A key aspect of PTSD is that a traumatic event is constantly reexperienced in the form of memories, dreams, a sense of reenactment, or physiological or psychological distress when a person faces cues that remind her of the trauma. Young children may relive trauma through repetitive play and believe their lives will be shortened or that they can foresee negative events. Someone with PTSD generally experiences increased arousal and avoids stimuli linked to the traumatic event. These symptoms must last longer than 1 month and must cause significant impairment in functioning. PTSD is chronic if symptoms last longer than 3 months (APA, 2000).

Joline appeared to meet some diagnostic criteria for PTSD. The reported abuse involved a threat to physical integrity – Joline told the social worker she felt endangered and "dirty" as a result. She reportedly felt helpless during the abusive episodes, daring not to resist her father. Joline had nightmares about the abuse and anxiety when confronted with the fact she might have to face her father in court. She often avoided talking further about the abuse, was disinterested in activities that used to make her happy, and was detached from others. In addition, PTSD symptoms were evident in Joline's anger and concentration problems. These symptoms affected Joline's social and academic functioning so a consideration of PTSD seemed warranted. About 21–50% of sexually abused youths later develop PTSD (Kearney, Wechsler, Kaur, & Lemos-Miller, 2010).

Assessing youths who have endured sexual abuse and who experience symptoms of PTSD usually involves an interview. For obvious reasons, interviewers usually focus on the child and must do so carefully and without forcefulness. An interviewer must develop rapport with the child and provide a safe, confidential environment where the child feels comfortable expressing personal issues. Joline's psychologist met with Joline and the social worker, who already had a special rapport with the girl. Joline said she felt comfortable talking with the psychologist individually about her abuse after a few sessions. In the meantime, the legal case against Mr. Kennington was delayed because of Joline's unwillingness to testify.

The psychologist's first task was to clarify whether abuse occurred and, if so, what type. After much discussion and reassurance about confidentiality, Joline repeated her original version of events. She said her father entered her bedroom at night for several months, talked to her about her day, and began some form of physical contact. This initially involved body massages but later progressed to full-body caressing. Mr. Kennington later told Joline to reciprocate and directed her hand to his genital area. As these events progressed, Mr. Kennington told his daughter not to tell anyone about their "special time together." He made no overt threats, however.

Joline said no kissing or other activity took place. She admitted lying to police after her mother told her to "make the story as painful as possible." She complied but later confused her accounts of these nonexistent events. Joline claimed she told her mother several times what was going on before the police came but that her mother took no action until the night of her big argument with Mr. Kennington.

Clinicians may use rating scales to assess PTSD and related symptoms caused by sexual abuse. An example is the Trauma Symptom Checklist for Children,* which contains items related to anxiety, depression, anger, posttraumatic stress, dissociation,

---

and sexual concerns (Briere, 1996; Lanktree et al., 2008). Sample items from this measure include the following:

1. Bad dreams or nightmares
2. Remembering things that happened that I didn't like
3. Feeling scared of men/women
4. Can't stop thinking about something bad happening to me
5. Feeling afraid somebody will kill me

Assessing children following disclosure of abuse should focus on several elements (Crooks & Wolfe, 2007; Wolfe, 2007):

1. Behavior patterns that may lead to future revictimization (e.g., delinquency, school absences)
2. Symptoms of PTSD and general anxiety
3. Sexual and peer relationships
4. Causes and feelings about the past abuse
5. Level of general disorganization
6. Current family atmosphere

Joline had no disruptive behaviors, substance use, stealing, or aggression. Depressive symptoms of social withdrawal, guilt, and suicidal ideation were present, however. Joline said she felt her classmates looked at her "funny," that she caused her father's legal trouble, and that the family "might be better off if I was dead." The psychologist developed a verbal contract with Joline to ensure that she would speak to the psychologist if she had suicidal thoughts or before any suicide attempt.

Joline was anxious about testifying in court. This persisted for so long that Joline eventually refused to testify, and the charges against Mr. Kennington were dropped (he moved out of state thereafter and had no further contact with Joline or Mrs. Kennington). The psychologist suspected that Joline refused to testify as well because of her guilt about the situation. Joline blamed herself for some aspects of the abuse, even saying her father would not have faced legal trouble had she not lived in the apartment.

The psychologist discussed Joline's current relationship with her peers and family members. Joline said her friends and people at school were supportive but that she felt uncomfortable given recent media attention about the case. Her relationship with her mother was strained because Mrs. Kennington was upset that Joline would not testify in court. In addition, Joline remained angry at her mother for waiting so long to do anything about the abuse. The psychologist believed Joline was learning to adjust to the major changes in her life, but that she would have to work through many of her negative feelings.

Assessing sexually abused youths may include anatomical dolls. A therapist may use the dolls in cases where a child is unwilling or not verbal enough to describe abusive events. The child learns to draw the human body and identify different body parts. The doll is then introduced to the child who answers different questions about what an offender may or may not have done. Use of dolls facilitates memory for details of abusive events but is not helpful if a child completely forgot what happened. The use of dolls may reveal aggressive and sexual play among those abused. The use of dolls does not appear to entice children to make up stories of abuse, a source of great controversy in this area (Faller, 2005). Dolls were not used for Joline.

Risk Factors and Maintaining Variables

No child is immune from abuse but some factors may precipitate sexual abuse (Whitaker et al., 2008; Wolfe, Crooks, Lee, McIntyre-Smith, & Jaffe, 2003). These factors include low family income, isolated families, marital conflict, parental substance abuse, presence of a stepfather, patriarchal attitudes on the part of the father, lack of social contact on the part of the child, sexually restrictive family attitudes, and a poor mother-child relationship. This relationship may have several features:

1. A past situation in which a child lived away from her mother
2. Emotional detachment on the part of the mother
3. Poor supervision of the child
4. The mother's punitiveness regarding her child's sexual development

Some of these characteristics did not apply to Joline and her family. The family's socioeconomic status was middle class, Mr. Kennington was Joline's natural father, Joline did have several close friends, Joline and her mother were never separated, and the family was not isolated from others. The family lived in an urban environment and interacted regularly with other families. Whether the family as a whole had sexually restrictive attitudes was unclear, though this did seem to be true for Mrs. Kennington.

Some of the other listed characteristics *did* apply to Joline and her family. Mr. Kennington was reportedly traditional and conservative regarding family structure. He disapproved of his wife's career and time spent away from home and fought a lot with his wife about their lack of sex and affection. Joline and her mother clearly had a problematic relationship as well. The social worker believed that Mrs. Kennington resented her husband's affection for his daughter and postponed calling the police about the abuse to deliberately poison the father-daughter relationship. In addition, Mrs. Kennington seemed nervous about her daughter's potential sexual development, telling the social worker at one point that she felt uncomfortable talking to Joline about dating and sex.

Several preconditions often set the stage for sexual abuse (Wolfe, 2007). First, the perpetrator must be motivated to abuse a child sexually. Many people believe sexual abuse is about sexual gratification, but it often relates to desire for power and need to humiliate others. Joline's psychologist believed Mr. Kennington's recent occupational difficulties, loss of the older sons from the house, and arguments with his wife may have created a sense of lack of power assuaged by controlling his daughter. No one interviewed Mr. Kennington, however, so no direct evidence existed of this need for power or desire to humiliate Joline.

A second precondition for sexual abuse is that the perpetrator must overcome inhibitions regarding sexual activity with a child. The person may engage in alcohol use, deny negative consequences of the abuse, accept child pornography as a legitimate medium, attribute the behavior to poor self-control, or believe a parent may do as he wishes with a child. The last condition certainly applied to Joline but no evidence was available regarding the other factors. Whether Mr. Kennington believed sexual interactions with his daughter involved affection and were not abusive was unknown.

A third precondition for sexual abuse is that the perpetrator must overcome external obstacles to the sexual behavior. Major obstacles include discovery and arrest. This was not initially difficult for Mr. Kennington because his wife allowed him to spend considerable time alone with Joline and did not listen to Joline's complaints about the sexual activity. Mr. Kennington also apparently thought, wrongly so, that his appeals to Joline to remain silent about their "special time together" would prevent any trouble.

Finally, a perpetrator must overcome a child's resistance to sexual contact. Mr. Kennington took advantage of Joline's initial confusion about the difference between normal parent–child affection and exploitation. The extra attention he gave Joline may have placated the girl for some time before she reported the abuse to her mother.

Researchers have developed etiological models of PTSD. Continual avoidance of thoughts associated with trauma may exacerbate PTSD symptoms (Tull, Gratz, Salters, & Roemer, 2004). A person must fully assimilate these thoughts into his psyche for PTSD symptoms to abate. This model may have applied to Joline, who was initially hesitant about sharing her account of sexual events. Others claim that traumatic events trigger feelings of shame and guilt from self-blame (Leskela, Dieperink, & Thuras, 2002). These feelings may then trigger symptoms of PTSD such as physiological arousal and negative views about the future. Joline had many of these feelings that the psychologist thought maintained her PTSD symptoms.

Other etiological theories of PTSD involve a more integrated approach. Fletcher (2003) outlined such a model for childhood PTSD that includes traumatic events, emotional and biological responses, attributions, individual characteristics, and characteristics of the social environment. A traumatic event would typically involve death, injury, loss of physical integrity, suddenness, unpredictability, uncontrollability, chronic or severe exposure, close proximity, and/or social stigma. Several of these certainly applied to Joline.

Emotional responses of PTSD include fear, horror, and helplessness, whereas biological responses include changes in neurotransmitters such as norepinephrine, dopamine, serotonin, and acetylcholine. Attributions linked to PTSD include an appraisal of a traumatic situation as inescapable, belief that one's safety will always be threatened, or an attitude that one's future will forever be tainted by trauma (Fletcher, 2003). These beliefs were evident to some extent in Joline.

Individual characteristics that may help cause PTSD include a biological predisposition to negative reactivity to stressful events, psychological vulnerabilities based on past experiences, and inability to cope with stressors. Characteristics of the social environment may lead to PTSD as well. These characteristics include negative family reactions to trauma and to the person, poor community support, and financial difficulties.

Joline's coping skills were quite good given her circumstances, though she continued to display negative emotions and poor school performance. She also became upset about new changes in her life and remained upset for long periods. Joline's condition was aggravated by her strained relationship with her mother and the family's problematic financial situation. Positive community support from school officials, the family services department, Joline's friends, and the psychologist likely prevented the development of some long-term PTSD symptoms, however.

Developmental Aspects

Researchers have examined short- and long-term consequences of abuse in youth, and these appear to differ from age to age. From infancy to age 2.5 years, children who face general trauma (e.g., from a natural disaster) may show sleeping and toileting problems, exaggerated startle responses to loud noises, fussiness and dependent behavior, loss of important developmental skills regarding speech and movement, sudden immobility, intense fears of separation, avoidance of cues that remind the child of trauma, and social withdrawal or lack of responsiveness to others (Johnson, 2004; Miller-Perrin & Perrin, 2007; Monahon, 1993).

Reactions among very young sexually abused children may include inappropriate touching of other children, unusual attention to one's genital area (e.g., massaging), demonstration of sexual knowledge highly advanced for a child's age, or genital pain or sexually transmitted disease. The last symptom, of course, may occur at any age. A child's play may also involve reenactment of abusive trauma and the child, if verbal enough, may suddenly discuss issues surrounding the abuse.

Children aged 2.5–6 years who face general trauma may show separation anxiety, social withdrawal, nightmares, magical thinking to explain "bad" events, somatic complaints, unpleasant visual images, regressions in language and self-care skills, retelling of the traumatic event, involvement of traumatic events in play and with playmates, changes in mood and personality, and fear that trauma will recur. A child may become more sensitive to anniversaries that remind her of trauma. Sexually abused children in this age group may show sexualized play, sudden and specific fears of a particular gender or place, aggressive touching of others, and overconcern with masturbation and their genital area. Children aged 2.5–6 years have better memories of traumatic events than younger children (Johnson, 2004; Miller-Perrin & Perrin, 2007; Monahon, 1993).

Children aged 6–11 years who face general trauma may reenact the trauma in detailed stories and play. These children have specific fears and unwanted visual images, distractibility, poor concentration, guilt about their role in the traumatic event, and sensitivity to parental reactions. The reactions mentioned for younger children may apply to 6–11-year-olds as well. Sexually abused children in this age may show overt sexual behaviors, hint about their own sexual experience, verbally describe abuse, or act like younger sexually abused children. They have better recall than preschoolers so their memories of abuse are more detailed and long standing (Johnson, 2004; Miller-Perrin & Perrin, 2007; Monahon, 1993).

Adolescents who face general trauma can have several reactions that include

- delinquent, reckless, or risk-taking behavior;
- accident proneness;
- vengefulness;
- shame and guilt;
- a sense of humiliation;
- intense memories;
- depression and pessimism;
- problems in interpersonal relationships;
- extreme social involvement or withdrawal.

Joline's most prominent reactions were guilt, social withdrawal, embarrassment, depressive symptoms, and sexual repression. Joline was clearly uncomfortable talking about sexual issues, though this is often normal for a 12-year-old. She had a tense relationship with her mother, wanted to skip school, and sometimes avoided social outings with her friends. Joline continued to blame herself for her father's absence and occasionally thought about suicide.

Traumatized and sexually abused adults tend to marry and have children at a younger age than the general population, leave school, fear independence, and seek a different social group. Common long-term problems include anxiety and depression, feelings of isolation, substance abuse, sexual problems, poor self-esteem, and eating and sleeping disorders. Sexually abused women are at greater risk of revictimization through rape or spousal abuse (Barnes, Noll, Putnam, & Trickett, 2009).

Key developmental aspects of PTSD may indicate how severe the disorder will be. A child's level of cognitive and social development is certainly critical. Children with more advanced cognitive development may appraise an event as more traumatic, have more self-defeating thoughts, be more susceptible to depression, fear more abstract consequences of the trauma, and have better memories of the trauma than younger children. Older children and adolescents with better cognitive development tend to have better coping skills, however. Younger children with poor social skills may not develop a wide support network or effectively communicate their fears and worries about the future. Conversely, adolescents with good social skills can soften PTSD symptoms by talking with their friends and escaping aversive family situations.

Developmental differences can influence how a child reacts to traumatic events. Children react worse to traumatic events because they have less control (and less perceived control), more disorganized behavior, and greater sensitivity to reminders of the event than adolescents (Fletcher, 2003). Younger children are better at dissociating themselves from a traumatic event, however, and this may protect them somewhat from developing PTSD. This may explain why severely abused children sometimes develop dissociative identity (multiple personality) disorder.

Joline's cognitive and social development was generally good. This proved to be a double-edged sword, however. Her cognitive skills allowed her to understand that the sexual abuse was not her fault and that her mother, though not blameless, was a victim of these circumstances. Joline came to fear men in general, however, regarded sexual behavior and activity as somewhat repulsive, and continued to have unpleasant memories of the abuse. Joline's positive social development allowed her to build coping skills, rely on a support network, and become more self-reliant than before. Joline's ongoing attachment with her friends, however, came at the expense of a continually strained relationship with her mother and less concern for her academic performance.

Treatment

Clinicians who treat abused children often focus on the parents and child. Clinicians often target the remaining parent because the other has been removed from the family. Parent-oriented treatment often involves building better methods of discipline through modeling, role-playing, and instructions regarding time-outs and appropriate positive reinforcement. Other parent treatment components include cognitive therapy to modify irrational thoughts about a child's behavior, anger and self-control training, and general coping skills training (Cohen, Deblinger, Mannarino, & Steer, 2004). Joline's psychologist did not emphasize parent training because Mrs. Kennington had not engaged in overt abuse toward Joline and because she did not want to be an active participant in therapy. Some might argue that Mrs. Kennington's neglect of Joline's trauma was abusive itself, however, and worthy of intervention.

Child-oriented treatment for maltreated youths, especially those sexually abused, depends largely on a child's age. Play therapy may be most useful for preschool children without fully developed cognitive or social skills. Play therapy involves having a child interact with different recreational items that allow for expression in a comfortable setting. Examples of such items include dollhouses, puppets, paints, clay, and building materials. Play therapy is effective for overcoming resistance to therapy, enhancing communication about certain events, promoting creative thinking and fantasy, and releasing emotions (Schaefer & Kaduson, 2007). As a child engages in pretend play, a therapist can raise questions about hypothetical scenarios (e.g., inappropriate requests from others) and how the child might protect himself (e.g., tell others about "bad" touches).

Treatment for sexually abused preschoolers can also focus on having a child talk about traumatic events. This helps lower a child's apprehension and identify people a child can trust. Emotive imagery techniques help address nightmares.

A therapist asks a child to imagine teaming up with a favorite superhero to battle a nightmare villain. A therapist may educate a child about what touching behaviors are inappropriate and how to reject unwanted touches. These latter techniques were not necessary for Joline, however.

For school-age children who have been sexually abused, child-based treatment focuses on impulse and anger control, emotional expression, problem-solving training, gradual exposure to feared stimuli with relaxation training, improving self-esteem, increasing social activity to reduce isolation or depression, and cognitive therapy. Education about sexuality, sexual abuse, and personal safety is important as well (Tavkar & Hansen, 2011). Group therapy may be helpful for education, emotional expression, and building social support. Another treatment technique is to have a child write letters to hypothetical victims or family members to describe her feelings and achieve mastery of the feelings (Kress, Hoffman, & Thomas, 2008).

Joline's psychologist asked her to write a letter to a hypothetical 12-year-old girl abused by her father. The psychologist asked Joline to write about her feelings and give advice to the other child. Joline wrote several short letters about her feelings of guilt and sadness and fortunately told the other child that she should not blame herself for abuse. She gave advice about how to talk with friends, see a therapist, and live life "one day at a time." As Joline wrote the letters, the psychologist talked to her about her feelings and helped ease her guilt and anger.

A more controversial topic that arose during therapy was Joline's desire to write a letter to her father. Mrs. Kennington adamantly opposed this idea and insisted that Joline have no contact with Mr. Kennington. The psychologist offered a compromise, suggesting Joline write the letter but send it to the psychologist. Joline agreed and wrote a long, rambling letter about her anger toward her father, her hopes that he was okay, and her wish to see him again at some future time. Mrs. Kennington said Joline took several days to complete the letter, during which time she often cried. Mrs. Kennington saw this as a destructive process but the psychologist knew Joline needed to express these feelings to put the abusive events behind her. Joline's overall mood did improve somewhat following the letter-writing exercise.

Treatment with Joline also focused on her feelings of isolation, general fears of men, and questions about dating and sex. The psychologist engaged in cognitive therapy to reduce Joline's interpretation of others' actions as threatening or mean. This applied especially to others who were close to her, including her peers and her mother, and was a natural result of her father's betrayal. Joline often felt her friends looked at her strangely and did not want to interact with her. Joline came to recognize that others were perhaps uncomfortable around her because they did not know what to say. The psychologist suggested that three of Joline's close friends attend therapy, and this issue regarding her peers was largely resolved. Therapy did not help improve Joline's relationship with her mother, however.

The psychologist helped Joline identify "good" men in her life to help her see that abuse was not a part of every man's nature. Joline identified her brothers, pastor, and school guidance counselor as positive role models. The psychologist answered Joline's questions about dating and sex and discussed appropriate and inappropriate sexual contacts at length.

The initial treatment of youths with PTSD symptoms involves ending trauma and helping a child recover in a safe environment. Subsequent treatment may then resemble components for sexually abused children, including emotional expression, family therapy, and exposure to thoughts and cues surrounding the trauma. Joline persistently avoided the old apartment where her father molested her. When the psychologist thought Joline was ready, they toured the old apartment together. Joline identified different aspects of the place and entered her old bedroom last. She cried for an extended period but eventually became calm. Joline wrote another unsent letter to her father following this experience but kept this one confidential.

The long-term prognosis for those abused or with PTSD depends largely on their degree of emotional expression (catharsis), level of family and social support, exposure to cues that remind a person of trauma, and coping skills. Joline remained in therapy for 7 months after which she and her mother moved to a different city. By the end of treatment, Joline's grades at school improved and she adjusted well to past events and to her new life. The psychologist thought that Joline's long-term prognosis was good.

DISCUSSION QUESTIONS

1. About one in four girls and one in six boys are sexually abused by age 18 years. Why do you think sexual abuse is so prevalent?

2. If you were to interview a severely abused child, what themes would be most important to cover first? What characteristics about yourself should you think about when talking to an abused child?

3. What types of trauma are most likely to lead to PTSD? Why do some people experience PTSD following a terrible event and others do not? Explore personal, family, and social issues to address this question.

4. What events in your life might you describe as traumatic? What about the event made you feel that way?

5. Given Mrs. Kennington's behavior, do you feel Joline should stay with her mother after her father left? Explore advantages and disadvantages of this situation.

6. If you could speak to Joline about her situation, what would you most like to say? If you were a therapist and were abused in the past, would you self-disclose this as part of therapy to help your client? Defend your answer.

7. Can memories of past abuse be repressed and later remembered? Support your answer. What are judicial and other ramifications of this phenomenon?

8. Explore the utility or desirability of self-help groups for treating people who have been sexually abused. Discuss the pros and cons of using support groups rather than a trained professional who never experienced abuse personally.

Chapter 14

Mixed Case Two

Symptoms

Cindy Weller was a 14-year-old European American female referred to an out-patient clinic for youths with school refusal behavior. Cindy was in ninth grade at the time of her initial assessment. Mrs. Weller referred her daughter after a school official told her that Cindy had missed 28 days of school since the beginning of the academic year (It was now November.). Most of these days were partial absences involving a skipped afternoon. The principal referred Cindy's case to juvenile court in accordance with school policy. Cindy would face charges of truancy and her parents might face charges of educational neglect. The principal informed Mrs. Weller that, historically, the court looked more favorably on families who sought therapy. Mrs. Weller made an initial appointment at the clinic for Cindy, herself, and her ex-husband.

A clinical psychologist interviewed Cindy and her parents separately. The psychologist interviewed Cindy first but she was vague when providing information. When asked how many days she missed, Cindy testily said, "it wasn't that many." She was aware, however, of the school's policy to refer a student to court after 20 absences in a semester. Cindy was reassured of confidentiality and became more open. She said she did not like school and found it boring. She said she did not like her classmates, teachers, subjects, or new high school. The psychologist asked Cindy if she did like anything about school and she said that she enjoyed free time with her friends.

The psychologist also questioned Cindy about her activities outside school. Cindy said she and her friends would often skip school to "hang out and smoke weed" or stay at someone's house to watch television or play video games. This occurred about two to three times per week. She would sometimes cruise a local shopping mall or go back home to sleep. This routine was usually the same on weekends. The psychologist explored Cindy's drug use further and found that she sometimes used crack and powder cocaine in addition to marijuana. Outside of missing school, however, Cindy's drug use did not interfere significantly with her daily functioning. She never missed family or doctor appointments because she was intoxicated. Cindy did not place herself in dangerous situations because of her drug use. She did not ride in a car with intoxicated friends or drink alcohol when using other drugs.

The psychologist delved into past areas of Cindy's life as well. Cindy said her parents divorced about 1 year earlier following a period of intense fighting. She described how Mr. and Mrs. Weller argued and became physically violent with one another. Cindy called the police twice to intervene. Mr. and Mrs. Weller remained in close contact following the divorce, however, and often consulted one another about Cindy (note that both came to the clinic). Cindy said the divorce was a "good thing" and was glad her father was out of the house. She and her mother clearly did not get along, however. Cindy said she often argued with her mother and that Mrs. Weller "was counting the days until she could kick me out." Cindy thus avoided her home and interactions with her mother as much as possible.

Cindy insisted she needed time with her friends and hinted that she might never go back to school. Cindy was anxious about her performance in several classes, claiming she did not understand the work and could not see its relevance to her life. She said she felt "out of place" during many of her classes and skipped school to be with more supportive friends. She denied emotional distress outside school but the psychologist saw that Cindy was concerned about what would happen in court and that her mood was somewhat depressed. Cindy shrugged in response to several questions and was tearful when asked about future plans. She provided no ideas regarding treatment goals.

Mrs. Weller was eager to give information and criticism regarding Cindy. She placed blame for recent problems squarely on her daughter, whom she called troubled. She outlined Cindy's long history of school refusal behavior, reporting that her daughter missed 17 days in seventh grade and 50 days the previous year in eighth grade. The school district took no legal action until now, however. Mrs. Weller said she was surprised by the school's policy regarding absenteeism and complained about her upcoming loss of work time for court and therapy appearances.

When asked why Cindy refused school, Mrs. Weller shrugged and said her daughter was "becoming a drug addict." Mrs. Weller found marijuana and cocaine in her daughter's room the previous summer and briefly kicked Cindy out of the house before relenting and allowing her to come home. She thought Cindy skipped school to be friends and "party it up." Mrs. Weller also believed Cindy was about to join a gang and start shoplifting. She claimed Cindy no longer listened to her and was "out of control" and "headed for big trouble." She doubted the psychologist would be able to help.

Mr. Weller, who was quiet to this point, adopted a softer tone. He said his divorce from Mrs. Weller was difficult on Cindy and she was probably "rebelling" against him and his ex-wife. He admitted past accounts of marital conflict and physical violence and speculated that Cindy was "scarred" in some way. Mr. Weller said Cindy still argued frequently with him and his ex-wife, at times using obscene language. She sometimes threatened to run away from home and had done so twice. She stayed at a friend's house on both occasions for 4 days before returning. Mr. Weller agreed with his ex-wife that Cindy was "headed for big trouble."

The psychologist spoke with school officials with Mr. and Mrs. Weller's permission. A different clinical picture emerged. Several teachers described Cindy as anxious, depressed, and withdrawn. No one said she was disruptive in class but one teacher complained that Cindy seemed "out of it" and would shrink when asked a question. All said Cindy was failing class. Her guidance counselor, Mrs. Arias, said Cindy threatened to hurt herself at the beginning of the year if she did not get the class schedule she wanted. The threat was not deemed serious but Mrs. Arias voiced concern about Cindy's family and social life and said she was an "at risk" student.

Following this initial assessment process, the psychologist concluded that Cindy had internalizing, externalizing, and academic difficulties. School refusal behavior was thought to be the most serious and immediate problem. Other problems that would have to be addressed in therapy included depression, substance use, noncompliance, and family conflict.

Assessment

School refusal behavior refers to a child-motivated refusal to attend school or difficulties remaining in classes for an entire day. The behavior refers to children and adolescents aged 5–17 years who engage in one or more of the following (Kearney, 2007):

1. Miss school completely
2. Go to school but then leave during the course of the day
3. Go to school only after severe behavior problems such as tantrums in the morning
4. Go to school with great dread and ask repeatedly to be excused

Terms such as "school phobia" or "truancy" sometimes describe this population but the term "school refusal behavior" is preferred because it covers all youths with trouble going to school. School refusal behavior is different from school withdrawal in which a parent deliberately withholds a child from school for economic purposes or to prevent harm to the child (e.g., kidnapping by an ex-spouse).

Cindy's was secretly refusing school of her own volition. Her parents knew little about her absenteeism until school officials produced her records. Cindy's school refusal behavior was largely the second type: she often went to school but left during the day to be with her friends. Her problem going to school was chronic because absenteeism occurred intermittently for 3 years. This year, however, was worse than previous ones and significant interference in family and academic functioning was evident.

Most cases of school refusal behavior involve a complex pattern of internalizing and externalizing behaviors (Kearney, 2001). Common internalizing behaviors include fear, anxiety, depression, social withdrawal, suicidal ideation, fatigue, and somatic complaints. The latter often involves stomachaches, headaches, trembling, and nausea. Somatic complaints can be real or exaggerated to avoid school. Cindy had no somatic complaints. She did report general anxiety and depression when in school, however. This applied especially to situations where she had to interact with classmates she did not know or when she had to perform before others. Cindy was a follower and avoided situations where she would have to initiate social contact or be the center of attention.

Common externalizing behaviors in youths who refuse school include verbal and physical aggression, noncompliance, running away from home or school, and temper tantrums. Cindy was clearly noncompliant with many parent and teacher requests and had a history of leaving home and school. Mr. and Mrs. Weller said Cindy became verbally and physically abusive when she did not get her way. They recalled one incident when Cindy tried to push her mother down the stairs so she could leave the house and be with her friends.

The assessment of youths with school refusal behavior must therefore concentrate on many areas of functioning. Several self-report and parent-teacher questionnaires for internalizing problems were used in this case. Cindy's score was in the normal range on the Children's Depression Inventory (Kovacs, 2003) but she did endorse several items. These items involved poor schoolwork, feeling unloved, depressed mood, fatigue, and thoughts about suicide. The psychologist made a contract in which Cindy promised to contact him if she had serious thoughts or impulses regarding suicide.

Cindy reported moderate to high levels of general and social anxiety on the Multidimensional Anxiety Scale for Children (March, 1997) and Social Anxiety Scale for Children-Revised (La Greca, 1998). Cindy was most anxious around people she did not know well and was concerned about how others assessed her appearance and behavior (This is often normal for a 14-year-old, however.). This concern partially explained why she stayed close to her small group of friends who missed school. Cindy's scores on the Piers-Harris Self-Concept Scale for Children (Piers, Harris, & Herzberg, 2002) revealed personal reservations about her popularity, performance before others, inner strength, and intelligence.

Cindy completed the School Refusal Assessment Scale-Revised (Kearney, 2006), a measure of the strength of four functional conditions that surround school refusal behavior. This measure revealed that Cindy missed school primarily for tangible rewards such as visiting her friends, engaging in drug use, and watching television at home. A secondary concern was Cindy's desire to escape aversive social and evaluative situations at school, including meeting new people and performing athletically and academically before others. Cindy thus missed school for more than one reason. Treating youths who refuse school for multiple reasons, as Cindy did, is more difficult than treating youths who refuse school for only one reason.

The psychologist utilized parent-teacher questionnaires for general externalizing behaviors. Mr. and Mrs. Weller endorsed several Child Behavior Checklist items related to delinquent, aggressive, anxious, depressed, and socially problematic behavior. They noted Cindy's frequent noncompliance, arguing, swearing, crying, worrying, nervousness, and failure to get along with others. The parents' assessment confirmed Cindy's report of mixed internalizing and externalizing symptoms. Mr. and Mrs. Weller completed the parent version of the School Refusal Assessment Scale-Revised. They rated Cindy very high on the tangible reward dimension, convinced she refused school to have more fun outside school.

Cindy's guidance counselor, Mrs. Arias, completed the Teacher's Report Form. Her ratings closely mirrored those of Mr. and Mrs. Weller. She released Cindy's academic records that revealed good attendance for morning classes (computer science, English, social studies) but poor attendance for afternoon classes (choir, math, earth science, and physical education). Cindy was failing each class but her computer science, English, and social studies teachers said that Cindy only needed to finish some makeup work to boost her grade to a passing level.

The assessment of youths with school refusal behavior may involve direct observation of behavior. The psychologist observed Cindy twice from 6:00 A.M., when she was supposed to rise from bed, until 8:15 A.M., when she was supposed to enter her first class. These observations revealed substantial conflict between Mrs. Weller and Cindy, who had a tough time rising from bed and getting ready for school. Once she arrived at school, however, she went to class without incident. Mrs. Arias secretly observed Cindy on 2 days after she left her social studies class. Both times, Cindy ate lunch with three friends before slipping out of school. Mrs. Arias extended her observation to a third day, hoping to catch Cindy leaving school without permission. She did so and gave Cindy 4 days of detention.

Risk Factors and Maintaining Variables

The precursors to school refusal behavior are not always clear but major triggers include entering a new school building, onset of a stressful school year, disagreements with a teacher, trouble with peers, separation anxiety, and serious illness. Family variables can provoke school refusal behavior as well. Cindy's entry into high school was troubling – she was confused about finding her classes and knowing how to do her homework. She felt some of her teachers were distant and mostly concerned with the best students. In addition, she complained of the school's racial composition.

Many youths continue to refuse school for one or more of four reasons or functions (Kearney, 2001). First, youths may refuse school to avoid strange or negative emotions they feel when in school (avoidance of stimuli that provoke a sense of negative affectivity). This usually refers to younger children absent because they feel anxious or upset about the school setting. These children often cannot identify anything that makes them upset but sometimes report a feeling of malaise about the size and scope of the school building or about transitions between classes. These children also report aversive physical symptoms, such as stomachaches. They tend to be more sensitive, reactive to stressors, and dependent than children who do not refuse school. A child may have a specific phobia of a school-related object or situation but these cases are rare and not representative of those who miss school.

A second reason or function for school refusal behavior, and one that applied more to Cindy, is escape from aversive social and/or evaluative situations. This usually refers to adolescents who skip school to avoid situations that require social interaction or performance before others. These youths avoid people such as peers, teachers, and other school officials. In addition, they may avoid tests, oral presentations, writing before others, recitals, athletic settings, walking into class or hallways, eating in the cafeteria, group events, large crowds, or other settings involving social interaction or evaluation. These youths often show high social anxiety and personalization. They may assume two people whispering in a hallway are necessarily talking about them. Social anxiety in adolescents is common, of course, but problematic if it interferes with school attendance.

Cindy skipped school partly to escape aversive social and evaluative situations. She was nervous before others, especially when meeting new people. She worried about the consequences of returning to class full-time and getting strange looks from her classmates and teachers. Cindy found it easiest to skip school during the afternoon when several of her classes involved more social interaction and evaluation. Cindy liked to skip physical education class so she would not have to perform athletically before others. She skipped choir so she would not have to sing before others. She liked to skip math so she would not have to write and solve problems on the board. Cindy's school refusal behavior was not always limited to her afternoon classes, however. She skipped all her morning English classes that involved student oral reports. Cindy preferred to be with her small group of friends and often shied away from others.

A third reason many children refuse school is for attention from parents or other caregivers. This usually refers to younger children who show behavior problems in the morning to stay with parents at home. Common behaviors include refusal to get out of bed, locking oneself in a room or car, clinging, tantrums, and running away from the school setting. These children may show high levels of separation anxiety as well (school refusal is one symptom of separation anxiety disorder), but attention getting is the larger issue. These youths are fearful, noncompliant, manipulative, and dependent. This functional condition clearly did not apply now or in the past to Cindy, however. She wanted to be as far away from her parents as possible.

Some youths refuse school for tangible reinforcement. This refers to adolescents who skip school to pursue the many attractions of being out of school. These attractions include time with friends, sleeping, and watching television. These youths often have no anxiety about school but are more prone to symptoms of oppositional defiant or conduct disorder. Common behaviors associated with this function include aggression, substance use, lying, and running away from home.

Cindy certainly refused school for tangible reinforcement. This pattern began the previous year when Cindy skipped school to go shopping with her friends. The pattern was reinforced when Cindy found she could leave school without much consequence. School officials rarely notified her parents of her absences. Absenteeism is difficult to track in many large school settings like Cindy's. Problems like Cindy's may thus fester for some time.

The first two functional conditions – avoiding negative emotions or physical symptoms associated with school and escaping aversive social and/or evaluative situations – represent youths who refuse school to get away from something unpleasant at school (negative reinforcement). The latter two functional conditions – attention getting and tangible reinforcement – represent youths who refuse school to pursue something pleasant outside school (positive reinforcement). Many youths refuse school for more than one reason as well. A child may initially miss school to avoid social interactions but then discover positive aspects of staying home alone (e.g., watching television, talking on the telephone without interruption). Conversely, an adolescent may skip long periods of school to be with friends but then become anxious about having to return to new classes, peers, and teachers.

The complex scenario seemed to apply to Cindy. She refused school for tangible rewards outside school but was nervous about returning to classes she had not attended in some time. The psychologist thought Cindy was more willing to return to school than she admitted but that she worried about what would happen if she did return (e.g., intrusive questions by others). The psychologist also recognized that other behaviors might interfere with Cindy's return to full-time attendance. These behaviors included frequent drug use, deteriorating family relationships, and depressive symptoms. Comorbid problems such as these generally complicate the treatment of youths with chronic school refusal behavior.

Developmental Aspects

Several child factors and functions maintain school refusal behavior. Certain dysfunctional family dynamics, however, may set the stage for the development of school refusal behavior in the first place. A well-known dynamic is enmeshment or overinvolvement of family members in one another's lives. These families are marked by parental overindulgence and overprotectiveness, dependence, hostility, and withdrawal on the father's part. This pattern often leads to a child's separation anxiety and attention-getting behavior and can worsen when a child first enters school. Cindy was never particularly close to her parents. She misbehaved in the past to get her parents to stop fighting but currently avoided them when possible.

Another family pattern characteristic of youths who refuse school is isolation, which is marked by little outside contact on the part of its members. Children in an isolated family spend much of their recreational time with parents and may develop fewer friendships than most children their age. These families are also less likely to seek treatment for a child's behavior problem. This pattern relates to those who refuse school to escape aversive social and evaluative situations. Cindy's parents often isolated themselves from others and Cindy spent much of her time at home during her early school years. Even now, Mr. and Mrs. Weller remained in close contact and did not socialize much with others. Early family isolation may have led Cindy to develop social anxiety and become a follower. She thus spent time with only a small group of friends and ended up following those who skipped school.

A third family pattern common to those who refuse school is detachment. Detached family members are poorly involved in one another's lives and pay little attention to each member's wants and needs. Detached parents usually wait a long time before responding to a child's behavior problems. Poor communication patterns and little emotional expression are present. This pattern seemed especially pertinent to Cindy. Mr. and Mrs. Weller had little positive communication with their daughter. Mrs. Weller often let Cindy's misbehavior continue undisciplined until it affected her life. Mrs. Weller was initially unconcerned about Cindy's school attendance even though Cindy had a long history of school refusal behavior. She intervened only after receiving a notice from the school about upcoming legal action.

Conflict is another family pattern seen in youths with school refusal behavior. Verbal and physical fighting, poor problem-solving skills, and coercion mark this family type. Family antagonism may result from marital problems that lead to inconsistent child discipline and later problems such as school refusal behavior. Conversely, however, a child's school refusal behavior may trigger marital fighting because parents disagree about how to address the situation. Conflict is most characteristic of youths who refuse school for tangible reinforcement (Kearney, 2001). Conflict among family members was certainly a long-standing pattern in Cindy's case.

How might these family patterns interact to produce Cindy's school refusal behavior? One possible scenario is that Mr. and Mrs. Weller were relatively withdrawn people who stayed mostly to themselves and required Cindy to do the same. This might explain why Cindy initially developed few friends and later became anxious in new social situations. Family stressors and little outside social support may have created an atmosphere of conflict that deprived Cindy of parental attention. Much of her reinforcement then came from external sources. As her parents split up, Cindy became more interested in enjoying material things available to her friends (e.g., video games, drugs). Her friends began to skip school to enjoy these activities more, so Cindy went along. Following the divorce, Mrs. Weller became more detached from her daughter and even blamed her for some of the marital problems. As this detachment worsened, Cindy skipped school and pursued tangible rewards with even greater vigor. This allowed her to skip classes involving extensive contact with others.

What about the long-term prognosis for youths who refuse school? Adults who refused school as adolescents are at risk for occupational and marital problems, anxiety and depression, alcohol abuse, and criminal behavior. Those who drop out of school are less likely to attend college and achieve economic success (Kearney, 2008).

What is the likely long-term prognosis for Cindy? Her treatment program was moderately effective but her chronic school refusal behavior certainly places her at risk for further delinquent behavior and eventual school dropout. These effects could impair her long-term academic and financial success. Cindy's social avoidance, depression, substance use, and poor parental support might predispose her to problems in adulthood as well.

Treatment

Cindy's psychologist wanted to address her multiple behavior problems but focused primarily on reducing her school refusal behavior. This was done in the hope that some of her secondary behaviors (e.g., social anxiety, depression, substance use) would then decline. Different treatments for youths with school refusal behavior relate to the functions described earlier (Kearney & Albano, 2007). Some children refuse school to avoid negative emotions or physical symptoms experienced there. These children might benefit from relaxation training, breathing retraining, and gradual reexposure to the school setting. Relaxation training and breathing retraining help children control physical school-based anxiety symptoms such as muscle tension or hyperventilation. These children may be gradually reintroduced to their classroom and other settings to associate relaxation and normal breathing with school-related stimuli. This treatment did not apply to Cindy, however.

For youths who refuse school to escape aversive social and evaluative situations, as Cindy partially did, a treatment regimen of modeling, role-playing, and cognitive therapy may be useful. Modeling and role-playing help build social skills. Cindy's social skills were relatively good but she often withdrew and did not show the skills. The psychologist believed this withdrawal was due to Cindy's depressive behaviors and social anxiety. At the heart of these symptoms were cognitive distortions Cindy had about herself and her interactions with others.

The psychologist worked with Cindy to identify distorted thought processes that maintained her depression and social anxiety. Cindy was self-conscious about her appearance and behavior before others. She sometimes assumed others were negatively judging her even when she had no evidence to support this assumption. She believed the psychologist, on meeting her for the first time, thought about her messy hair, problematic complexion, and large nose. Cindy also thought others would judge her harshly, as her mother had in the past, when she tried new things on her own. She thus avoided new situations and rarely attempted to do things differently from before.

The psychologist helped Cindy try new ways of interacting with her environment. He gave Cindy substantial encouragement and invited her parents to do the same. Cindy was asked to engage in new situations involving school (e.g., talking to others outside her group), church (e.g., joining the youth group), and family (e.g., initiating more conversations with her mother). Cindy examined her thoughts during each situation and changed irrational thoughts. She learned to attend to positive *and* negative feedback received when meeting people the first time. These efforts were designed to help her think more realistically, increase her activity level, and reduce her social anxiety and withdrawal. Cindy gradually took more social risks and engaged others more actively over several weeks.

Parent training in contingency management may be useful for youths who refuse school for attention. Parents are encouraged to set regular morning and evening routines for a child, issue commands more clearly, actively reward pro-social or school attendance behaviors, and punish or ignore inappropriate school refusal behaviors. This treatment program is used primarily for younger children but certain aspects can be applied to adolescents as well.

Cindy's psychologist helped Mrs. Weller improve the clarity of her statements to her daughter. She was encouraged to say, in unequivocal terms, what she wanted Cindy to do regarding chores, curfew, and school attendance. Cindy and her mother agreed on times Cindy should rise from bed, go to school, arrive home from school, and associate with friends. Mr. and Mrs. Weller praised Cindy for her positive behaviors and avoided sarcastic or hurtful comments. The psychologist saw that Mr. Weller was able to improve his relationship with Cindy. Mrs. Weller's attitude toward her daughter remained negative, however, and her relationship with Cindy remained strained.

Family therapy may be useful for youths who refuse school for tangible reinforcement. This approach emphasizes contracting and problem-solving, communication, and peer refusal skills. The psychologist's first goal was to reestablish Cindy's full-time school attendance so the family's initial treatment sessions involved contracting. The written contracts had conditions under which Cindy would attend school in exchange for the opportunity to do chores at home for money. Cindy could earn the chance to vacuum the house and clean the bathrooms for money if she attended school full time for 1 week. If she missed any amount of school, then she would have to complete the chores without payment. If she then refused to do the chores, she was grounded for the weekend. A clinic staff member contacted the school daily and informed Mr. and Mrs. Weller of any absence on Cindy's part.

Cindy had great trouble complying with these initial contracts. She left school on four different occasions in the first two weeks. The psychologist then warned Cindy that one of her parents or a school official would escort her from class to class if she did not attend. Cindy still missed 15 afternoon classes over the next 2 weeks. Mr. Weller and Mrs. Arias, the guidance counselor, then took turns walking Cindy to each of her afternoon classes. Cindy attended school under this condition and received the contract rewards. This procedure was later phased out though Mrs. Arias asked Cindy's teachers to keep an eye on her as she went from class to class.

The psychologist focused as well on Cindy's peer refusal skills. This involved behaviors and statements Cindy could use to decline offers to skip school without feeling rejected. Cindy was encouraged to avoid lingering in hallways where she was likely to face such offers. Her lunchtime was changed to avoid temptations by certain peers to leave school. The psychologist helped Cindy form statements to respond to those who wanted her to skip class. Cindy was encouraged to say no because she wanted to earn money for chores by attending school (i.e., adhere to the contract). Another goal was to reduce Cindy's time with people who skipped school. Cindy compensated for this, however, by spending extra time with her friends on the weekends.

The psychologist also worked with Cindy and her parents to improve their problem-solving and communication skills. The Wellers learned to define current problems, develop solutions, communicate with one another respectfully, and implement and evaluate solutions. Much of this process occurred as the family formed school attendance contracts. These procedures generally eased family tensions but produced no major improvements in overall communication. Family members continued to interrupt one another.

The psychologist addressed Cindy's drug use as well. Cindy was educated about the harmful effects of marijuana and cocaine and the psychologist designed a schedule so Cindy could reduce her drug use comfortably over time. This led to little success, however. Cindy slightly *increased* her drug use, albeit mostly on the weekends. The lone bright spot was that Cindy continued to abstain from alcohol.

Cindy's treatment lasted 4 months during which time her school attendance gradually improved. By the end of therapy, she attended school about 90% of the time and all her grades except two were passing. Her passing grades included English because Cindy finished her oral presentation assignments. Her social anxiety and depression generally declined. The family's interactions and problem-solving abilities remained mediocre, however. Cindy left therapy when Mrs. Weller decided it was no longer necessary – in other words, she no longer faced legal action. Informal telephone contact with Cindy 6 months later revealed her overall functioning to be fair. Her school attendance was stable but her relationship with her parents remained distant. Cindy's level of drug use had not changed.

DISCUSSION QUESTIONS

1. Does Cindy meet diagnostic criteria for any DSM–IV–TR disorder? If so, which one(s)? Defend your answer. What are the advantages and disadvantages of assigning a mental disorder to a case such as this one involving several behavior problems?

2. Explore the issue of comorbidity or the occurrence of several problems in an individual. What childhood problems are most closely related?

3. Compare Cindy's behavior problems to the others described in this casebook. Compare her social anxiety to Bradley's in Chapter 2, her depression to Anna's in Chapter 3, her substance use to Jennifer's in Chapter 9, and her family conflict to the Simington family in Chapter 10. Discuss which case was more serious and why. How might a specific treatment be used differently for Cindy compared to the others listed here? How might Cindy's prognosis differ from these other cases?

4. How might you change your assessment protocol for a youth with several behavior problems? What questions become more pertinent?

5. How might you change your treatment program for a youth with several behavior problems? How should dual therapy procedures be conducted? Why and how might family therapy become more crucial?

6. Cindy's case appeared to be chronic. How might you alter your assessment or treatment of a youth if you know her problems have lasted a year or longer?

7. What procedures would you recommend to *prevent* chronic or multiple problems such as Cindy's? What procedures would you recommend *following* therapy for a youth with chronic or several behavior problems?

8. Which treatments for children are most effective, and why?

Chapter 15

Mixed Case Three

Symptoms

Athena Galvez was a 17-year-old multi-ethnic (Hispanic, Asian, and European American) female referred to an inpatient psychiatric unit for self-mutilation and other bizarre behaviors. Athena was in tenth grade at the time of her referral but had attended school only sporadically in the last 2 weeks. Her parents, Mr. and Mrs. Galvez, brought Athena to the hospital following recommendations from her clinical psychologist and her school counselor. Athena scraped her legs with pieces of glass and was a danger to herself. Athena's parents found her bleeding through socks from cuts on her ankles.

The psychologist made the referral based on other immediate concerns as well. Athena's speech was occasionally incoherent and she sometimes uttered phrases that made sense to her but to no one else. Athena told the psychologist that her "dead mother was floating on the ceiling" despite the fact that her mother was alive and lived with her. When asked to clarify, Athena said she worried about her mother's death, but her statement still seemed extreme. The psychologist was also concerned about Athena's apathy because she seemed depressed and no longer cared about going to school or tending to her hygiene. Athena was increasingly disheveled and nonresponsive over the past several weeks.

Athena's school counselor said Athena engaged in strange behaviors since the beginning of the academic year. Teachers sometimes found Athena standing in the middle of the hallway during class periods, looking at the ceiling and counting. When asked what she was doing, Athena either would not reply or say she needed to "count all the tiles in the ceiling to make sure no one could get through." The counselor said Athena admittedly spent large amounts of time in the bathroom washing her hands or counting the tiles there as well. Athena was a bright student who usually did well in school. Her grades at the beginning of the school year were good but had declined since. Currently she was passing only three of six classes and was in danger of retention for the third time in her young academic life. The counselor reported no direct signs or admissions of self-mutilation, however.

Athena's hospitalization was spurred by the fact that she drove her parents' car nearly 80 miles per hour down a busy street 3 weeks earlier. Athena received a ticket for this event and later faced her confused and livid parents. Athena said she had an overwhelming urge to speed down the street. Athena became withdrawn when asked what compelled her. The psychologist asked Athena if she engaged in this behavior at other times. Athena shrugged, tacitly admitting she had done so.

Athena's current behavior concerned her psychologist even more because of her past bizarre behavior. Athena was placed in an inpatient psychiatric ward 19 months earlier for digging into her legs with a pair of scissors, trying to speak in a foreign language (though usually poorly and inaudibly), walking on desks at school, and saying "strange spirits are all around me." Athena often pointed to empty space and moved her finger as if to follow something. When asked what she was doing, Athena said she was "tracing the spirit." During this time, as with her current episode, Athena's schoolwork and hygiene declined dramatically within a 2-month span.

During this strange series of events 19 months earlier, Athena had engaged in other dangerous behaviors. She stole her mother's credit card and charged nearly $3,000 worth of goods at a shopping mall within 4 hours. She would sometimes stand on the roof of her house in the middle of the night and had unprotected sex with three of her classmates within 7 days, one of them another female. Her parents said this last incident was highly unusual because Athena had no prior sexual experience and often referred to sex as "ugly." What made the behavior even more unusual was the fact that Athena had a compelling sexual urge she felt needed satisfaction but did not report any sexual desire since that time.

Athena was scared and initially nonresponsive when in the inpatient ward for the first time. The psychiatrist who evaluated Athena said she was withdrawn, somewhat stereotypic in her behavior (she twirled her hair and spun in her chair), and insisted on having her bed near a window. The staff thought Athena wanted to be near a window to damage the glass and use shards to cut herself, so they supervised her in a room where no glass or sharp objects were available.

Athena gradually became more social and less likely to harm herself the longer she stayed in the unit during her first hospitalization. She participated in group therapy sessions, took antidepressant, antipsychotic, and other mood-stabilizing medications willingly, and became social with others during mealtimes. Her only unusual behavior was a general "spaciness" in the form of staring at the ceiling, pointing to nothing in particular, and moving her head from side to side. When asked why she did so, Athena said she "had to do it." Athena was discharged 9 days later when her mood was stable and she was no longer a danger to herself.

Following her release from the hospital, Athena went back to school, continued her medication, reinitiated contact with a few friends and family members, and agreed to see a clinical psychologist. Her parents reported some minor misbehavior during Athena's first 7 months out of the unit but nothing intolerable or unmanageable. Their first indication of trouble, however, came about 12 months ago when Athena's mood became more irritable and vacillating.

She had trouble sleeping and convinced her parents that her medication was to blame. After stopping the medication, however, Athena's behavior deteriorated. Her mood often shifted between sullenness and effervescence. These mood changes did not relate to any specific environmental event and often occurred on a daily basis. Athena was not always appropriate in her hygiene, dressed unusually, and sometimes insisted that her bed be near the window so she could "see the birds in the morning and other things at night." Athena's current behaviors, especially self-mutilation, apathy, counting, hand washing, and pointing, had evolved over the past 6 months.

In the same inpatient unit where she was before, Athena's new psychiatrist considered her patient's behavior and medication history as well as reports from Athena's psychologist, school counselor, and parents. She placed Athena under strict supervision and gave her a sedative to relax. Given available information, the psychiatrist thought that Athena potentially met criteria for a psychotic, mood, personality, and/or anxiety disorder.

Assessment

A specific definition of psychosis refers to hallucinations and delusions with a lack of insight into the troublesome nature of the symptoms. Hallucinations involve sensations in the absence of actual stimuli; examples include seeing things not actually there or hearing voices when no one is around. Delusions are bizarre thoughts held despite clear evidence to the contrary. A common example is a persecutory delusion where a person erroneously believes someone or something is out to harm her. A broader definition of psychosis includes symptoms other than hallucinations or delusions. Examples include disorganized speech patterns, catatonic behavior, and negative symptoms such as blunted affect or poor hygiene. Schizophrenia is a severe condition that affects many areas of cognitive and social functioning and significantly interferes with one's ability to work, concentrate, and care for oneself.

Does Athena have schizophrenia? The answer is difficult to pinpoint because Athena seemed to have some but not all elements of this disorder. Her reports of seeing her mother floating on the ceiling and her occasional disconnectedness from others were troubling. In addition, Athena displayed negative symptoms such as apathy and nonresponsiveness but these could have been due to normal or abnormal mood changes, substance use, or organic factors. Her stereotypic behavior was unusual as well, though perhaps not to the level of a psychotic reaction.

The assessment of people with schizophrenia often involves interviews and observations. The child version of the Schedule for Affective Disorders and Schizophrenia (SADS) (Ambrosini, 2000) may be used to assess bizarre behaviors such as those seen in Athena. If a person is incoherent or overly suspicious, however, then family members and close friends may provide the most information. A thorough history of symptoms, sudden changes in behavior, and past family disorder should be covered. If a person is able, then psychological testing may be given; the adolescent version of the Minnesota Multiphasic Personality Inventory (MMPI-A) (Butcher et al., 1992) contains a schizophrenia scale. Medical assessment is crucial to rule out competing organic causes such as brain injury, thyroid abnormalities, and drug use. Athena's psychiatrist administered a brief unstructured interview to assess current symptoms and relied heavily on the psychologist's case history report.

Does Athena have a mood disorder? Mood disorders involve depression and/or mania. Several depressive symptoms were evident in Athena. She was socially isolated, nonresponsive, and potentially suicidal in her behavior. A manic episode is "a distinct period during which there is an abnormally and persistently elevated, expansive, or irritable mood" [(American Psychiatric Association (APA), 2000, p. 357]. Other common symptoms of mania include inflated self-esteem or grandiosity, decreased need for sleep, pressured speech, racing thoughts, distractibility, increased involvement in goal-directed activities or psychomotor agitation, and excessive involvement in pleasurable but potentially dangerous activities (APA, 2000, p. 357).

Athena had some of these symptoms to a degree. Her mood was often irritable and changed quickly from happiness to sadness to anger and back again. Her parents said they were always "walking on eggshells" around Athena because they were unsure of her current mood or afraid something would trigger an explosive reaction on her part. Athena also had spurts of impulsivity that were potentially dangerous, such as driving fast and engaging in at least one sexual spree. She had trouble sleeping as well. Athena did not have grandiosity or racing thoughts, however.

Assessment of mania or bipolar disorder (alternating phases of mania and depression) may include structured diagnostic interviews such as the SADS (child version) or psychological testing. Family member reports about everyday behaviors are particularly important as well. The psychiatrist asked Athena's parents to describe their daughter's daily behavior and found that Athena was angry and defiant when told what to do, would vacillate between nonresponsiveness and talkativeness, and had trouble concentrating. She occasionally had episodes of euphoria and alcohol use with peers.

Does Athena have a personality disorder? A personality disorder is an "enduring pattern of inner experience and behavior that deviates markedly from the expectations of the individual's culture, is pervasive and inflexible, has an onset in adolescence or early adulthood, is stable over time, and leads to distress or impairment" (APA, 2000, p. 685). Personality disorders include broad classes of behaviors that are (1) odd or eccentric, (2) dramatic or overly emotional, and (3) anxious or avoidant. The first class includes paranoid, schizoid, and schizotypal personality disorders.

Paranoid personality disorder involves distrust and suspicion of others as well as intense jealousy, doubts about others' loyalty, and reluctance to confide in people. Schizoid personality disorder involves detachment from others, little emotional reaction, indifference, and flat affect. Schizotypal personality disorder involves severe interpersonal deficits and lack of friends because of strange behaviors. Such behaviors often include ideas of reference (i.e., attributing personal meaning to almost all events), magical thinking, superstitiousness, bizarre fantasies or preoccupations, strange perceptual experiences, and odd thinking and speech.

Athena's "spirit tracing" and foreign language-speaking behaviors were obviously bizarre and may have been part of a personality disorder. Vacillating behavior may also indicate borderline personality disorder. Assessment of personality disorders often involves psychological testing such as the MMPI-A or Millon Adolescent Personality Inventory (Millon, Green, & Meagher, 1993) as well as interviews and observations.

Does Athena have obsessive-compulsive disorder (OCD)? OCD consists of (1) obsessions or recurrent and intrusive ideas, thoughts, impulses, or images, and (2) compulsions or repetitive behaviors, such as hand washing, that occur in response to an obsession. Compulsions help reduce anxiety from an obsession; incessant worry about leaving the stove on (obsession) could be temporarily relieved by checking (compulsion). Obsessions and resulting compulsions often recur in a time-consuming cycle. The psychiatrist considered a diagnosis of OCD for Athena given her propensity to count ceiling tiles and wash her hands. Sometimes her counting related to a specific thought process such as worry about "people coming through the ceiling," but sometimes not.

The assessment of OCD involves interview (e.g., the Anxiety Disorders Interview Schedule for Children; see Chapter 2), self-monitoring, observation, clinician ratings [e.g., the Children's Yale-Brown Obsessive Compulsive Scale (Scahill et al., 1997)], and self-report instruments such as the Short Leyton Obsessional Inventory for Children and Adolescents (Bamber, Tamplin, Park, Kyte, & Goodyer, 2002). Athena's psychologist asked her to self-monitor her checking behavior but Athena's compliance in this regard was spotty.

Risk Factors and Maintaining Variables

Genetic and other biological factors influence psychotic conditions such as schizophrenia as well as severe mood disorders. The closer one is genetically to someone with schizophrenia, the more at risk he is for contracting the disorder. Children with a parent or twin with schizophrenia are particularly more vulnerable than the general population to develop the disorder themselves (Shih, Belmonte, & Zandi, 2004).

Other biological factors influence psychosis as well. Certain brain changes or damage to the limbic system, amygdala, or prefrontal cortex may relate to negative symptoms of schizophrenia. People with schizophrenia sometimes had prenatal complications and lower birth weight (Welham, Isohanni, Jones, & McGrath, 2009). Such problems may relate to enlarged brain ventricles (spaces) sometimes seen in people with negative schizophrenia. Vulnerability in the developing brain, perhaps from a genetic predisposition, may produce symptoms of schizophrenia following onset of key environmental stressors such as viruses or family instability. Impaired neuropsychological deficits in memory and attention and excess dopamine relate to overt symptoms of schizophrenia as well (Murray, Lappin, & Di Forti, 2008).

Athena's parents reported difficulties during Mrs. Galvez's pregnancy with Athena. A high-risk obstetrician supervised Mrs. Galvez's pregnancy and childbirth, and Athena was 8 weeks premature and weighed only 5 pounds. She was a sickly infant who often contracted colds during day care. Her health since toddlerhood was not overly problematic but key brain changes may have already occurred. No family history of schizophrenia existed but Mr. Galvez admitted he was hospitalized in college for severe depression and occasionally took antidepressant medication. Mrs. Galvez reported no personal psychopathology but said her mother suffered from early dementia. Both parents conceded there was much family conflict concerning Athena's behaviors. Poor communication and a hostile interaction style – expressed emotion – often occur in families of those with schizophrenia (Aguilera, Lopez, Breitborde, Kopelowicz, & Zarate, 2010).

Risk factors for severe mood disorders may be similar to those for psychotic reactions. A key similarity is severe depression in a close family member, as was the case with Athena. A strong genetic predisposition and possible changes in the neurotransmitters serotonin and norepinephrine influence mood disorders. Environmentally, youths with bipolar disorder tend to have little support from family members or friends and often experience impaired affect regulation and social interaction (Belardinelli et al., 2008).

Athena's social interactions with others seemed to predispose her to a severe mood disorder. Her strange behaviors often precluded close friendships and Athena said several years had passed since she had a best friend. She ventured out with peers only occasionally and sometimes engaged in deviant or dangerous acts such as drinking alcohol when doing so. Her parents were not always supportive of her and lecturing or detachment was common in the family.

Researchers have investigated precursors to personality disorders among youths as well. In contrast to psychotic and severe mood disorders, these precursors are more psychological or environmental than biological. Several general themes seem related to the development of personality disorders (Geiger & Crick, 2010; Shiner, 2005):

1. Hostile, paranoid world view

2. Intense, unstable, and inappropriate emotion to restricted, flat affect

3. Impulsivity to rigidity

4. Overly close relationships to distant or avoidant relationships

5. Negative sense of self or lack of self to exaggerated sense of self

6. Peculiar thought processes and behaviors

7. Lack of concern for social norms and needs of others

Several of these themes applied to Athena. Her emotional state varied often and involved different affective states such as anger, sadness, and joy. Her affect was sometimes flat as well. Emotional regulation relates to early attachment and perhaps this was problematic for Athena. Changes in the limbic system, described earlier as a predispositional factor for schizophrenia, have been implicated as well.

Schizotypal and schizoid personality disorders may occur along a spectrum of abnormal behavior that includes schizophrenia.

Another precursor to personality disorders that pertained to Athena was her impulsive behavior. Athena's inability to control certain aspects of her behavior resembled symptoms of attention deficit/hyperactivity disorder and her difficulty concentrating in school may be another connection. Athena's relationships with others were generally distant and avoidant, her self-image was unstable, and she certainly had peculiar thought processes and behaviors. Other precursors did not apply to Athena, however. She was not hostile or paranoid regarding others and did not lack concern for others. She wanted close friends but said others seemed to distance themselves from her.

Many of the precursors mentioned for anxiety in Chapter 2 apply to OCD, including physiological reactivity, negative cognitions, stressful life events, and familial modeling. A genetic predisposition for OCD may overlap with Tourette's syndrome (Cavanna, Servo, Monaco, & Robertson, 2009). Children with OCD often have family members with obsessive-compulsive symptoms or tics. Abnormalities in various brain areas have been implicated as well, particularly the basal ganglia, left anterior cingulate, and frontal cortex. Serotonin and neuro-endocrine changes also occur in youths with OCD (Cameron, 2007). No family history of OCD or tics was reported in Athena's case, though potential brain changes mentioned earlier could have applied to her.

Developmental Aspects

Psychotic conditions may develop in one of two main ways. Many psychoses such as schizophrenia occur in episodes that contain three main stages. A prodromal stage involves gradual deterioration in behavior over several months. A person has greater apathy regarding everyday events and self-care, more peculiar behaviors such as odd speech or thoughts, trouble concentrating and remembering, and greater emotional changes and distance from others. The prodromal stage may devolve into an active or acute stage where full-blown symptoms of schizophrenia such as delusions or hallucinations occur. An intense environmental stressor such as job loss or end of a relationship may trigger these symptoms, which often require extensive inpatient treatment. Following treatment, a person may enter a residual phase where she returns to a better level of functioning that resembles the early prodromal phase. This stage process does not neatly apply to all episodes or to all people with schizophrenia, however.

The stage process was messy for Athena. A prodromal phase could be marked between the time she stopped taking her medication to the time she entered the hospital for the second time, but whether her behaviors significantly deteriorated over time or whether her strange behaviors simply continued at the same level was unclear. The only behaviors that became significantly worse were her apathy and skin cutting that escalated in weeks before hospitalization. A clear active phase was not evident in Athena because no overt delusions or hallucinations occurred. Athena returned to her initial state immediately after her first hospitalization, which involved some strange behaviors but nothing harmful (see Treatment).

Another way to consider psychoses developmentally is to evaluate longitudinal studies conducted with this population. Such studies often involve "high-risk" studies where children of parents with schizophrenia are followed over time to identify precursors to the disorder. Schizophrenia is a neurodevelopmental disorder that has biological bases in genetic predispositions, prenatal events, and brain and biochemical changes. Some believe schizophrenia may evolve as a lifelong disorder with telltale signs in childhood or one that suddenly escalates in late adolescence or early adulthood. Telltale childhood signs of later schizophrenia include hyperresponsiveness to stress, motor difficulties, and classroom misbehaviors but these signs also occur in many youths who do not eventually develop schizophrenia (Schiffman et al., 2009).

Athena did show some of these early signs. She was often in trouble at school for failure to remain seated and often cried for extended periods when something stressful happened at school. Her parents said Athena underwent an evaluation in second grade for attention deficit/hyperactivity and learning disorders but did not qualify for special education because her misbehaviors were thought to be manageable through classroom intervention. Even recently, Athena continued to react to stressors in odd and sometimes explosive ways. Many adolescents with schizophrenia continue to have significant problems with their disorder, even into adulthood. Good prognosis relates to absence of strange behaviors before an episode of full-blown schizophrenia and low level of impairment following the first hospitalization (Singh, 2007). Neither applied to Athena, however, who may continue to have problems functioning as an adult.

The developmental progression of mania or bipolar disorder may involve some early telltale signs as well. Children who eventually develop bipolar disorder are often irritable, aggressive, hyperactive, easily distracted, and labile in mood. They are sometimes described as euphoric, grandiose, paranoid, and having racing thoughts and fast speech in early adolescence (Miklowitz & Cicchetti, 2010). As these youths reach mid to late adolescence, some have clearer episodes of mania and depression but many do not.

Many of these early symptoms overlap with those reported for schizophrenia and did apply to Athena. She was often an irritable child who wanted her way and had trouble concentrating on schoolwork because she was distracted. Her overactivity in school was frustrating to her teachers but not to the point that medication or psychologist-directed behavior modification was required. Athena was never aggressive, however, and was never truly grandiose or paranoid. Other early signs such as euphoria and pressured thoughts and speech were seen only occasionally in Athena. Good prognostic factors for bipolar disorder include later onset, medication maintenance, and delayed relapse (Geller & DelBello, 2003; Geller, Tillman, Bolhofner, & Zimerman, 2008). Athena's long-term outcome with respect to these problems is unclear given her mixed symptoms.

With respect to personality disorders, general trends in behavior across the early life span may predict later problems. A child whose temperament involves greater behavioral inhibition may be more likely to develop an anxious or avoidant personality disorder. A child who had been dependent on a parent early in life because of health problems may be predisposed to dependent personality disorder. A child whose attachment to parents was problematic may be predisposed to a personality disorder (e.g., schizoid, borderline) involving emotional dysregulation. Research in this area is limited, however. Athena's parents did indulge, tolerate, and even reinforce some of her early odd behaviors. Her mother encouraged her daughter's tendency to wear unusual clothing and both parents acquiesced to Athena's dramatic and inappropriate behavior in public.

Many children engage in minor ritualistic behaviors such as counting or having to have things "just so." These behaviors often fade during middle childhood as a child becomes more social and interested in various appropriate activities (Evans, Milanak, Medeiros, & Ross, 2002). Strong biological predispositions or parental modeling or reinforcement of obsessive-compulsive behavior may induce some children to continue early ritualistic patterns and eventually develop OCD. Athena had no early ritualistic patterns, however. She sometimes had odd or pressured thoughts or speech but nothing indicated recurrent, intrusive, and overly bizarre thoughts in childhood.

Treatment

Treatment for youths with psychotic conditions and/or severe mood disorders often involves inpatient hospitalization, medication, and outpatient therapy to maintain adherence to a medical regimen and address personal and family issues to prevent relapse (Findling & Schulz, 2005). All applied to Athena. During her stay in the inpatient unit, Athena attended group and individual therapy sessions with staff members and other patients. These sessions concentrated on reconnecting with others and improving Athena's willingness to interact and share recent personal experiences. Athena gradually became more responsive to others during her hospitalization but her level of spontaneously initiated conversation was only moderate.

Athena's self-cutting was a priority as well. Her clinical psychologist regularly visited Athena in the unit to discuss this issue, though Athena had trouble articulating why she engaged in this behavior. The psychologist asked about antecedents to the behavior or what mood states or events preceded cutting. Athena said the self-mutilation occurred when she felt agitated and that cutting helped her focus and calm herself. Sometimes this occurred after an argument with her parents but more often occurred when she felt anxious or irritated for no reason.

Athena received four medications to address her symptoms and antecedents to her self-mutilation. The first was a mood-stabilizing drug, carbamazepine (Tegretol), which can help reduce agitation and aggression by producing a calming, sedating effect. The second medication was an atypical antipsychotic drug, olanzapine (Zyprexa), the third was an antidepressant drug, paroxetine (Paxil), and the fourth was an anti-anxiety drug, lorazepam (Ativan). Athena and her parents learned about the dosages, side effects, and need for compliance regarding each medication. Athena was released from the hospital when her psychiatrist was convinced that her mood was stable and that she was no longer at imminent risk for harming herself by cutting or any other means.

Following her release from the hospital, Athena went to a residential facility that served as a precursor to living again with her parents. At this facility, a group home for seven adolescents with similar behavior and mood problems, Athena took her medications, participated in group therapy sessions, completed various chores, and regularly visited with her parents. The purpose of this placement was to closely monitor Athena's mood and medication side effects, increase her social interactions and support, and help her function again as a regular teenager. Athena was at the group home for 4 weeks, gradually spending more time at her parents' house (e.g., weekends) before her discharge. During her stay at the group home, Athena participated in group activities and befriended two of the residents. Her medication was adjusted as needed and she and her parents resumed treatment with the clinical psychologist.

Psychological intervention for adolescents with psychoses and/or severe mood disorders often focuses on family members (Hall & Bean, 2008). This involves extensive education about the adolescent's disorder as well as communication and problem-solving skills training to help family members resolve conflicts effectively and prevent relapse. Education about the disorder includes information on specific symptoms, understanding that the adolescent is highly vulnerable to relapse, and accepting the fact that medication is likely a long-term necessity to address symptoms. More advanced family-focused treatment aims to distinguish an adolescent's personality from symptoms of the psychotic or mood disorder and help family members recognize and cope with stressful events that could trigger relapse.

Athena's education about her symptoms and disorders was less necessary given the family's long-term knowledge of them. More pertinent, however, was providing the family with a strategy to solve problems as they occurred instead of acquiescing or fighting. Each family member defined problems from the past week in specific form (e.g., Athena came home late from school; my mom yelled at me for no reason) and wrote potential solutions. The psychologist then established a process whereby family members met at home to discuss the issue. Potential solutions were then compared and an overall solution acceptable to everyone was chosen, implemented, and evaluated. The psychologist added communication skills training to this process; each family member made a statement and others paraphrased the statement before responding.

Athena's family initially had difficulty in treatment because they were so used to avoiding conflict or having large fights. Athena and her parents were motivated, however, by a desire to avert another episode of bizarre behavior and hospitalization. Their attendance at therapy and efforts to implement the procedures were good. Their ability to establish house rules and consequences and immediately address problems as they arose developed considerably. A nice side effect of treatment was that stress in the home was reduced, which allowed Athena's parents to better monitor their daughter's mood and medication usage.

The medication was occasionally problematic because Athena complained about the number of medications she was prescribed. Her psychologist, psychiatrist, and parents gave her substantial praise and other rewards for continuing her medical regimen.

The psychologist later worked with the Galvez family to sort Athena's genuine personality from more bizarre symptoms. This was less successful because Athena's parents complained to the psychiatrist about the need for medication change whenever Athena became more sullen. The psychologist pointed out that everyone, especially adolescents, experience subtle mood changes during a day or week and that a completely even mood was unrealistic. The psychologist helped the family identify behaviors that were unacceptable or worthy of concern. These included instances of self-harm, severe noncompliance, explosive or highly impulsive or dangerous behavior, and odd rituals.

Athena's situation was stable during the next year. She no longer displayed self-mutilating behavior and, though her speech remained peculiar at times, made few substantially bizarre statements. Her mood was generally consistent but sometimes she became agitated. Her ritualistic behaviors largely faded as well. Athena was occasionally impulsive and needed considerable help finishing high school. She and her family remained in therapy and Athena continued to live with her parents. Athena understood she needed long-term care and family support, especially because she was still unsure what direction her life would take next.

DISCUSSION QUESTIONS

1. What diagnosis you would give Athena, if any? Examine the DSM-IV-TR carefully to see whether Athena truly meets criteria for the disorders mentioned in this chapter. Identify what you think is the most primary diagnosis for her case.

2. Which of Athena's behaviors could be construed as normal adolescent behavior? If you remove these behaviors from consideration, does Athena meet criteria for a mental disorder?

3. Think about possible reasons an adolescent would engage in self-mutilation. Even if a teenager had no diagnosable mental disorder, why might she deliberately harm herself? What could be done to address this situation?

4. When assessing someone with delusions and hallucinations, what questions do you think you could or should ask? Regarding someone who hears voices, what information would you want to know?

5. Discuss the importance of family members for treating adolescents with severe behavior problems. Do you think family members can influence adolescents with such problems or are the problems more amenable to psychological or pharmacological treatment? Should Athena have gone home after her hospitalization?

6. What are ethical issues in medicating adolescents with schizophrenia or severe bipolar disorder? What might happen should an adolescent not wish to take such medication?

7. People with schizophrenia are often portrayed in the media as dangerous. Why might this be the case and what can mental health professionals do to dispel such a myth?

8. How might you reduce the stigma Athena may face from her peers because of her mental status?

9. Which child in this casebook would you most want to work with, and why?

References

Abramson, L. Y., Alloy, L. B., Hankin, B. L., Haeffel, G. J., MacCoon, D. G., & Gibb, B. E. (2002). Cognitive vulnerability-stress models of depression in a self-regulatory and psychobiological context. In I. H. Gotlib & C. L. Hammen (Eds.), *Handbook of depression* (pp. 268–294). New York: Guilford.

Achenbach, T. M., & Rescorla, L. A. (2001). *Manual for the ASEBA school-age forms & profiles*. Burlington, VT: University of Vermont Research Center for Children, Youth, & Families.

Aguilera, A., Lopez, S. R., Breitborde, N. J. K., Kopelowicz, A., & Zarate, R. (2010). Expressed emotion and sociocultural moderation in the course of schizophrenia. *Journal of Abnormal Psychology, 119*, 875–885.

Ahn, M. S., & Frazier, J. A. (2004). Diagnostic and treatment issues in childhood-onset bipolar disorder. *Essential Psychopharmacology, 6*, 25–44.

Alegria, M., Woo, M., Cao, Z., Torres, M., Meng, X. L., & Striegel-Moore, R. (2007). Prevalence and correlates of eating disorders in Latinos in the United States. *International Journal of Eating Disorders, 40*(Suppl), S15–S21

Alexander, G. M. (2003). An evolutionary perspective of sex-typed toy preferences: Pink, blue, and the brain. *Archives of Sexual Behavior, 32*, 7–14.

Ambrosini, P. J. (2000). Historical development and present status of the schedule for affective disorders and schizophrenia for school-age children (K-SADS). *Journal of the American Academy of Child and Adolescent Psychiatry, 39*, 49–58.

American Academy of Child and Adolescent Psychiatry. (2001). Summary of the practice parameter for the use of stimulant medications in the treatment of children, adolescents, and adults. *Journal of the American Academy of Child and Adolescent Psychiatry, 40*, 1352–1355.

American Psychiatric Association. (2000). *Diagnostic and statistical manual of mental disorders* (4th ed., text rev.). Washington, DC: American Psychiatric Association.

Anastopoulos, A. D., Smith, T. F., Garrett, M. E., Morrissey-Kane, E., Schatz, N. K., Sommer, J. L., Kollins, S. H., & Ashley-Koch, A. (2011). Self-regulation of emotion, functional impairment, and comorbidity among children with AD/HD. *Journal of Attention Disorders, 15*, 583–592.

Anderluh, M. B., Tchanturia, K., Rabe-Hesketh, S., & Treasure, J. (2003). Childhood obsessive-compulsive personality traits in adult women with eating disorders: Defining a broader eating disorder phenotype. *American Journal of Psychiatry, 160*, 242–247.

Anderson, D. A., Lundgren, J. D., Shapiro, J. R., & Paulosky, C. A. (2004). Assessment of eating disorders: Review and recommendations for clinical use. *Behavior Modification, 28*, 763–782.

Andrist, L. C. (2003). Media images, body dissatisfaction, and disordered eating in adolescent women. *American Journal of Maternal Child Nursing, 28*, 119–123.

Anthony, K. K., & Schanberg, L. E. (2007). Assessment and management of pain syndromes and arthritis pain in children and adolescents. *Rheumatic Diseases Clinics of North America, 33*, 625–660.

Armstrong, T. D., & Costello, E. J. (2002). Community studies on adolescent substance use, abuse, or dependence and psychiatric comorbidity. *Journal of Consulting and Clinical Psychology, 70*, 1224–1239.

Babin, P. R. (2003). Diagnosing depression in persons with brain injuries: A look at theories, the DSM-IV and depression measures. *Brain Injury, 17*, 889–900.

Bailer, U. F., & Kaye, W. H. (2003). A review of neuropeptide and neuroendocrine dysregulation in anorexia and bulimia nervosa. *Current Drug Targets, CNS and Neurological Disorders, 2*, 53–59.

Balluffi, A., Kassam-Adams, N., Kazak, A., Tucker, M., Dominguez, T., & Helfaer, M. (2004). Traumatic stress in parents of children admitted to the pediatric intensive care unit. *Pediatric Critical Care Medicine, 5*, 547–553.

Bamber, D., Tamplin, A., Park, R. J., Kyte, Z. A., & Goodyer, I. (2002). Development of a short Leyton Obsessional Inventory for Children and Adolescents. *Journal of the American Academy of Child and Adolescent Psychiatry, 41*, 1246–1252.

Barker, P. (2007). *Basic family therapy* (7th ed.). Ames, IA: Blackwell.

Barkley, R. A. (2000). *Taking charge of ADHD: The complete, authoritative guide for parents.* New York: Guilford.

Barkley, R. A. (2003). Issues in the diagnosis of attention-deficit/hyperactivity disorder in children. *Brain and Development, 25*, 77–83.

Barnes, H. L., & Olson, D. H. (1985). Parent-adolescent communication and the circumplex model. *Child Development, 56*, 438–447.

Barnes, J. E., Noll, J. G., Putnam, F. W., & Trickett, P. K. (2009). Sexual and physical revictimization among victims of severe childhood sexual abuse. *Child Abuse and Neglect, 33*, 412–420.

Bayley, N. (2005). *Bayley Scales of Infant and Toddler Development*, 3rd ed. San Antonio, TX: Harcourt.

Bearden, C. E., Soares, J. C., Klunder, A. D., Nicoletti, M., Dierschke, N., Hayashi, K. M., Narr, K. L., Brambilla, P., Sassi, R. B., Axelson, D., Ryan, N., Birmaher, B., & Thompson, P. M. (2008). Three-dimensional mapping of hippocampal anatomy in adolescents with bipolar disorder. *Journal of the American Academy of Child and Adolescent Psychiatry, 47*, 515–525.

Beauchaine, T. P., Webster-Stratton, C., & Reid, M. J. (2005). Mediators, moderators, and predictors of 1-year outcomes among children treated for early-onset conduct problems: A latent growth curve analysis. *Journal of*

Consulting and Clinical Psychology, 73, 371–388.

Beck, A. T. (2005). The current state of cognitive therapy: A 40-year retrospective. *Archives of General Psychiatry, 62,* 953–959.

Beidel, D. C., Turner, S. M., & Morris, T. L. (2000). *Social Phobia And Anxiety Inventory for Children: Manual.* North Tonawanda, NY: Multi-Health Systems.

Beitchman, J. H., Wilson, B., Johnson, C. J., Atkinson, L., Young, A., Adlaf, E., Escobar, M., & Douglas, L. (2001). Fourteen-year follow-up of speech/language-impaired and control children: Psychiatric outcome. *Journal of the American Academy of Child and Adolescent Psychiatry, 40,* 75–82.

Berkman, N. D., Lohr, K. N., & Bulik, C. M. (2007). Outcomes of eating disorders: A systematic review of the literature. *International Journal of Eating Disorders, 40,* 293–309.

Berlardinelli, C., Hatch, J. P., Olvera, R. L., Fonseca, M., Caetano, S. C., Nicoletti, M., Pliszka, S., & Soares, J. C. (2008). Family environment patterns in families with bipolar children. *Journal of Affective Disorders, 107,* 299–305.

Berninger, V. W., Nielsen, K. H., Abbott, R. D., Wijsman, E., & Raskind, W. (2008). Writing problems in developmental dyslexia: Under-recognized and under-treated. *Journal of School Psychology, 46,* 1–21.

Beyers, J. M., Toumbourou, J. W., Catalano, R. F., Arthur, M. W., & Hawkins, J. D. (2004). A cross-national comparison of risk and protective factors for adolescent substance use: The United States and Australia. *Journal of Adolescent Health, 35,* 3–16.

Biederman, J., & Faraone, S. V. (2005). Attention-deficit hyperactivity disorder. *Lancet, 366,* 237–248.

Biederman, J., Petty, C. R., Dolan, C., Hughes, S., Mick, E., Monuteaux, M. C., & Faraone, S.V. (2008). The long-term longitudinal course of oppositional defiant disorder and conduct disorder in ADHD boys: Findings from a controlled 10-year prospective longitudinal follow-up study. *Psychological Medicine, 38,* 1027–1036.

Billstedt, E., Gillberg, C., & Gillberg, C. (2005). Autism after adolescence: Population-based 13- to 22-year follow-up study of 120 individuals with autism diagnosed in childhood. *Journal of Autism and Developmental Disorders, 35,* 351–360.

Birmaher, B., & Axelson, D. (2006). Course and outcome of bipolar spectrum disorder in children and adolescents: A review of the existing literature. *Development and Psychopathology, 18,* 1023–1035.

Birmaher, B., Axelson, D., Strober, M., Gill, M. K., Valeri, S., Chiappetta, L., Ryan, N., Leonard, H., Hunt, J., Iyengar, S., & Keller, M. (2006). Clinical course of children and adolescents with bipolar spectrum disorders. *Archives of General Psychiatry, 63,* 175–183.

Bishop, D. V. M., & Snowling, M. J. (2004). Developmental dyslexia and specific language impairment: Same or different? *Psychological Bulletin, 130,* 858–886.

Bogels, S. M., & Brechman-Toussaint, M. L. (2006). Family issues in child anxiety: Attachment, family functioning, parental rearing and beliefs. *Clinical Psychology Review, 26,* 834–856.

Bolte, S., & Poustka, F. (2002). The relation between general cognitive level and adaptive behavior domains in individuals with autism with and without co-morbid mental retardation. *Child Psychiatry and Human Development, 33,* 165–172.

Brennan, P. A., Hall, J., Bor, W., Najman, J. M., & Williams, G. (2003). Integrating biological and social processes in relation to early-onset persistent aggression in boys and girls. *Developmental Psychology, 39,* 309–323.

Briere, J. (1996). *Trauma symptom checklist for children.* Lutz, FL: Psychological Assessment Resources.

Bryson, S. A., Corrigan, S. K., McDonald, T. P., & Holmes, C. (2008). Characteristics of children with autism spectrum disorders who received services through community mental health centers. *Autism, 12,* 65–82.

Bulik, C. M., Slof-Op't Landt, M. C. T., van Furth, E. F., & Sullivan, P. F. (2007). The genetics of anorexia nervosa. *Annual Review of Nutrition, 27,* 263–275.

Butcher, J. N., Williams, C. L., Graham, J. R., Archer, R. P., Tellegen, A., Ben-Porath, Y. S., & Kaemmer, B. (1992). *Minnesota Multiphasic Personality Inventory—Adolescent.* Minneapolis, MN: NCS Assessments.

Cadoret, R. J., Langbehn, D., Caspers, K., Troughton, E. P., Yucuis, R., Sandhu, H. K., & Philibert, R. (2003). Associations of the serotonin transporter promoter polymorphism with aggressivity, attention deficit, and conduct disorder in an adoptee population. *Comprehensive Psychiatry, 44,* 88–101.

Calhoon, M. B., Sandow, A., & Hunter, C. V. (2010). Reorganizing the instructional reading components: Could there be a better way to design remedial reading programs to maximize middle students with reading disabilities' response to treatment? *Annals of Dyslexia, 60,* 57–85.

Cameron, C. L. (2007). Obsessive-compulsive disorder in children and adolescents. *Journal of Psychiatric and Mental Health Nursing, 14,* 696–704.

Cappadocia, M. C., Desrocher, M., Pepler, D., & Schroeder, J. H. (2009). Contextualizing the neurobiology of conduct disorder in an emotion dysregulation framework. *Clinical Psychology Review, 29,* 506–518.

Caraceni, A., Cherny, N., Fainsinger, R., Kaasa, S., Poulain, P., Radbruch, L., & De Conno, F. (2002). Pain measurement tools and methods in clinical research in palliative care: Recommendations of an expert working group of the European association of palliative care. *Journal of Pain and Symptom Management, 23,* 239–255.

Carter, B. D., Kronenberger, W. G., Baker, J., Grimes, L. M., Crabtree, V. M., Smith, C., & McGraw, K. (2003). Inpatient pediatric consultation-liaison: A case-controlled study. *Journal of Pediatric Psychology, 28,* 423–432.

Casey, R. L., & Brown, R. T. (2003). Psychological aspects of hematologic diseases. *Child and Adolescent Psychiatric Clinics of North America, 12,* 567–584.

Cavanna, A. E., Servo, S., Monaco, F., & Robertson, M. M. (2009). The behavioural spectrum of Gilles de la Tourette syndrome. *Journal of Neuropsychiatry and Clinical Neurosciences, 21,* 13–23.

Chambliss, C. R., Heggen, J., Copelan, D. N., & Pettignano, R. (2002). The assessment and management of chronic pain in children. *Paediatric Drugs, 4,* 737–746.

Charach, A., Volpe, T., Boydell, K. M., & Gearing, R. E. (2008). A theoretical approach to medication adherence for children and youth with psychiatric disorders. *Harvard Review of Psychiatry, 16,* 126–135.

Charman, T. (2005). Outcome at 7 years of children diagnosed with autism at age 2: Predictive validity of assessments conducted at 2 and 3 years of age and pattern of symptom change over time. *Journal of Child Psychology and Psychiatry, 46,* 500–513.

Chassin, L., Beltran, I., Lee, M., Haller, M., & Villalta, I. (2010). Vulnerability to substance use disorders in childhood and adolescence. In R. E. Ingram & J. M. Price (Eds.), *Vulnerability to psychopathology: Risk across the lifespan* (2nd ed., pp. 113–140). New York: Guilford.

Chassin, L., Ritter, J., Trim, K. S., & King, K. M. (2003). Adolescent substance use disorders. In E. J. Mash & R. A. Barkley (Eds.), *Child psychopathology* (2nd ed., pp. 199–230). New York: Guilford.

Chorpita, B. F., Moffitt, C. E., & Gray, J. (2005). Psychometric properties of the Revised Child Anxiety and Depression Scale in a clinical sample. *Behaviour Research and Therapy, 43,* 309–322.

Cohen, J. A., Deblinger, E., Mannarino, A. P., & Steer, R. A. (2004). A multisite, randomized controlled trial for children with sexual abuse-related PTSD symptoms. *Journal of the American Academy of Child and Adolescent Psychiatry, 43,* 393–402.

Conners, C. K. (2008). *Conners third edition (Conners 3).* Los Angeles, CA: Western Psychological Services.

Conners, C. K. (1999). *Conners ADHD/DSM-IV Scales.* North Tonawanda, NY: Multi-Health Systems.

Conners, C. K. (2004). *Conners continuous performance test II version 5.* North Tonawanda, NY: Multi-Health Systems.

Coon, K. B., Waguespack, M. M., & Polk, M. J. (1994). *Dyslexia screening instrument.* San Antonio, TX: Pearson.

Cooper, M. J. (2005). Cognitive theory in anorexia nervosa and bulimia nervosa: Progress, development and future directions. *Clinical Psychology Review, 25,* 511–531.

Crooks, C. V., & Wolfe, D. A. (2007). Child abuse and neglect. In E. J. Mash & R. A. Barkley (Eds.), *Assessment of childhood disorders* (4th ed., pp. 639–684). New York: Guilford.

Davidson, M. A. (2008). ADHD in adults: A review of the literature. *Journal of Attention Disorders, 11,* 628–641.

Daviss, W. B., Racusin, R., Fleischer, A., Mooney, D., Ford, J. D., & McHugo, G. J. (2000). Acute stress disorder symptomatology during hospitalization for pediatric injury. *Journal of the American Academy of Child and Adolescent Psychiatry, 39,* 569–575.

Diler, R. S., Uguz, S., Seydaoglu, G., Erol, N., & Avci, A. (2007). Differentiating bipolar disorder in Turkish prepubertal children with attention-deficit hyperactivity disorder. *Bipolar Disorders, 9,* 243–251.

Dilsaver, S. C., & Akiskal, H. S. (2004). Preschool-onset mania: Incidence, phenomenology and family history. *Journal of Affective Disorders, 82S,* S35–S43.

Duffy, A., Alda, M., Crawford, L., Milin, R., & Grof, P. (2007). The early manifestations of bipolar disorder: A longitudinal prospective study of the offspring of bipolar patients. *Bipolar Disorders, 9,* 828–838.

Dunn, L. M., & Dunn, D. M. (2006). *PPVTTM-4: Peabody picture vocabulary test,* 4th ed. Bloomington, MN: Pearson.

Durand, V. M., & Merges, E. (2009). Functional communication training to treat challenging behavior. In W. T. O'Donohue & J. E. Fisher (Eds.), *General principles and empirically supported techniques of cognitive behaviour therapy* (pp. 320–327). Hoboken, NJ: Wiley.

Eaton, W. W., Shao, H., Nestadt, G., Lee, B. H., Bienvenu, O. J., & Zandi, P. (2008). Population-based study of first onset and chronicity in major depressive disorder. *Archives of General Psychiatry, 65,* 513–520.

Eberhart, N. K., & Hammen, C. L. (2006). Interpersonal predictors of onset of depression during the transition to adulthood. *Personal Relationships, 13,* 195–206.

Eckert, M. (2004). Neuroanatomical markers for dyslexia: A review of dyslexia structural imaging studies. *The Neuroscientist, 10,* 362–371.

Edmonds, M. S., Vaughn, S., Wexler, J., Reutebuch, C., Cable, A., Tackett, K. K., & Schnakenberg, J. W. (2009). A synthesis of reading interventions and effects on reading comprehension outcomes for older struggling readers. *Review of Educational Research, 79,* 262–300.

Ehrensaft, M. K. (2005). Interpersonal relationships and sex differences in the development of conduct problems. *Clinical Child and Family Psychology Review, 8,* 39–63.

Eisen, A. R., Spasaro, S. A., Brien, L. K., Kearney, C. A., & Albano, A. M. (2004). Parental expectancies and childhood anxiety disorders: Psychometric properties of the Parental Expectancies Scale. *Journal of Anxiety Disorders, 18,* 89–109.

Eisler, I., Dare, C., Hodes, M., Russell, G., Dodge, E., & Le Grange, D. (2005). Family therapy for adolescent anorexia nervosa: The results of a controlled comparison of two family interventions. *Focus, 3,* 629–640.

Elkins, I. J., McGue, M., & Iacono, W. G. (2007). Prospective effects of attention-deficit/hyperactivity disorder, conduct disorder, and sex on adolescent substance use and abuse. *Archives of General Psychiatry, 64,* 1145–1152.

Elliot, D. L., Goldberg, L., Moe, E. L., DeFrancesco, C. A., Durham, M. B., & Hix-Small, H. (2004). Preventing substance use and disordered eating: Initial outcomes of the ATHENA (athletes targeting healthy exercise and nutrition alternatives) program. *Archives of Pediatric and Adolescent Medicine, 158,* 1043–1049.

Evans, D. W., Milanak, M. E., Medeiros, B., & Ross, J. L. (2002). Magical beliefs and rituals in young children. *Child Psychiatry and Human Development, 33,* 43–58.

Eyberg, S. M., Nelson, M. M., & Boggs, S. R. (2008). Evidence-based psychosocial treatments for children and adolescents with disruptive behavior. *Journal of Clinical Child and Adolescent Psychology, 37,* 215–237.

Eyberg, S. M., & Pincus, D. (1999). *Eyberg Child Behavior Inventory and Sutter-Eyberg Behavior Inventory-Revised: Professional manual.* Odessa, FL: Psychological Assessment Resources.

Faedda, G. L., Baldessarini, R. J., Glovinsky, I. P., & Austin, N. B. (2004). Pediatric bipolar disorder: Phenomenology and course of illness. *Bipolar Disorders, 6,* 305–313.

Fairburn, C. G., & Harrison, P. J. (2003). Eating disorders. *Lancet, 361,* 407–416.

Faller, K. C. (2005). Anatomical dolls: Their use in assessment of children who may have been sexually abused. *Journal of Child Sexual Abuse, 14,* 1–21.

Faraone, S. V., Lasky-Su, J., Glatt, S. J., Van Eerdewegh, P., & Tsuang, M. T. (2006). Early onset bipolar disorder: Possible linkage to chromosome 9q34. *Bipolar Disorders, 8,* 144–151.

Faraone, S. V., Perlis, R. H., Doyle, A. E., Smoller, J. W., Goralnick, J. J., Holmgren, M. A., & Sklar, P. (2005). Molecular genetics of attention-deficit/hyperactivity disorder. *Biological Psychiatry, 57,* 1313–1323.

Findling, R. L., & Schulz, S. C. (Eds.). (2005). *Juvenile-onset schizophrenia.*

Baltimore, MD: Johns Hopkins University Press.

Fletcher, K. E. (2003). Childhood posttraumatic stress disorder. In E. J. Mash & R. A. Barkley (Eds.), *Child psychopathology* (2nd ed., pp. 330–371). New York: Guilford.

Fox, L., Carta, J., Strain, P. S., Dunlap, G., & Hemmeter, M. L. (2010). Response to intervention and the pyramid model. *Infants and Young Children, 23,* 3–13.

Frick, P. J. (2006). Developmental pathways to conduct disorder. *Child and Adolescent Psychiatric Clinics of North America, 15,* 311–331.

Frick, P. J., Cornell, A. H., Barry, C. T., Bodin, S. D., & Dane, H. E. (2003). Callous-unemotional traits and conduct problems in the prediction of conduct problem severity, aggression, and self-report of delinquency. *Journal of Abnormal Child Psychology, 31,* 457–470.

Frick, P. J., & White, S. F. (2008). The importance of callous-unemotional traits for developmental models of aggressive and antisocial behavior. *Journal of Child Psychology and Psychiatry, 49,* 359–375.

Friedberg, R. D., McClure, J. M., & Garcia, J. H. (2009). *Cognitive therapy techniques with children and adolescents: Tools for enhancing practice.* New York: Guilford.

Garcia-Lopez, L.-J., Olivares, J., Beidel, D., Albano, A. M., Turner, S., & Rosa, A. I. (2006). Efficacy of three treatment protocols for adolescents with social anxiety disorder: A 5-year follow-up assessment. *Journal of Anxiety Disorders, 20,* 175–191.

Garner, D. M. (1997). Psychoeducational principles in treatment. In D. M. Garner & P. E. Garfinkel (Eds.), *Handbook of treatment for eating disorders* (2nd ed., pp. 145–177). New York: Guilford.

Garner, D. M., & Keiper, C. D. (2010). Anorexia and bulimia. In J. C. Thomas & M. Hersen (Eds.), *Handbook of clinical psychology competencies* (pp. 1429–1460). New York: Springer.

Garrett, A. J., Mazzocco, M. M. M., & Baker, L. (2006). Development of the metacognitive skills of prediction and evaluation in children with or without math disability. *Learning Disabilities Research and Practice, 21,* 77–88.

Geiger, T. C., & Crick, N. R. (2010). Developmental pathways to personality disorders. In R. E. Ingram & J. M. Price (Eds.), *Vulnerability to psychopathology: Risk across the lifespan* (2nd ed., pp. 57–112). New York: Guilford.

Geller, B., Craney, J. L., Bolhofner, K., DelBello, M. P., Williams, M., & Zimerman, B. (2001). One-year recovery and relapse rates of children with a prepubertal and early adolescent bipolar disorder phenotype. *American Journal of Psychiatry, 158,* 303–305.

Geller, B., & DelBello, M. P. (2003). *Bipolar disorder in childhood and early adolescence.* New York: Guilford.

Geller, B., Tillman, R., Bolhofner, K., & Zimerman, B. (2008). Child bipolar I disorder: Prospective continuity with adult bipolar I disorder; characteristics of second and third episodes; predictors of 8-year outcome. *Archives of General Psychiatry, 65,* 1125–1133.

Geller, B., Tillman, R., Craney, J. L., & Bulhofner, K. (2004). Four-year prospective outcome and natural history of mania in children with a prepubertal and early adolescent bipolar disorder phenotype. *Archives of General Psychiatry, 61,* 459–467.

Gersten, R., Fuchs, L. S., Williams, J. P., & Baker, S. (2001). Teaching reading comprehension strategies to students with learning disabilities: A review of research. *Review of Educational Research, 71*, 279–320.

Gilliam, J. E. (2002). *Conduct Disorder Scale.* Austin, TX: Pro-Ed.

Goldstein, B. I., Strober, M. A., Birmaher, B., Axelson, D. A., Esposito-Smythers, C., Goldstein, T. R., Leonard, H., Hunt, J., Gill, M. K., Iyengar, S., Grimm, C., Yang, M., Ryan, N. D., & Keller, M. B. (2008). Substance use disorders among adolescents with bipolar spectrum disorders. *Bipolar Disorders, 10*, 469–478.

Gordis, E. B., & Margolin, G. (2001). The family coding system: Studying the relation between marital conflict and family interaction. In P. K. Kerig & K. M. Lindahl (Eds.), *Family observational coding systems: Resources for systemic research* (pp. 111–125). Mahwah, NJ: Lawrence Erlbaum.

Gracious, B. L., Youngstrom, E. A., Findling, R. L., & Calabrese, J. R. (2002). Discriminative validity of a parent version of the Young Mania Rating Scale. *Journal of the American Academy of Child and Adolescent Psychiatry, 41*, 1350–1359.

Granic, I., Hollenstein, T., Dishion, T. J., & Patterson, G. R. (2003). Longitudinal analysis of flexibility and reorganization in early adolescence: A dynamic systems study of family interactions. *Developmental Psychology, 39*, 606–617.

Granic, I., & Patterson, G. R. (2006). Toward a comprehensive model of antisocial development: A dynamic systems approach. *Psychological Review, 113*, 101–131.

Gray, L. (2008). Chronic abdominal pain in children. *Australian Family Physician, 37*, 398–400.

Greimel, E., Herpertz-Dahlmann, B., Gunther, T., Vitt, C., & Konrad, K. (2008). Attentional functions in children and adolescents with attention-deficit/hyperactivity disorder with and without comorbid tic disorder. *Journal of Neural Transmission, 115*, 191–200.

Griswold, K. S., Aronoff, H., Kernan, J. B., & Kahn, L. S. (2008). Adolescent substance use and abuse: Recognition and management. *American Family Physician, 77*, 331–336.

Guarda, A. S. (2008). Treatment of anorexia nervosa: Insights and obstacles. *Physiology and Behavior, 94*, 113–120.

Hall, S. D., & Bean, R. A. (2008). Family therapy and childhood-onset schizophrenia: Pursuing clinical and bio/psycho/social competence. *Contemporary Family Therapy, 30*, 61–74.

Hammen, C., & Rudolph, K. D. (2003). Childhood mood disorders. In E. J. Mash & R. A. Barkley (Eds.), *Child psychopathology* (pp. 233–278). New York: Guilford.

Hara, H. (2007). Autism and epilepsy: A retrospective follow-up study. *Brain and Development, 29*, 486–490.

Harrison, P. L., & Oakland, T. (2003). *Adaptive behavior assessment system*, 2nd ed. San Antonio, TX: Pearson.

Hawke, J. L., Wadsworth, S. J., & DeFries, J. C. (2006). Genetic influences on reading difficulties in boys and girls: The Colorado twin study. *Dyslexia, 12*, 21–29.

Hayward, C., Wilson, K. A., Lagle, K., Kraemer, H. C., Killen, J. D., & Taylor, C. B. (2008). The developmental psychopathology of social anxiety in adolescents. *Depression and Anxiety, 25*, 200–206.

Henggeler, S. W. (2011). Efficacy studies to large-scale transport: The development and validation of multisystemic therapy programs. *Annual Review of Clinical Psychology, 7*, 351–381.

Heyman, R. E., Chaudhry, B. R., Treboux, D., Crowell, J., Lord, C., Vivian, D., & Waters, E. B. (2001). How much observational data is enough? An empirical test using marital interaction coding. *Behavior Therapy, 32,* 107–122.

Hintze, J. M., Stoner, G., & Bull, M. H. (2000). Analogue assessment: Research and practice in evaluating emotional and behavioral problems. In E. S. Shapiro & T. R. Kratochwill (Eds.), *Behavioral assessment in schools* (2nd ed., pp. 104–138). New York: Guilford.

Hirshfeld-Becker, D. R., Micco, J., Henin, A., Bloomfield, A., Biederman, J., & Rosenbaum, J. (2008). Behavioral inhibition. *Depression and Anxiety, 25,* 357–367.

Hodapp, R. M., & Dykens, E. M. (2003). Mental retardation (intellectual disabilities). In E. J. Mash & R. A. Barkley (Eds.), *Child psychopathology* (2nd ed., pp. 486–519). New York: Guilford.

Huang, C. H., & Santangelo, S. L. (2008). Autism and serotonin transporter gene polymorphisms: A systematic review and meta-analysis. *American Journal of Medical Genetics Part B, 147,* 903–913.

Hudziak, J. J. (2008). *Developmental psychopathology and wellness: Genetic and environmental influences.* Washington, DC: American Psychiatric Publishing.

Hyde, J. S., Mezulis, A. H., & Abramson, L. Y. (2008). The ABCs of depression: Integrating affective, biological, and cognitive models to explain the emergence of the gender difference in depression. *Psychological Review, 115,* 291–313.

Ivanov, I., Schulz, K. P., London, E. D., & Newcorn, J. H. (2008). Inhibitory control deficits in childhood and risk for substance use disorders: A review. *American Journal of Drug and Alcohol Abuse, 34,* 239–258.

Jaffee, S. R., Caspi, A., Moffitt, T. E., & Taylor, A. (2004). Physical maltreatment victim to antisocial child: Evidence of an environmentally mediated process. *Journal of Abnormal Psychology, 113,* 44–55.

James, R., Blair, R., Monson, J., & Frederickson, N. (2001). Moral reasoning and conduct problems in children with emotional and behavioural difficulties. *Personality and Individual Differences, 31,* 799–811.

Jarvis, P. E., & Barth, J. T. (1994). *The Halstead-Reitan neuropsychological battery: A guide to interpretation and clinical applications.* Odessa, FL: Psychological Assessment Resources.

Johnson, C. F. (2004). Child sexual abuse. *Lancet, 364,* 462–470.

Johnson, C. J., Beitchman, J. H., & Brownlie, E. B. (2010). Twenty-year follow-up of children with and without speech-language impairments: Family, educational, occupational, and quality of life outcomes. *American Journal of Speech-Language Pathology, 19,* 51–65.

Johnston, L. D., O'Malley, P. M., Bachman, J. G., & Schulenberg, J. E. (2009). *Monitoring the future: National results on adolescent drug use: Overview of key findings,* 2008. Bethesda, MD: National Institute on Drug Abuse.

Johnstone, S. J., Barry, R. J., & Clarke, A. R. (2007). Behavioural and ERP indices of response inhibition during a stop-signal task in children with two subtypes of attention-deficit hyperactivity disorder. *International Journal of Psychophysiology, 66,* 37–47.

Judd, L. L., Akiskal, H. S., Schettler, P. J., Endicott, J., Maser, J., Solomon, D. A., Leon, A. C., Rice, J. A., & Keller, M. B. (2002). The long-term natural history of the weekly symptomatic status of bipolar I disorder. *Archives of General Psychiatry, 59,* 530–537.

Kagan, J. (2001). Temperamental contributions to affective and behavioral profiles in childhood. In S. G. Hofmann & P. M. DiBartolo (Eds.), *From social* anxiety to social phobia: Multiple perspectives (pp. 216–234). Needham Heights, MA: Allyn and Bacon.

Kandel, D. B. (2003). Does marijuana use cause the use of other drugs? *Journal of the American Medical Association, 289*, 482–483.

Kapornai, K., & Vetro, A. (2008). Depression in children. *Current Opinion in Psychiatry, 21*, 1–7.

Kashdan, T. B., & Herbert, J. D. (2001). Social anxiety disorder in childhood and adolescence: Current status and future directions. *Clinical Child and Family Psychology Review, 4*, 37–61.

Kaufman, J., Birmaher, B., Brent, D., Rao, U., Flynn, C., Moreci, P., Williamson, D., & Ryan, N. (1997). Schedule for affective disorders and schizophrenia for school-aged children—Present and lifetime version (K-SADS-PL): Initial reliability and validity data. *Journal of the American Academy of Child and Adolescent Psychiatry, 36*, 980–988.

Kaufman, J., Martin, A., King, R. A., & Charney, D. (2001). Are child-, adolescent-, and adult-onset depression one and the same disorder? *Biological Psychiatry, 49*, 980–1001.

Kazak, A. E., Simms, S., & Rourke, M. T. (2002). Family systems practice in pediatric psychology. *Journal of Pediatric Psychology, 27*, 133–143.

Kearney, C. A. (2001). *School refusal behavior in youth: A functional approach to assessment and treatment*. Washington, DC: American Psychiatric Association.

Kearney, C. A. (2005). *Social anxiety and social phobia in youth: Characteristics, assessment, and psychological treatment*. New York: Springer.

Kearney, C. A. (2006). Confirmatory factor analysis of the School Refusal Assessment Scale-Revised: Child and parent versions. *Journal of Psychopathology and Behavioral Assessment, 28*, 139–144.

Kearney, C. A. (2007). Forms and functions of school refusal behavior in youth: An empirical analysis of absenteeism severity. *Journal of Child Psychology and Psychiatry, 48*, 53–61.

Kearney, C. A. (2008). School absenteeism and school refusal behavior in youth: A contemporary review. *Clinical Psychology Review, 28*, 451–471.

Kearney, C. A., & Albano, A. M. (2007). *When children refuse school: A cognitive-behavioral therapy approach/therapist's guide* (2nd ed.). New York: Oxford University Press.

Kearney, C. A., & Drake, K. (2002). Social phobia. In M. Hersen (Ed.), *Clinical behavior therapy: Adults and children* (pp. 326–344). New York: Wiley.

Kearney, C. A., & Vecchio, J. (2002). Contingency management. In M. Hersen & W. Sledge (Eds.), *The encyclopedia of psychotherapy*. New York: Academic.

Kearney, C. A., Wechsler, A., Kaur, H., & Lemos-Miller, A. (2010). Posttraumatic stress disorder in maltreated youth: A review of contemporary research and thought. *Clinical Child and Family Psychology Review, 13*, 46–76.

Kessler, R. C., Adler, L. A., Barkley, R., Biederman, J., Conners, C. K., Faraone, S. V., Greenhill, L. L., Jaeger, S., Secnik, K., Spencer, T., Ustun, T. B., & Zaslavsky, A. M. (2005). Patterns and predictors of attention-deficit/hyperactivity disorder persistence into adulthood: Results from the national comorbidity survey replication. *Biological Psychiatry, 57*, 1442–1451.

Kessler, R. C., Berglund, P., Demler, O., Jin, R., Merikangas, K. R., & Walters, E. E. (2005). Lifetime prevalence and age-of-onset distributions of DSM-IV disorders in the national comorbidity survey replication. *Archives of General Psychiatry, 62,* 593–602.

Key, J. D., Brown, R. T., Marsh, L. D., Spratt, E. G., & Recknor, J. C. (2001). Depressive symptoms in adolescents with a chronic illness. *Children's Health Care, 30,* 283–292.

Khouzam, H. R., El-Gabalawi, F., Pirwani, N., & Priest, F. (2004). Asperger's disorder: A review of its diagnosis and treatment. *Comprehensive Psychiatry, 45,* 184–191.

Kieling, C., Goncalves, R. R., Tannock, R., & Castellanos, F. X. (2008). Neurobiology of attention deficit hyperactivity disorder. *Child and Adolescent Psychiatric Clinics of North America, 17,* 285–307.

Kloos, A., Weller, E. B., & Weller, R. A. (2008). Biologic basis of bipolar disorder in children and adolescents. *Current Psychiatry Reports, 10,* 98–103.

Knappe, S., Lieb, R., Beesdo, K., Fehm, L., Low, N. C. P., Gloster, A. T., & Wittchen, H.-U. (2009). The role of parental psychopathology and family environment for social phobia in the first three decades of life. *Depression and Anxiety, 26,* 363–370.

Konarski, J. Z., McIntyre, R. S., Kennedy, S. H., Rafi-Tari, S., Soczynska, J. K., & Ketter, T. A. (2008). Volumetric neuroimaging investigations in mood disorders: Bipolar disorder versus major depressive disorder. *Bipolar Disorders, 10,* 1–37.

Koopman, H. M., Baars, R. M., Chaplin, J., & Zwinderman, K. H. (2004). Illness through the eyes of the child: The development of children's understanding of the causes of illness. *Patient Education and Counseling, 55,* 363–370.

Kovacs, M. (2003). *Children's Depression Inventory (CDI): Technical manual update.* North Tonawanda, NY: Multi-Health Systems.

Kowatch, R. A., Youngstrom, E. A., Danielyan, A., & Findling, R. L. (2005). Review and meta-analysis of the phenomenology and clinical characteristics of mania in children and adolescents. *Bipolar Disorders, 7,* 483–496.

Kress, V. E., Hoffman, R., & Thomas, A. M. (2008). Letters from the future: The use of therapeutic letter writing in counseling sexual abuse survivors. *Journal of Creativity in Mental Health, 3,* 105–118.

Kroner-Herwig, B., Morris, L., & Heinrich, M. (2008). Biopsychosocial correlates of headache: What predicts pediatric headache occurrence? *Headache, 48,* 529–544.

Krug, D. A., Arick, J. R., & Almond, P. J. (2008). *Autism screening instrument for educational planning (ASIEP-3).* Austin, TX: Pro-Ed.

Kupka, R. W., Luckenbaugh, D. A., Post, R. M., Leverich, G. S., & Nolen, W. A. (2003). Rapid and non-rapid cycling bipolar disorder: A meta-analysis of clinical studies. *Journal of Clinical Psychiatry, 64,* 1483–1494.

Lachar, D., & Gruber, C. P. (2000). *Personality Inventory for Children-second edition (PIC-2) manual.* Los Angeles, CA: Western Psychological Services.

La Greca, A. M. (1998). *Social anxiety scales for children and adolescents: Manual and instructions for the SASC, SASC-R, SAS-A (adolescents), and parent versions of the scales.* Miami, FL: Author.

Lahey, B. B., Loeber, R., Burke, J. D., & Applegate, B. (2005). Predicting future antisocial personality disorder in males from a clinical assessment in childhood. *Journal of Consulting and Clinical Psychology, 73,* 389–399.

Lanktree, C. B., Gilbert, A. M., Briere, J., Taylor, N., Chen, K., Maida, C. A., & Saltzman, W. R. (2008). Multi-informant assessment of maltreated children: Convergent and discriminant validity of the TSCC and TSCYC. *Child Abuse and Neglect, 32,* 621–625.

Larson, K., Russ, S. A., Kahn, R. S., & Halfon, N. (2011). Patterns of comorbidity, functioning, and service use of US children with ADHD, 2007. *Pediatrics, 127,* 462–470.

Laszloffy, T. A. (2002). Rethinking family development theory: Teaching with the systemic family development (SFD) model. *Family Relations, 51,* 206–214.

Legenbauer, T., Vogele, C., & Ruddel, H. (2004). Anticipatory effects of food exposure in women diagnosed with bulimia nervosa. *Appetite, 42,* 33–40.

Lehn, H., Derks, E. M., Hudziak, J. J., Heutink, P., van Beijsterveldt, T. C. E. M., & Boomsma, D. I. (2007). Attention problems and attention-deficit/hyperactivity disorder in discordant and concordant monozygotic twins: Evidence of environmental mediators. *Journal of the American Academy of Child and Adolescent Psychiatry, 46,* 83–91.

Leibenluft, E., & Rich, B. A. (2008). Pediatric bipolar disorder. *Annual Review of Clinical Psychology, 4,* 163–187.

Lejuez, C. W., Hopko, D. R., Acierno, R., Daughters, S. B., & Pagoto, S. L. (2011). Ten year revision of the brief behavioral activation treatment for depression: Revised treatment manual. *Behavior Modification, 35,* 111–161.

Leonard, B. E., McCarten, D., White, J., & King, D. J. (2004). Methylphenidate: A review of its neuropharmacological, neuropsychological and adverse clinical effects. *Human Psychopharmacology: Clinical and Experimental, 19,* 151–180.

Leskela, J., Dieperink, M., & Thuras, P. (2002). Shame and posttraumatic stress disorder. *Journal of Traumatic Stress, 15,* 223–226.

Leskovec, T. J., Rowles, B. M., & Findling, R. L. (2008). Pharmacological treatment options for autism spectrum disorders in children and adolescents. *Harvard Review of Psychiatry, 16,* 97–112.

Levy, P. A. (2009). Inborn errors of metabolism: Part 1: Overview. *Pediatrics in Review, 30,* 131–138.

Li, C., Pentz, M. A., & Chou, C. P. (2002). Parental substance use as a modifier of adolescent substance use risk. *Addiction, 97,* 1537–1550.

Luby, J., & Belden, A. (2006). Defining and validating bipolar disorder in the preschool period. *Development and Psychopathology, 18,* 971–988.

Luby, J. L., Heffelfinger, A. K., Mrakotsky, C., Brown, K. M., Hessler, M. J., Wallis, J. M., & Spitznagel, E. L. (2003). The clinical picture of depression in preschool children. *Journal of the American Academy of Child and Adolescent Psychiatry, 42,* 340–348.

Lyon, G. R., Fletcher, J. M., & Barnes, M. C. (2003). Learning disabilities. In E. J. Mash & R. A. Barkley (Eds.), *Child psychopathology* (2nd ed., pp. 520–586). New York: Guilford.

Maia, A. P., Boarati, M. A., Kleinman, A., & Fu-I, L. (2007). Preschool bipolar disorder: Brazilian children case reports. *Journal of Affective Disorders, 104,* 237–243.

Malone, P. S., Lamis, D. A., Masyn, K. E., & Northrup, T. F. (2010). A dual-process discrete-time survival analysis model: Application to the gateway drug hypothesis. *Multivariate Behavioral Research, 45,* 790–805.

March, J. (1997). *Multidimensional Anxiety Scale for Children.* North Tonawanda, NY: Multi-Health Systems.

March, J. S., Silva, S., Petrycki, S., Curry, J., Wells, K., Fairbank, J., Burns, B., Domino, M., McNulty, S., Vitiello, B., & Severe, J. (2007). The treatment for adolescents with depression study

(TADS): Long-term effectiveness and safety outcomes. *Archives of General Psychiatry, 64,* 1132–1143.

Martin, C. L., & Ruble, D. (2004). Children's search for gender cues: Cognitive perspectives on gender development. *Current Directions in Psychological Science, 13,* 67–70.

Martinez-Gonzalez, M. A., Gual, P., Lahortiga, F., Alonso, Y., de Irala-Estevez, J., & Cervera, S. (2003). Parental factors, mass media influences, and the onset of eating disorders in a prospective population-based cohort. *Pediatrics, 111,* 315–320.

Mash, E. J., & Dozois, D. J. A. (2003). Child psychopathology: A developmental-systems perspective. In E. J. Mash & R. A. Barkley (Eds.), *Child psychopathology* (2nd ed., pp. 3–71). New York: Guilford.

Masi, G., Perugi, G., Millepiedi, S., Mucci, M., Toni, C., Bertini, N., Pfanner, C., Berloffa, S., & Pari, C. (2006). Developmental differences according to age at onset in juvenile bipolar disorder. *Journal of Child and Adolescent Psychopharmacology, 16,* 679–685.

Matsui, D. (2007). Current issues in pediatric medication adherence. *Paediatric Drugs, 9,* 283–288.

Matthys, W., & Lochman, J. E. (2010). *Oppositional defiant disorder and conduct disorder in children.* Malden, MA: Wiley.

Mayes, S. D., Calhoun, S. L., Murray, M. J., Morrow, J. D., Yurich, K. K. L., Mahr, F., Cothren, S., Purichia, H., Bouder, J.N., & Petersen, C. (2009). Comparison of scores on the checklist for autism spectrum disorder, childhood autism rating scale, and Gilliam Asperger's disorder scale for children with low functioning autism, high functioning autism, Asperger's disorder, ADHD, and typical development.

Journal of Autism and Developmental Disorders, 39, 1682–1693.

McCloskey, L. A., & Lichter, E. L. (2003). The contribution of marital violence to adolescent aggression across different relationships. *Journal of Interpersonal Violence, 18,* 390–412.

McDermott, S., Durkin, M. S., Schupf, N., & Stein, Z. A. (2007). Epidemiology and etiology of mental retardation. In J. W. Jacobsen, J. A. Mulick, & J. Rojahn (Eds.), *Handbook of intellectual and developmental disabilities* (pp. 3–40). New York: Springer.

McIntosh, V. V. W., Carter, F. A., Bulik, C. M., Frampton, C. M. A., & Joyce, P. R. (2011). Five-year outcome of cognitive behavioral therapy and exposure with response prevention for bulimia nervosa. *Psychological Medicine, 41,* 1061–1071.

McQuaid, E. L., Howard, K., Kopel, S. J., Rosenblum, K., & Bibace, R. (2002). Developmental concepts of asthma: Reasoning about illness and strategies for prevention. *Applied Developmental Psychology, 23,* 179–194.

Mehl, R. C., O'Brien, L. M., Jones, J. H., Dreisbach, J. K., Mervis, C. B., & Gozal, D. (2006). Correlates of sleep and pediatric bipolar disorder. *Sleep, 29,* 193–197.

Merline, A. C., O'Malley, P. M., Schulenberg, J. E., Bachman, J. G., & Johnston, L. D. (2004). Substance use among adults 35 years of age: Prevalence, adulthood predictors, and impact of adolescent substance use. *American Journal of Public Health, 94,* 96–102.

Miklowitz, D. J., & Cicchetti, D. (2006). Toward a life span developmental psychopathology perspective on bipolar disorder. *Development and Psychopathology, 18,* 935–938.

Miklowitz, D. J., & Cicchetti, D. (Eds.). (2010). *Understanding bipolar disorder:*

A developmental psychopathology perspective. New York: Guilford.

Miller, G. A. (2001). *Adolescent SASSI-A2 Substance Abuse Subtle Screening Inventory*. Springville, IN: SASSI Institute.

Miller-Perrin, C. L., & Perrin, R. D. (2007). *Child maltreatment: An introduction* (2nd ed.). Thousand Oaks, CA: Sage.

Millon, T., Green, C. J., & Meagher, R. B. (1993). *Millon Adolescent Personality Inventory*. Minneapolis, MN: NCS Assessments.

Monahon, C. (1993). *Children and trauma: A parent's guide to helping children heal*. New York: Lexington.

Moos, R. H., & Moos, B. S. (1986). *Family Environment Scale manual* (2nd ed.). Palo Alto, CA: Consulting Psychologists Press.

Muck, R., Zempolich, K. A., Titus, J. C., Fishman, M., Godley, M. D., & Schwebel, R. (2001). An overview of the effectiveness of adolescent substance abuse treatment models. *Youth and Society, 33*, 143–168.

Mufson, L., Dorta, K. P., Wickramaratne, P., Nomura, Y., Olfson, M., & Weissman, M. M. (2004). A randomized effectiveness trial of interpersonal psychotherapy for depressed adolescents. *Archives of General Psychiatry, 61*, 577–584.

Muhle, R., Trentacoste, S. V., & Rapin, I. (2004). The genetics of autism. *Pediatrics, 113*, e472–486.

Murray, R. M., Lappin, J., & Di Forti, M. (2008). Schizophrenia: From developmental deviance to dopamine dysregulation. *European Neuropsychopharmacology, 18*, S129–S134.

Nelson, H. D., Nygren, P., Walker, M., & Panoscha, R. (2006). Screening for speech and language delay in preschool children: Systematic evidence review for the US preventive services task force. *Pediatrics, 117*, e298–e319.

Newberg, A. R., Catapano, L. A., Zarate, C. A., & Manji, H. K. (2008). Neurobiology of bipolar disorder. *Expert Review of Neurotherapeutics, 8*, 93–110.

Newman, B., Reinecke, D., & Ramos, M. (2009). Is a reasonable attempt reasonable? Shaping versus reinforcing verbal attempts of preschoolers with autism. *Analysis of Verbal Behavior, 25*, 67–72.

Nigg, J. T., Goldsmith, H. H., & Sachek, J. (2004). Temperament and attention deficit hyperactivity disorder: The development of a multiple pathway model. *Journal of Clinical Child and Adolescent Psychology, 33*, 42–53.

Nihira, K., Leland, H., & Lambert, N. (1993). *AAMR Adaptive Behavior Scale—Residential and Community* (2nd ed.). Austin, TX: Pro-Ed.

Nobile, M., Cataldo, G., Marino, C., & Molteni, M. (2003). Diagnosis and treatment of dysthymia in children and adolescents. *CNS Drugs, 17*, 927–946.

Odgers, C. L., Caspi, A., Broadbent, J. M., Dickson, N., Hancox, R. J., Harrington, H., Poulton, R., Sears, M. R., Thomson, W. M., & Moffitt, T. E. (2007). Prediction of differential adult health burden by conduct problem subtypes in males. *Archives of General Psychiatry, 64*, 476–484.

Olfson, M. (2004). New options on the pharmacological management of attention-deficit/hyperactivity disorder. *American Journal of Managed Care, 10*, S117–S124.

Olson, D. H., Portner, J., & Lavee, Y. (1987). Family Adaptability and Cohesion Evaluation Scales (FACES III). In N. Fredman & R. Sherman (Eds.), *Handbook of measurements for marriage and family therapy* (pp. 180–185). New York: Brunner Mazel.

Olsson, M., Hansson, K., & Cederblad, M. (2008). A follow-up study of adolescents with conduct disorder: Can long-term outcome be predicted from psychiatric assessment data? *Nordic Journal of Psychiatry, 62,* 121–129.

Orth, U., Robins, R. W., & Roberts, B. W. (2008). Low self-esteem prospectively predicts depression in adolescence and young adulthood. *Journal of Personality and Social Psychology, 95,* 695–708.

Papadopoulos, F. C., Ekbom, A., Brandt, L., & Ekselius, L. (2009). Excess mortality, causes of death and prognostic factors in anorexia nervosa. *British Journal of Psychiatry, 194,* 10–17.

Paul, I., Bott, C., Heim, S., Eulitz, C., & Elbert, T. (2006). Reduced hemispheric asymmetry of the auditory n260m in dyslexia. *Neuropsychologia, 44,* 785–794.

Pavuluri, M. N., Birmaher, B., & Naylor, M. W. (2005). Pediatric bipolar disorder: A review of the past 10 years. *Journal of the American Academy of Child and Adolescent Psychiatry, 44,* 846–871.

Perlis, R. H., Miyahara, S., Marangell, L. B., Wisniewski, S. R., Ostacher, M., DelBello, M. P., Bowden, C. L., Sachs, G. S., & Nierenberg, A. A. (2004). Long-term implications of early onset in bipolar disorder: Data from the first 1000 participants in the systematic treatment enhancement program for bipolar disorder (STEP-BD). *Biological Psychiatry, 55,* 875–881.

Piers, E. V., Harris, D. B., & Herzberg, D. S. (2002). *Piers-Harris Children's Self-Concept Scale (PHCSCS-2)* (2nd ed.) Austin, TX: Pro-Ed.

Pliszka, S. R. (2005). The neuropsychopharmacology of attention deficit/hyperactivity disorder. *Biological Psychiatry, 57,* 1385–1390.

Papolos, D., Hennen, J., Cockerham, M. S., Thode, H. C., & Youngstrom, E. A. (2006). The child bipolar questionnaire: A dimensional approach to screening for pediatric bipolar disorder. *Journal of Affective Disorders, 95,* 149–158.

Poulin, F., & Dishion, T. J. (2008). Methodological issues in the use of peer sociometric nominations with middle school youth. *Social Development, 17,* 908.

Pratt, H. D., & Patel, D. R. (2007). Learning disorders in children and adolescents. *Primary Care, 34,* 361–374.

Quay, H. C., & Peterson, D. R. (1996). *Revised behavior problem checklist: PAR edition.* Odessa, FL: Psychological Assessment Resources.

Raine, A. (2002). The role of prefrontal deficits, low autonomic arousal, and early health factors in the development of antisocial and aggressive behavior in children. *Journal of Child Psychology and Psychiatry, 43,* 417–434.

Ramus, F. (2004). Neurobiology of dyslexia: A reinterpretation of the data. *Trends in Neurosciences, 27,* 720–726.

Rapoff, M. A. (2006). Management of adherence and chronic rheumatic disease in children and adolescents. *Best Practice and Research Clinical Rheumatology, 20,* 301–314.

Raven, J. C. (2000). *Raven's progressive matrices.* San Antonio, TX: Harcourt.

Remschmidt, H., & Global ADHD Working Group. (2005). Global consensus on ADHD/HKD. *European Child and Adolescent Psychiatry, 14,* 127–137.

Reyes, J. C., Robles, R. R., Colon, H. M., Negron, J. L., Matos, T. D., & Calderon, J. M. (2011). Polydrug use and attempted suicide among Hispanic adolescents in Puerto Rico. *Archives of Suicide Research, 15,* 151–159.

Reynolds, C. R., & Kamphaus, R. W. (2004). *Behavior assessment system for children-2.* Circle Pines, MN: American Guidance Service.

Reynolds, W. M. (2004). *Reynolds Adolescent Depression Scale-2: Professional manual.* Lutz, FL: Psychological Assessment Resources.

Rice, M. L., Warren, S. F., & Betz, S. K. (2005). Language symptoms of developmental language disorders: An overview of autism, down syndrome, fragile X, specific language impairment, and Williams syndrome. *Applied Psycholinguistics, 26,* 7–27.

Robin, A. L., & Foster, S. L. (2002). *Negotiating parent-adolescent conflict: A behavioral-family systems approach.* New York: Guilford.

Rodenburg, R., Meijer, A. M., Dekovic, M., & Aldenkamp, A. P. (2007). Parents of children with enduring epilepsy: Predictors of parenting stress and parenting. *Epilepsy and Behavior, 11,* 197–207.

Rogers, G., Joyce, P., Mulder, R., Sellman, D., Miller, A., Allington, M., Olds, R., Wells, E., & Kennedy, M. (2004). Association of a duplicated repeat polymorphism in the 5'-untranslated region of the DRD4 gene with novelty seeking. *American Journal of Medical Genetics Part B, 126,* 95–98.

Roid, G. (2003). *Stanford-Binet Intelligence Scales* (5th ed.). Chicago, IL: Riverside.

Roid, G., & Miller, L. J. (1997). *Leiter International Performance Scale-revised.* Wood Dale, IL: Stoelting.

Rosen, D. S. (2010). Clinical report—Identification and management of eating disorders in children and adolescents. *Pediatrics, 126,* 1240–1253.

Rubin, K. H., Burgess, K. B., Kennedy, A. E., & Stewart, S. L. (2003). Social withdrawal in childhood. In E. J. Mash & R. A. Barkley (Eds.), *Child psychopathology* (2nd ed., pp. 372–406). New York: Guilford.

Rucklidge, J. J. (2008). Retrospective parent report of psychiatric histories: Do checklists reveal specific prodromal indicators for postpubertal-onset pediatric bipolar disorder? *Bipolar Disorders, 10,* 56–66.

Rushton, J. L., Forcier, M., & Schectman, R. M. (2002). Epidemiology of depressive symptoms in the national longitudinal study of adolescent health. *Journal of the American Academy of Child and Adolescent Psychiatry, 41,* 199–205.

Sanna, K., Pollock-Wurman, R., Ebeling, H., Hurtig, T., Joskitt, L., Mattila, M.-L., Jussila, K., & Moilanen, I. (2009). Psychometric Evaluation of Social Phobia and Anxiety Inventory for Children (SPAI-C) and Social Anxiety Scale for Children-Revised (SASC-R). *European Child and Adolescent Psychiatry, 18,* 116–124.

Sawyer, M. G., Whitham, J. N., Roberton, D. M., Taplin, J. E., Varni, J. W., & Baghurst, P. A. (2004). The relationship between health-related quality of life, pain and coping strategies in juvenile idiopathic arthritis. *Rheumatology, 43,* 325–330.

Scahill, L., Riddle, M., McSwiggin-Hardin, M., Ort, S., King, R., Goodman, W., Cicchetti, D., & Leckman, J. (1997). Children's Yale-Brown Obsessive Compulsive Scale: Reliability and Validity. *Journal of the American Academy of Child and Adolescent Psychiatry, 36,* 844–852.

Schaefer, C. E., & Kaduson, H. G. (Eds.). (2007). *Contemporary play therapy: Theory, research, and practice.* New York: Guilford.

Scharff, L., & Simons, L. E. (2008). Functional abdominal pain. In G. A. Walco & K. R. Goldschneider (Eds.), *Pain in children: A practical guide for primary care* (pp. 163–171). Totowa, NJ: Humana.

Schatschneider, C., Wagner, R. K., & Crawford, E. C. (2008). The importance of measuring growth in response to intervention models: Testing a core assumption. *Learning and Individual Differences, 18,* 308–315.

Schenkel, L. S., West, A. E., Harral, E. M., Patel, N. B., & Pavuluri, M. N. (2008). Parent-child interactions in pediatric bipolar disorder. *Journal of Clinical Psychology, 64,* 422–437.

Schepis, T. S., Adinoff, B., & Rao, U. (2008). Neurobiological processes in adolescent addictive disorders. *American Journal of Addiction, 17,* 6–23.

Schiavenato, M. (2008). Facial expression and pain assessment in the pediatric patient: The primal face of pain. *Journal for Specialists in Pediatric Nursing, 13,* 89–97.

Schiffman, J., Sorensen, H. J., Maeda, J., Mortensen, E. L., Victoroff, J., Hayashi, K., Michelsen, N. M., Ekstrom, M., & Mednick, S. (2009). Childhood motor coordination and adult schizophrenia spectrum disorders. *American Journal of Psychiatry, 166,* 1041–1047.

Schopler, E., Reichler, R., & Renner, B. (1988). *The Childhood Autism Rating Scale (CARS).* Los Angeles, CA: Western Psychological Services.

Schoppe, S. J., Mangelsdorf, S. C., & Frosch, C. A. (2001). Coparenting, family process, and family structure: Implications for preschoolers' externalizing behavior problems. *Journal of Family Psychology, 15,* 526–545.

Schrimsher, G. W., Billingsley, R. L., Jackson, E. F., & Moore, B. D. (2002). Caudate nucleus volume asymmetry predicts attention-deficit hyperactivity disorder (ADHD) symptomatology in children. *Journal of Child Neurology, 17,* 877–884.

Schweinsburg, A. D., Schweinsburg, B. C., Nagel, B. J., Eyler, L. T., & Tapert, S. F. (2011). Neural correlates of verbal learning in adolescent alcohol and marijuana users. *Addiction, 106,* 564–573.

Shalev, R. S. (2004). Developmental dyscalculia. *Journal of Child Neurology, 19,* 765–771.

Shastry, B. S. (2007). Developmental dyslexia: An update. *Journal of Human Genetics, 52,* 104–109.

Shaywitz, S. E., & Shaywitz, B. A. (2005). Dyslexia (specific reading disability). *Biological Psychiatry, 57,* 1301–1309.

Shiels, K., & Hawk, L. W. (2010). Self-regulation of ADHD: The role of error processing. *Clinical Psychology Review, 30,* 951–961.

Shih, R. A., Belmonte, P. L., & Zandi, P. P. (2004). A review of the evidence from family, twin and adoption studies for a genetic contribution to adult psychiatric disorders. *International Review of Psychiatry, 16,* 260–283.

Shiner, R. L. (2005). A developmental perspective on personality disorders: Lessons from research on normal personality development in childhood and adolescence. *Journal of Personality Disorders, 19,* 202–210.

Silani, G., Frith, U., Demonet, J. F., Fazio, F., Perani, D., Price, C., Frith, C. D., & Paulesu, E. (2005). Brain abnormalities underlying altered activation in dyslexia: A voxel based morphometry study. *Brain, 128,* 2453–2461.

Silverman, W. K., & Albano, A. M. (1996). *Anxiety disorders interview schedule for DSM-IV: Child version.* San Antonio, TX: The Psychological Corporation.

Silverman, W. K., Saavedra, L. M., & Pina, A. A. (2001). Test-retest reliability of anxiety symptoms and diagnoses with the anxiety disorders interview schedule for DSM-IV: Child and parent versions. *Journal of the American Academy of Child and Adolescent Psychiatry, 40*, 937–944.

Simons-Morton, B., Haynie, D. L., Crump, A. D., Eitel, P., & Saylor, K. E. (2001). Peer and parent influences on smoking and drinking among early adolescents. *Health Education and Behavior, 28*, 95–107.

Singh, S. P. (2007). Outcome measures in early psychosis: Relevance of duration of untreated psychosis. *British Journal of Psychiatry, 50*, s58–s63.

Skinner, H., Steinhauer, P., & Sitarenios, G. (2000). Family assessment measure (FAM) and process model of family functioning. *Journal of Family Therapy, 22*, 190–210.

Snowling, M. J., & Hulme, C. (2011). Evidence-based interventions for reading and language difficulties: Creating a virtuous circle. *British Journal of Educational Psychology, 81*, 1–23.

Spanier, G. (2001). *Dyadic Adjustment Scale*. North Tonawanda, NY: Multi-Health Systems.

Sparrow, S. S., Cicchetti, D. V., & Balla, D. A. (2005). *Vineland Adaptive Behavior Scales-second edition*. Bloomington, MN: Pearson.

Spence, S. H., & Reinecke, M. A. (2004). Cognitive approaches to understanding, preventing and treating child and adolescent depression. In M. A. Reinecke & D. A. Clark (Eds.), *Cognitive therapy across the lifespan* (pp. 358–395). New York: Cambridge University Press.

Steele, M. M., & Doey, T. (2007). Suicidal behaviour in children and adolescents. Part 1: Etiology and risk factors. *Canadian Journal of Psychiatry, 52*(6), 21S–33S.

Stein, D., Kaye, W. H., Matsunaga, H., Orbach, I., Har-Even, D., Frank, G., McConaha, C. W., & Rao, R.

(2002). Eating-related concerns, mood, and personality traits in recovered bulimia nervosa subjects: A replication study. *International Journal of Eating Disorders, 32*, 225–229.

Stein, M. B., & Stein, D. J. (2008). Social anxiety disorder. *Lancet, 371*, 1115–1125.

Sturge-Apple, M. L., Davies, P. T., & Cummings, E. M. (2010). Typologies of family functioning and children's adjustment during the early school years. *Child Development, 81*, 1320–1335.

Tavkar, P., & Hansen, D. J. (2011). Interventions for families victimized by child sexual abuse: Clinical issues and approaches for child advocacy center-based services. *Aggression and Violent Behavior, 16*, 188–199.

Thorell, L. B., & Wahlstedt, C. (2006). Executive functioning deficits in relation to symptoms of ADHD and/or ODD in preschool children. *Infant and Child Development, 15*, 503–518.

Thurber, S., Hollingsworth, D. R., & Miller, L. (1996). The Hopelessness Scale for Children: Psychometric properties with hospitalized adolescents. *Journal of Clinical Psychology, 52*, 543–545.

Tims, F. M., Dennis, M. L., Hamilton, N., Buchan, B. J., Diamond, G., Funk, R., & Brantley, L. B. (2002). Characteristics and problems of 600 adolescent cannabis abusers in outpatient treatment. *Addiction, 97* (Suppl 1), 46–57

Todd, R. D., Huang, H., Todorov, A. A., Neuman, R. J., Reiersen, A. M., Henderson, C. A., & Reich, W. C. (2008). Predictors of stability of attention-deficit/hyperactivity disorder subtypes from childhood to young adulthood. *Journal of the American Academy of Child and Adolescent Psychiatry, 47*, 76–85.

Tompson, M. C., Pierre, C. B., Boger, K. D., McKowen, J. W., Chan, P. T., & Freed, R. D. (2010). Maternal depression, maternal expressed emotion, and youth psychopathology. *Journal of Abnormal Child Psychology, 38,* 105–117.

Toriello, H. V. (2008). Role of the dysmorphologic evaluation in the child with developmental delay. *Pediatric Clinics of North America, 55,* 1085–1098.

Toumbourou, J. W., Stockwell, T., Neighbors, C., Marlatt, G. A., Sturge, J., & Rehm, J. (2007). Interventions to reduce harm associated with adolescent substance use. *Lancet, 369,* 1391–1401.

Treasure, J., Sepulveda, A. R., MacDonald, P., Whitaker, W., Lopez, C., Zabala, M., Kyriacou, O., & Todd, G. (2008). The assessment of the family of people with eating disorders. *European Eating Disorders Review, 16,* 247–255.

Troisi, A., Massaroni, P., & Cuzzolaro, M. (2005). Early separation anxiety and adult attachment style in women with eating disorders. *British Journal of Clinical Psychology, 44,* 89–97.

Tull, M. T., Gratz, K. L., Salters, K., & Roemer, L. (2004). The role of experiential avoidance in posttraumatic stress symptoms and symptoms of depression, anxiety, and somatization. *Journal of Nervous and Mental Disease, 192,* 754–761.

Vakalahi, H. F. (2001). Adolescent substance use and family-based risk and protective factors: A literature review. *Journal of Drug Education, 31,* 29–46.

Vargas, D. L., Nascimbene, C., Krishnan, C., Zimmerman, A. W., & Pardo, C. A. (2005). Neuroglial activation and neuroinflammation in the brains of patients with autism. *Annals of Neurology, 57,* 67–81.

Vervaet, M., Audenaert, K., & van Heeringen, C. (2003). Cognitive and behavioural characteristics are associated with personality dimensions in patients with eating disorders. *European Eating Disorders Review, 11,* 363–378.

Vismara, L. A., & Rogers, S. J. (2010). Behavioral treatments in autism spectrum disorder: What do we know? *Annual Review of Clinical Psychology, 6,* 447–468.

Walters, G. D. (2002). The heritability of alcohol abuse and dependence: A meta-analysis of behavior genetic research. *American Journal of Drug and Alcohol Abuse, 28,* 557–584.

Warden, D., & MacKinnon, S. (2003). Prosocial children, bullies and victims: An investigation of their sociometric status, empathy and social problem-solving strategies. *British Journal of Developmental Psychology, 21,* 367–385.

Warner, T. D., Behnke, M., Eyler, F. D., & Szabo, N. J. (2011). Early adolescent cocaine use as determined by hair analysis in a prenatal cocaine exposure cohort. *Neurotoxicology and Teratology, 33,* 88–99.

Watts, M. (2007). High expressed emotion, severe mental illness and substance use disorder. *British Journal of Nursing, 16,* 1259–1262.

Wechsler, D. (2002). *Wechsler Preschool and Primary Scale of Intelligence-third edition.* San Antonio, TX: The Psychological Corporation.

Wechsler, D. (2003). *Wechsler Intelligence Scale for Children-fourth edition integrated.* San Antonio, TX: Psychological Corporation.

Weiss, M., Worling, D., & Wasdell, M. (2003). A chart review study of the inattentive and combined types of ADHD. *Journal of Attention Disorders, 7,* 1–9.

Welham, J., Isohanni, M., Jones, P., & McGrath, J. (2009). The antecedents of schizophrenia: A review of birth cohort studies. *Schizophrenia Bulletin, 35,* 603–623.

Weller, E. B., Calvert, S. M., & Weller, R. A. (2003). Bipolar disorder in children and adolescents: Diagnosis and treatment. *Current Opinion in Psychiatry, 16,* 383–388.

Weller, E. B., Weller, R. A., Fristad, M. A., Rooney, M. T., & Schecter, J. (2000). Children's interview for psychiatric syndromes (ChIPS). *Journal of the American Academy of Child and Adolescent Psychiatry, 39,* 76–84.

Whitaker, D. J., Le, B., Hanson, R. K., Baker, C. K., McMahon, P. M., Ryan, G., Klein, A., & Rice, D. D. (2008). Risk factors for the perpetration of child sexual abuse: A review and meta-analysis. *Child Abuse and Neglect, 32,* 529–548.

White, W., & Savage, B. (2005). All in the family: Alcohol and other drug problems, recovery, advocacy. *Alcoholism Treatment Quarterly, 23,* 3–37.

Wilens, T. E. (2007). The nature of the relationship between attention-deficit/hyperactivity disorder and substance use. *Journal of Clinical Psychiatry, 68*(Suppl 11), 4–8

Wilens, T. E., Biederman, J., Brown, S., Tanguay, S., Monuteaux, M. C., Blake, C., & Spencer, T. J. (2002). Psychiatric comorbidity and functioning in clinically referred preschool children and school-age youths with ADHD. *Journal of the American Academy of Child and Adolescent Psychiatry, 41,* 262–268.

Wilens, T. E., Biederman, J., Forkner, P., Ditterline, J., Morris, M., Moore, H., Galdo, M., Spencer, T. J., & Wozniak, J. (2003). Patterns of comorbidity and dysfunction in clinically referred preschool and school-age children with bipolar disorder. *Journal of Child and Adolescent Psychopharmacology, 13,* 495–505.

Wilkinson, G. S., & Robertson, G. J. (2006). *Wide range achievement test 4.* Lutz, FL: Psychological Assessment Resources.

Willoughby, M. T. (2003). Developmental course of ADHD symptomatology during the transition from childhood to adolescence: A review with recommendations. *Journal of Child Psychology and Psychiatry, 44,* 88–106.

Wilson, C. T., Fairburn, C. C., Agras, W. S., Walsh, B. T., & Kraemer, H. (2002). Cognitive-behavioral therapy for bulimia nervosa: Time course and mechanisms of change. *Journal of Consulting and Clinical Psychology, 70,* 267–274.

Wilson, G. T., Becker, C. B., & Heffernan, K. (2003). Eating disorders. In E. J. Mash & R. A. Barkley (Eds.), *Child psychopathology* (2nd ed., pp. 687–715). New York: Guilford.

Wilson, S. T., Stanley, B., Oquendo, M. A., Goldberg, P., Zalsman, G., & Mann, J. J. (2007). Comparing impulsiveness, hostility, and depression in borderline personality disorder and bipolar II disorder. *Journal of Clinical Psychiatry, 68,* 1533–1539.

Winston, F. K., Kassam-Adams, N., Vivarelli-O'Neill, C., Ford, J., Newman, E., Baxt, C., Stafford, P., & Cnaan, A. (2002). Acute stress disorder symptoms in children and their parents after pediatric traffic injury. *Pediatrics, 109,* e90.

Winters, K. C., Fahnhorst, T., & Botzet, A. (2007). Adolescent substance use and abuse. In E. J. Mash & R. A. Barkley (Eds.), *Assessment of childhood disorders* (4th ed., pp. 184–209). New York: Guilford.

Wolfe, D. A., Crooks, C. V., Lee, V., McIntyre-Smith, A., & Jaffe, P. G. (2003). The effects of children's exposure to domestic violence:

A meta-analysis and critique. *Clinical Child and Family Psychology Review, 6,* 171–187.

Wolfe, V. V. (2007). Child sexual abuse. In E. J. Mash & R. A. Barkley (Eds.), *Assessment of childhood disorders* (4th ed., pp. 685–748). New York: Guilford.

Wong, B. Y. L. (Eds.). (2004). *Learning about learning disabilities* (3rd ed.). New York: Elsevier.

Wong, B. Y. L. (2008). *The ABCs of learning disabilities* (2nd ed.). Boston, MA: Elsevier/Academic.

Wright, D. A., Bobashev, G., & Folsom, R. (2007). Understanding the relative influence of neighborhood, family, and youth on adolescent drug use. *Substance Use and Misuse, 42,* 2159–2171.

Young, M. E., & Fristad, M. A. (2007). Evidence based treatments for bipolar disorder in children and adolescents. *Journal of Contemporary Psychotherapy, 37,* 157–164.

Youngstrom, E. (2007). Pediatric bipolar disorder. In E. J. Mash & R. A. Barkley (Eds.), *Assessment of childhood disorders* (4th ed., pp. 253–304). New York: Guilford.

Youngstrom, E. A., Findling, R. L., Danielson, C. K., & Calabrese, J. R. (2001). Discriminative validity of parent report of hypomanic and depressive symptoms on the General Behavior Inventory. *Psychological Assessment, 13,* 267–276.

Zacny, J., Bigelow, G., Compton, P., Foley, K., Iguchi, M., & Sannerud, C. (2003). College on problems of drug dependence taskforce on prescription opioid non-medical use and abuse: Position statement. *Drug and Alcohol Dependence, 69,* 215–232.

Index